D0052999

Everybody's frightened a bit. But how many of us just go through the fear and do it anyway?

I was reading this book called *You Can't Afford the Luxury of a Negative Thought.* It impressed me a lot. It says fear is the energy behind doing your best work.

I thought, "Wow, that's a positive way to look at it." I think it's very important to be positive about everything in your life that's negative. You can turn a twist on it.

I can either complain about my mother not believing in me, or I can tell you it served me in some way to become who I am.

I can say, "I am terribly frightened and fear is terrible and awful and it makes me uncomfortable, so I won't do that because it's uncomfortable." Or I could say what it says in this book, "Get used to being uncomfortable. It is uncomfortable doing something that's risky."

But, so what? Do you want to stagnate and just be comfortable?

—Barbra Streisand

"Thank you for your wonderful book. I've surrounded myself with every conceivable work on self knowledge, realization, universal consciousness and the rest from Jung to Alice M. Baily. You have created a work of unique simplicity which offers a way of thinking and living in which motives are high but realistic and available. I love it."

—Pauline Collins
Tony Award Winner
Academy Award Nominee

"Pithy quotes and upbeat prose will chase away those negative thoughts."

—Detroit Free Press

"*You Can't Afford the Luxury of a Negative Thought* is as complete a discourse on personal growth as one can find among the numerous self-help books available today."

—Tim Janulewicz
St. Joseph News-Press/Gazette

"The book is much too big, much too full of great stuff to select any one thing to quote here. Suffice to say that if you were to flip through it at a bookstore, you'd surely want to take it home."

—The Union Leader
Manchester, NH

"This is the best book I've ever read. I read it at home. I put it in the car and read a page or two before going to work. I read a few pages before going to bed. I've carried it around so much the pages are starting to fall out. I really do enjoy it."

—Pally H., Gaffney, SC

"Thanks for all the pleasant, happy thoughts."

—Mrs. B., Adelphi, MD

"I'm just calling to tell you I'm reading your book and enjoying it tremendously. I found out about it in a cancer support group. My daughter just ordered two books from you because of me. I think it is one of the finest things of its type I've read in a long time."

—Lorraine O., Livermore, CA

"I'd like to order a case. I'll be waiting for the books to share them with my friends and I'm so happy that this book is out. God bless all of you."

—Myrna B., Coronado, CA

"This is the fourth book I've ordered from you. I think it's a phenomenal book. It's kind of become my Bible. I just love the fact that it's so easy and humorous to read and so gentle. The book doesn't take itself seriously. So, thank you for writing it."

—Roni S., Pleasantown, CA

"I read your book. It was NEEDED. I will recommend your book to others."

—Anita H., Red Bluff, CA

"Your book came highly recommended from a friend who has two copies and is always lending them out so she's thinking about buying a third for herself."

—Patricia H., Livermore, CA

"I appreciate it and tell all my friends. Thank you."

—John Z., San Diego, CA

"Sincere thanks and God reward you."

—Father John M., Little Rock, AR

"The book is fantastic! My husband recently had cancer surgery and usually will *not* read anything but 'technical' (engineering) books. He is now reading your book and loves it. Thank you very much."

—Donna D., Burney, CA

"I saw your book in a bookstore in a shopping mall and I was blown away by how fantastic it was and is! I'm a 12-step person. Thank you for the book. Thank you for everything that's gone into it."

—Jim R., Arleta, CA

"We'd like to get this as soon as we can. It's a great book; we all love it here. We're just dying to get our hands . . . no, we're living to get our hands on more because everybody here wants more. We're looking forward to getting our order soon."

*—Clybourn Chiropractic Health Center,
Chicago, IL*

"I love the book. Thank you. God bless!"

—Juliana L., Bayonne, NJ

"By now, I'm sure you're aware of the world-changing events that are occurring in the Persian Gulf. The war here affects not only us soldiers in the region, but also our friends and families half-way around the world. There aren't too many amenities of home we can have—those are just dreamt-of, almost forgotten luxuries. But one of the most important things I brought with me is your book, *You Can't Afford the Luxury of a Negative Thought*. Over the period of time my unit has been here, your book has helped me keep my focus, raise my spirits, and just clarify my sense of purpose. Every day, when I wake, I read a section of the book, and I feel I can handle any challenge that comes my way throughout the day.

"I just want to thank you again for such a wonderful book, and I'd like to have a bookmark, and if at all possible, the audio cassette package that you speak of at the end of the book. The book is loved by my entire unit—it's frayed and worn, but it keeps its universal appeal . . . ."

—SPC Yael Pacls, NY

A companion workbook for
You Can't Afford the Luxury of a Negative Thought
is available.

It is entitled
Focus on the Positive: The You Can't Afford the Luxury of a Negative Thought Workbook.
$11.95

❦ ❦ ❦

Also available is an audio cassette of
You Can't Afford the Luxury of a Negative Thought.
Read by the author,
unabridged
$24.95

You Can't Afford the Luxury of a Negative Thought

Peter McWilliams

Prelude Press
8159 Santa Monica Boulevard
Los Angeles, California 90046

1-800-LIFE-101

ISBN 0-931580-20-X

Editor: Jean Sedillos
Desktop publishing: Todd Charleville, Carol Taylor
Production: Paurvi Trivedi

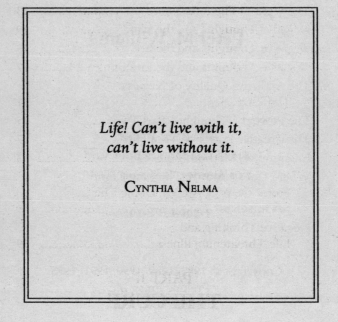

Life! Can't live with it,
can't live without it.

Cynthia Nelma

Contents

To love oneself
is the beginning
of a lifelong romance.

Oscar Wilde

You Can't Afford the Luxury of a Negative Thought

'Tis the good reader that makes the good book;
in every book he finds passages which seem
to be confidences or asides
hidden from all else
and unmistakably meant for his ear;
the profit of books is according to
the sensibility of the reader;
the profoundest thought or passion
sleeps as in a mine,
until it is discovered by an
equal mind and heart.

EMERSON

The way a book is read—
which is to say,
the qualities a reader brings to a book—
can have as much to do
with its worth as anything
the author puts into it.

NORMAN COUSINS

Introduction

This is not a book just for people with life-threatening illnesses. It's a book for anyone afflicted with one of the primary diseases of our time: negative thinking.

I come before you a certified expert on the subject: I'm a confirmed negaholic. I don't just see a glass that's half-full and call it half-empty; I see a glass that's completely full and worry that someone's going to tip it over.

Negative thinking is always expensive—dragging us down mentally, emotionally, and physically—hence I refer to any indulgence in it as a luxury. When, however, we have the symptoms of a life-threatening illness—be it AIDS, heart trouble, cancer, high blood pressure, or any of the others—negative thinking is a luxury we can no longer afford.

I remember a bumper sticker from the 1960s—"Death Is Nature's Way of Telling You to Slow Down." Well, the signs of a life-threatening illness are nature's way of telling you to—as we say in California—lighten up.

Be easier on yourself. Think better of yourself. Learn to forgive yourself and others.

This is a book about getting behind on your worrying. Way, way behind. The further behind on your worrying you get, the further ahead you'll be.

My favorite quote on worry: "Worrying is the interest paid on a debt you may not owe."

This is not so much a book to be read as it is a book to be *used*. It doesn't have to be read cover to

The quotations
when engraved
upon the memory
give you good thoughts.
They also make you
anxious to read
the authors
and look for more.

SIR WINSTON CHURCHILL

cover. I like to think you can flip it open at any time to any page and get something of value from it. This is especially true of the second—and longest—section of the book.

This book has two sections: ***The Disease*** and ***The Cure.***

The disease is not any specific illness, but what I believe to be a precursor of all life-threatening illnesscs—negative thinking.

The cure is not a wonder drug or a vaccination or The Magic Bullet. The cure is very simple: (1) spend more time focusing on the positive things in your life *(Accentuate the Positive);* (2) spend less time thinking negatively *(Eliminate the Negative);*

and (3) enjoy each and every moment you can *(Latch on to the Affirmative).*

That's it. Simple, but far from easy.

It's the aim of this book to make the process simple and, if not easy, at least easier.

Please don't use anything in this book against yourself. Don't interpret anything I say in ***The Disease*** as blame. When I use the word *responsibility,* for example, I simply mean you have the *ability* to *respond.* (And you *are* responding or you wouldn't be reading this book.)

And please don't take any of the suggestions in ***The Cure*** as "musts," "shoulds," or "have-tos." Think of them as joyful activity, creative play, curious exploration—not as additional burdens in an already burdensome life.

This book is not designed to replace proper medical care. Please use this book *in conjunction with* whatever course of treatment your doctor or health-care provider prescribes. If you have a life-threatening illness, you will have to take some life-supporting actions, and naturally these include proper medical attention.

You are far more powerful than you ever dreamed.

You are a marvelous, wonderful, worthwhile person—just because you are. That's the point of view I'll be taking. Please join me for a while—an hour, a week, a lifetime—at that viewing point.

We are, perhaps,
uniquely among the
earth's creatures,
the worrying animal.
We worry away our lives,
fearing the future,
discontent with the present,
unable to take in
the idea of dying,
unable to sit still.

Lewis Thomas

PART I

THE DISEASE

Thinking is
an experimental dealing
with small quantities of energy,
just as a general
moves miniature figures
over a map
before setting his troops
in action.

SIGMUND FREUD

The Power of Thoughts (Part One)

A simple thought. A few micromilliwatts of energy flowing through our brain. A seemingly innocuous, almost ephemeral event. And yet, a thought—or, more accurately, a carefully orchestrated series of thoughts—has a significant impact on our mind, our body, and our emotions.

Thoughts cause responses in the body. Think of a lemon. Imagine cutting it in half. Imagine removing the seeds with the point of a knife. Smell the lemon. Now, imagine squeezing the juice from the lemon into your mouth. Imagine digging your teeth into the center of the lemon. Chew the pulp. Feel those little things (whatever those little things are called) breaking and popping inside your mouth. Most people's salivary glands respond to the very *thought* of a lemon.

For some people, thinking about the sound of fingernails on a chalkboard is physically uncomfortable. Try this—imagine an emery board or a double-sided piece of sandpaper. Imagine putting it in your mouth. Bite down on it. Now move your teeth from side to side. Goose bumps?

Thoughts influence our emotions. Think of something you love. What do you feel? Now think of something you hate. What do you feel? Now, something you love again. We don't have to change our emotions—we change our thoughts, and our emotions follow along.

Every good thought you think
is contributing its share
to the ultimate result
of your life.

GRENVILLE KLEISER

Now imagine your favorite place in nature. Where is it? A beach? A meadow? A mountaintop? Take your time. Imagine lying on your back, your eyes closed. Feel the sun on your face. Smell the air. Hear the sounds of creation. Become a part of it. Feel more relaxed?

Most people who took the time to try these little experiments know what I'm talking about.

Those who thought, "This stuff is stupid. I'm not going to try anything as silly as this!" are left with the emotional and physiological consequences of *their* thoughts—perhaps irritability, impatience, or even hostility. A few—because of their *thoughts* about books containing sentences such as "Now imagine your favorite place in nature"—put this book down, never to pick it up again. These people (bless their independent hearts!) proved the point as well as those who followed along with the "suggested" thoughts. The point: thoughts have power over our mind, our body, and our emotions.

Positive thoughts (joy, happiness, fulfillment, achievement, worthiness) have positive results (enthusiasm, calm, well-being, ease, energy, love). Negative thoughts (judgment, unworthiness, mistrust, resentment, fear) produce negative results (tension, anxiety, alienation, anger, fatigue).

To know why something as minuscule as a thought can have such a dramatic effect on our mind, body, and emotions, it helps to understand the automatic reaction human beings have whenever they perceive danger: the Fight or Flight Response.

And we are here
as on a darkling plain
Swept with confused alarms
of struggle and flight,
Where ignorant armies
clash by night.

MATTHEW ARNOLD

The Fight or Flight Response

Human beings have been around for a long, long time. One of the main reasons the human animal has survived as long and as successfully as it has is its highly developed, integrated, and instantaneous response to perceived danger: the Fight or Flight Response.

Let's consider our not-too-distant ancestor, Zugg. Zugg is far more advanced than a simple caveman—he has learned to manipulate tools, to till the fields, and to build shelters. Zugg is out tilling his field one day when he hears a twig snap in the underbrush.

Zugg, because he has a fairly well-developed mind, remembers that one time when he heard a twig snap, a wild animal came out of the underbrush and ate his sister, Zuggrina. His mind immediately associates twig snapping with ravenous wild animals. Without even having to think about it, he prepares.

He focuses all his attention on the geographical area of the snap. His brain concentrates on the input of his senses. His mind whirls through possible defense strategies and paths of retreat. His emotions flare: a heady combination of fear and anger. Adrenalin, sugar, and other stimulants surge into his system. Blood is diverted from comparatively unimportant functions of the body—such as digesting food, fighting infections, and healing wounds—and rushes to the skeletal muscles, especially his arms and legs. The eyes narrow; the muscles tense.

I'll moider de bum.

Tony Two-Ton Galento

He is ready.

Ready for what? To do battle or to run; to combat or to escape, "to take a stand and fight or take off out of here," as Joni Mitchell put it.

Hence, the Fight or Flight Response. It's an automatic, physiological response to danger—either real or perceived.

The Fight or Flight Response has been an essential tool for the survival of our species. Back in Zugg's time, the more laid-back humans were, for the most part, eaten. These gentler folk might hear a twig snap and say, "Hark, a twig snapping. Isn't that a lovely sound?" The next thing they knew they were dinner. This group did not, uh, persevere.

But Zugg and his kind? Victorious. They got through the animal wars, and then, having seemingly nothing better to do, spent the last 5,000 years fighting one another in human wars. People with the most intensely honed Fight or Flight Responses lived to fight another day, and, more importantly from a genetic point of view, lived to reproduce another night.

The Zuggrinas played an important role in all this, too. The offspring of the women who could defend their young the fiercest and/or grab their young and run the fastest survived. The most protected children—who were most likely to make it to adulthood and reproduce—were the ones with the genetically strongest Fight or Flight Response.

In the past few hundred years—in the Western world, at least—the need for the Fight or Flight Response has, for all practical purposes, disappeared.

When was the last time you had to *physically* fight or flee *to save your life?*

I'm talking about *you*, not people you read about in the newspapers or see on TV.*

*One of the easiest ways to negate new information is to apply it to someone else—preferably someone you don't know and, even more preferably, to a fictional character. "What about James Bond (or Rambo or Road Warrior or Roarunner)? He fights for his life *all the time*." Yes, but you're not James Bond (etc.). In fact, *nobody* is. Please apply everything in this book to *your* life, not the fictional lives of television, movies, and novels, or the almost-fictional lives of "real people" reported in

Give them great meals
of beef and iron and steel,
they will eat like wolves
and fight like devils.

SHAKESPEARE

The Fight or Flight Response, ironically, now works *against* our survival in these newfangled civilized times. The veneer of civilization is thin—a few hundred years papered over millions of years of biological evolution. The "beast" within is still strong.

The Press (both print and electronic). Also, please avoid the temptation to apply this information to "the average person." There is no such person, and even if there were, he or she is not you. You are a unique individual. Use this book to take an honest, perceptive look at yourself—the good, the bad, the ugly, and the beautiful—and learn to accept and love it all.

When we are cut off in traffic, are spoken to unkindly, fear that our job may be in danger, get a rent increase, hear Nostradamus's revised doomsday predictions, are told the restaurant lost our reservation, or have a flat tire, the Fight or Flight Response kicks in with full force as though our lives depended on slugging it out or running away *in that very moment.*

Worse, the Fight or Flight Response is activated whenever we *think* about being cut off in traffic, *think* that our job may be in danger, *think* about getting a rent increase, *think* about Nostradamus's dire predictions, *think* about the restaurant losing the reservation, or *think* about having a flat tire.

Even if none of these "disasters" (only one of which could be genuinely life-threatening) comes to pass, just *thinking* that any one of them *might* happen is enough to trigger the Fight or Flight Response.

The Fight or Flight Response is alive and well.

And it's killing us.

The mind
is its own place,
and in itself can make
heaven of Hell,
a hell of Heaven.

MILTON

Negative Thoughts and the Mind

When the Fight or Flight Response is triggered, the mind immediately focuses on the area of perceived danger. It is intent on finding what's wrong. It's *looking* for danger, evil, enemies, wild beasts.

It's a good bet that our friend Zugg didn't spend too much time appreciating the color of the sky or the fragrance of the flowers as he squinted in the direction of the twig snap. No. He was looking for trouble. His mind *automatically filtered out* anything that didn't pertain to the perceived danger. If the evidence wasn't bad, it was no good.

The mind is a marvelous filtering mechanism. It shelters us from large amounts of unnecessary information. If it didn't, we would probably go mad. We simply cannot pay conscious attention to every single detail being collected by our five senses.

Without moving it, be aware of your tongue. Were you aware of it before I asked? Probably not. The sensation was there, but your mind filtered it out—you didn't need that information. Look carefully at the paper on this page. What's the texture like? Had you noticed that before? Unless you are in the printing or paper trade, probably not. Are there any smells in the room? How about noises? Ticking clock? Air conditioner? Feel the sensation of your body against whatever you're sitting (or lying) on. Have you forgotten about your tongue again?

When the Fight or Flight Response is activated,

> *Wisdom entereth not*
> *into a malicious mind.*
>
> RABELAIS

we begin to look for everything wrong with a situation, person, place, or thing. And, boy, do we find it! There's always *something* wrong. We're living in a material world. Material things are, almost by definition, imperfect.

So there's our mind, automatically filtering out the positive while automatically focusing on the negative. Sounds like the perfect recipe for misery.

But it gets worse.

Zugg's mind, you will recall, also reviewed past moments of his life in which snapping twigs played a devastating part. There was, of course, that terrible time with Zuggrina. Poor Zuggrina. Then there was that time with OggaBooga. Poor OggaBooga.

Zugg is now looking not just for twig-snap memories, but for memories of *all* wild beasts devouring *anything.* He even thinks back to times he *thought* about wild beasts devouring anything. He is searching his memory for real and imaginary images of mutilation, and there are plenty to be found.

We often do the same thing. If someone cuts us off in traffic, our mind goes reeling back to all the rude and inconsiderate people we've ever seen driving cars, then to all the rude and inconsiderate people we've ever seen anywhere, then to all the rude and inconsiderate people we've seen in movies, on TV, or in the theater of our imagination.

If someone is five minutes late for an appointment, we often spend four minutes and fifty-nine seconds of that five minutes remembering every other time the person was late, all people who were ever late, and every situation—either real or imagined—of being disappointed or feeling unloved.

The mind—an incredibly perceptive tool—is looking both within and without for negativity. It finds it. That thought triggers a more intense Fight or Flight Response, which demands an even more enthusiastic negative mental search, which discovers even more hideous evidence, which kicks off a stronger Fight or Flight Response, which . . . .

Get the idea? It's known as a temper tantrum or losing one's cool or an anxiety attack or getting steamed—or life as we know it in this (and most likely the next) century.

Most of the time
we think we're sick,
it's all in the mind.

Thomas Wolfe

Negative Thoughts and the Body

The Fight or Flight Response puts a body through its paces. All the resources of the body are mobilized for immediate, physical, demanding action—fight or flee.

All the other bodily functions are put on hold—digestion, assimilation, cell production, body maintenance, circulation (except to certain fight-or-flee skeletal muscles), healing, and immunological defenses.

In addition, the body is pumping chemicals—naturally produced drugs, if you will—into the system. The muscles need energy and they need it *fast*.

Zugg was luckier than we are in this respect. Often he would actually *use* these chemicals by running them off, climbing them off, or fighting them off. In our civilized world, we usually don't. At most we bang our fists or throw stuff (which only hurts our hands and breaks things).

Occasionally we yell, but that's not physical enough. Our body has armed itself to *fight or flee for its life*—but usually we just sit and seethe.

The repeated and unnecessary triggering of the Fight or Flight Response puts enormous physiological stress on the body.

It make us more vulnerable to disease (the immune system being told, "Hold off on attacking those germs—we have wild beasts to fight!"), digestive trouble (ulcers and cancers at the far side of it),

I don't do anything
that's bad for me.
I don't like to be made
nervous or angry.
Any time you get upset
it tears down
your nervous system.

MAE WEST

poor assimilation (preventing necessary nutrients from entering the system), slower recovery from illnesses (conquering a disease is less urgent than conquering a wild beast), reduced cell production, sore muscles, fatigue, and a general sense, as Keats put it, "that if I were underwater I would scarcely kick to come to the top."

Sound bad? It gets worse.

The emergency chemicals, unused, eventually break down into other, more toxic substances. Our body must then mobilize—yet again—to get rid of the poisons.

The muscles stay tense for a long time after the response is triggered—especially muscles around the stomach, chest, lower back, neck, and shoulders. (Most people have chronic tension in at least one of these areas.) We feel jittery, nervous, uptight.

The mind always tries to find reasons for things. If the body's feeling tense, it wonders, "What is there to feel tense about?" Seldom do we conclude (correctly), "Oh, this is just the normal aftereffect of the Fight or Flight Response. Nothing to be concerned about." Usually we start scanning the environment (inner and outer) for something out of place. And, as I mentioned before, there will *always* be something out of place.

The mind's a remarkable mechanism. Given a task, the mind will fulfill it with astounding speed and accuracy. When asked, "What's wrong?" it will compile and cross-reference a list of grievances with blinding swiftness and precision. Everything everyone (including ourselves) should have done but didn't and shouldn't have done but did is reviewed, highlighted, indexed, and prioritized. All this elaborate mental labor sparked by a sensation in the body.

Naturally, this review of negative events prompts a new round of Fight or Flight Responses, which promotes more tension in the body, which promotes more mental investigation into What's Wrong?

Do you see how this downward mind/body spiral can continue almost indefinitely?

It's not surprising, then, that some people make a decision deep inside themselves that life is just not worth living.

To hate and to fear
is to be psychologically ill.
It is, in fact,
the consuming illness
of our time.

H. A. Overstreet

Negative Thoughts and the Emotions

The primary emotions generated by the Fight or Flight Response are anger (the emotional energy to fight) and fear (the emotional energy to flee).

Anger and fear—and variations on them—are most often the feelings we call *negative.*

Consider these lists:

ANGER	**FEAR**
• hostility	• terror anxiety
• resentment	• timidity
• guilt (anger at oneself)	• shyness (fear of others)
• rage	• withdrawal
• seething	• reticence
• depression	• apprehension
• hurt (you're usually upset with someone else, or yourself, or both)	• grieving (fear that you'll never love or be loved again)

Any others you'd care to add from your own repertoire could probably be considered a variation of anger or fear—or a combination of the two.

Zugg, while deciding what to do, probably experienced a good deal of both. Anger ("Win one for

Anger is one
of the sinews of the soul;
he that wants it hath
a maimed mind.

THOMAS FULLER

1642

Zuggrina!") and fear ("What happened to Zuggrina ain't gonna happen to me!").

The problem with these emotions—in addition to their obvious unpleasantness—is that they tend to mar logical, rational, life-supportive decisions.

In his passionate anger for sibling revenge, Zugg might wade into the tall grass, spear in hand, and discover a whole gathering of wild beasts. Perhaps the beasts didn't even know Zugg was around. Maybe they were just breaking twigs to roast weenies, but when Zugg appeared they decided on a quick change of menu.

How often have you waded into a confrontation, only to find that, as the saying goes, you had stirred up a hornet's nest?* On the other hand, Zugg could have, at the first sound of a snap, run away. (Remember the movie *Monty Python and the Holy Grail?* Whenever King Arthur's men were in even the slightest danger, their battle cry—as they fled in all different directions—was, "Run away! Run away!") This meant that every time a rabbit snapped a twig or two gophers were going for it in the underbrush, Zugg would abandon his plowing and head for the high country. He would eventually abandon his field, vowing never to return to such a wild and savage place again.

How many fields have you abandoned in your life? The field of a challenging new career? The field of a more fulfilling place to live? The field of relationships? The field of your dreams?

Because people are afraid of fear, they give up acre after acre of their own life. Some find the snapping of twigs so uncomfortable that they abandon the territory of life altogether.

*While on vacation, I received a traffic ticket from a particularly obnoxious police officer. A ticket *plus* insults! Too much was enough. I stormed over to the local police station and reported the offending public servant to his superior. While listening to my story, the police captain tapped away at his computer. I thought he was taking some sort of formal report. Oh, boy. The nasty policeman was really in trouble now. What the captain was doing, however, was looking up my driving record. He discovered an unpaid traffic ticket from a vacation seven years before. I was placed under arrest. The anger quickly turned to fear. My anger cost me $110 and several hours in the cooler. Now I know why they call it the cooler.

Habit with him was
all the test of truth,
"It must be right:
I've done it from my youth."

George Crabbe

The Addictive Quality of Negative Thinking

For many, negative thinking is a habit which, over time, becomes an addiction. It's a disease, like alcoholism, compulsive overeating, or drug abuse.

A lot of people suffer from this disease because negative thinking is addictive to each of The Big Three—the mind, the body, and the emotions. If one doesn't get you, the others are waiting in the wings.

The mind becomes addicted to being "right." In this far-less-than-perfect world, one of the easiest ways to be right is to predict failure—especially for ourselves. The mind likes being right. When asked, "Would you rather be right or be happy?" some people—who really take the time to consider the ramifications of being "wrong"—have trouble deciding.

The body becomes addicted to the rush of chemicals poured into the blood stream by the Fight or Flight Response. Some people can't resist the physical stimulation of a serious session of negative thinking. They get off on the rush of adrenalin.

The emotions become addicted to the sheer *intensity* of it all. The Fight or Flight Response may not trigger pleasant feelings, but at least they're not boring. As the emotions become accustomed to a higher level of stimulation, they begin demanding more and more intensity. It's not unlike the slash-

To fall into a habit
is to begin to cease to be.

Miguel de Unamuno

and-gash movies—too much is no longer enough. Remember when the shower scene from *Psycho* was considered the ultimate in blood and gore? Now it's *Friday the 13th, Part Seven.* (Seven?!)

Negative thinking must be treated like any addiction—with commitment to life, patience, discipline, a will to get better, forgiveness, self-love, and the knowledge that recovery is not just possible but, following certain guidelines, inevitable.

We should be taught not to wait
for inspiration to start a thing.
Action always generates inspiration.
Inspiration seldom generates action.

FRANK TIBOLT

¶ *Most people live, whether physically, intellectually or morally, in a very restricted circle of their potential being.* ¶ *They make use of a very small portion of their possible consciousness, and of their soul's resources in general, much like a man who, out of his whole bodily organism, should get into a habit of using and moving only his little finger.* ¶ *Great emergencies and crises show us how much greater our vital resources are than we had supposed.*

WILLIAM JAMES

The Power of Thoughts (Part Two)

What I've discussed thus far is pretty much accepted, mainline medical fact. The most "controversial" subject I've presented is the idea that negative thinking is an addictive disease.

With that possible exception, if your local physician were to read the first chapters of this book, he or she would probably nod knowingly and agree that they are fairly accurate. (Thirty years ago, of course, most of the medical establishment wouldn't admit that thoughts had any causal effect on organic illness. If you mentioned such a notion, physicians would have thought you were nuts. We all live and learn.) Now I'm going to explore some thinking about thoughts they don't teach at Harvard Medical School.

You can take the next few pages with as many grains of salt as you please. The accepted medical theory—that thoughts contribute to symptomatic illness, and that improving one's thoughts can help improve one's health—is all I need to illustrate the premise of this book.

The rest is, well, interesting, fun, provocative, stupid, enlightening—use your own adjectives to describe it. Even if it's just the rantings of a Detroit boy transplanted to California by way of New York, it doesn't negate the fact that, in anyone's book—medical or metaphysical—if a life-threatening illness threatens, you can't afford the luxury of a negative thought.

There is nothing I love as much as a good fight.

Franklin D. Roosevelt

JANUARY 22, 1911*

* After making this statement, Roosevelt went on to fight polio, fought to become president, and led the Allies in probably the biggest fight of this century—World War II. If he loved a good fight, he certainly got what he loved.

The Creative Power of Thoughts

Thoughts are powerful. All the spectacular and terrible creations of humanity began as a thought—an idea. From the idea came the plan; from the plan came the action; from the action came the object. Whatever you're sitting or reclining on began as a thought. The room you're in—and almost everything in it—began as a thought.

All the wars and fighting the world has known began with thoughts. (Usually, "You have it, I want it," "You're doing this, I want you to do that," or "I just don't like you.")

All the good, fine, noble, and creative acts of humanity were conceived as a spark in a single human consciousness. The Eiffel Tower, the Mona Lisa, the Magna Carta, the Declaration of Independence, movies, books, and television began in the mind. (Granted, some of it should have stayed there. As someone once said, "In every journalist is a novel, and that is precisely where it should remain.")

Even the creation of a human being begins as a thought. As the old saying goes, "I knew you before you were a twinkle in your father's eye."

Victor Hugo described it this way: "An invasion of armies can be resisted, but not an idea whose time has come." Often misquoted as "There is nothing so powerful as an idea whose time has come," it has been used so often, it's become a

Enlighten the people generally,
and tyranny and oppressions
of body and mind
will vanish like evil spirits
at the dawn of day.

THOMAS JEFFERSON

cliché. (There is nothing less powerful than a cliché whose time has passed.)

Everything created by humans—both good and bad—began as a thought. (The categorization of "good" and "bad," of course, is just another thought.) The only difference between a thought and a physical reality is time, passion (love or hate), and physical activity.

The amount of time, passion, and physical activity varies from project to project. Sometimes it's seconds; sometimes it's years; sometimes the thought must be passed from generation to generation. Some of the great cathedrals took a century and four generations of stone cutters to complete.

On the other hand, there was the Hundred Years' War.

Leonardo da Vinci invented the helicopter four hundred years before one ever flew. Two hundred years ago, Thomas Jefferson envisioned a nation free from religious persecution, of people "with certain unalienable rights, that among these are life, liberty, and the pursuit of happiness." We're still working on that one.*

To illustrate the power of thought: Imagine the corner of this page turned over. Let it be an idea in your mind. Now reach up and fold it over. There. A thought was passed from my mind to your mind, and you turned that thought into a physical reality. (If you're not the first person to read this book you might have wondered, "Why is the corner of this page turned over?" Now you know.)

Some people are particularly good at turning ideas into realities. Edison was one. Imagine: the phonograph, movies, an improved telephone, and the electric light all from one man. Henry Ford wanted to make a cheap, reliable automobile and invented the assembly line to do it.

Without thoughts, things that involve any sort of human action simply don't happen. Where we are is the result of a lifetime of thinking—both positive and negative.

If you're pleased with some parts of your life, then your thinking in those areas has been what

*Please see my book, *Ain't Nobody's Business If You Do.*

> *Great men*
> *are they who see*
> *that spiritual is stronger*
> *than any material force,*
> *that thoughts rule the world.*
>
> EMERSON

you would call generally "positive." If you're not pleased with other parts of your life, then your thoughts about those areas have probably not been as positive as they could have been. The good news is that thoughts can be changed, and with that change come changes in your life.

If you persist in your thoughts of wealth, for example, you focus on wealth—an overall state of being that is open, accepting, abundant, and flowing—and this focus on wealth tends to produce physical manifestations of wealth: houses, cars, cash, and your own special edition of *Lifestyles of the Rich and Famous.*

"But," some protest, "I think about money *all*

the time and I still don't have any." What they mean is that they *worry* about money all the time. Worry is a form of fear, in this case a fear of poverty. Holding an ongoing series of thoughts about poverty creates a focus on poverty, which creates a lack of everything but bills—which causes more worry, which creates more poverty.

Our thoughts create our reality—not instantly, necessarily, as in "Poof! There it is"—but eventually. Where we put our focus—our inner and outer vision—is the direction we tend to go. That's our desire, our intention. The *way* we get there—well, there are many methods.

Follow your desire
as long as you live;
do not lessen the time
of following desire,
for the wasting of time
is an abomination
to the spirit.

PTAHHOTEP

2350 B.C.

Intention vs. Method

If I were in New York and wanted to go to Toledo (God knoweth why—a writer has to stretch reality sometimes to come up with examples), what are some of the ways I could get there?

Plane? Car? Train? Bus? Bike? Walk? Hitch-hike? Pogo stick? Crawl? Roll? Skip? Hop? Somersault? You, no doubt, have some other ways I haven't mentioned. (Somersault. What a strange-looking word.)

In this example, Toledo would be the *intention.* The many ways of traveling there are the *methods*.

Each intention we have can be fulfilled by any number of methods. The idea is to hold your intention clearly in mind, and then be open to whatever methods appear—even unexpected ones.

For example, in traveling from New York to Toledo, what general direction should you take? West, right? That would be the generally accepted method—directionally speaking. Some might even argue that it is the *only* direction that would get you to Toledo. But what if you went east, and kept going east? Could you eventually find yourself in Toledo? Sure.

As Niels Bohr said, "The opposite of a correct statement is a false statement. But the opposite of a profound truth may well be another profound truth." Some people say the way to get more money is to hoard it. Others say the way to get more money is to give it away. Some say health is gained through more rest. Others say it's obtained

It is common sense
to take a method and try it.
If it fails,
admit it frankly
and try another.
But above all,
try something.

Franklin D. Roosevelt

by more activity. Be open to all methods, even *seemingly* contradictory ones.

Back to Toledo. Which direction is the faster route from New York to Toledo, east or west? It can only be west, right? Not necessarily. If I went west doing somersaults and you went east on the Concorde, who do you suppose would get to Toledo faster? (Hint: I am not listed in *Guinness' Book of World Records* as Mr. Somersault.)

Again, keep open to various methods and behaviors, and remember: life often offers surprising solutions.

For the last time, back to Toledo. All silly examples aside, if I really wanted to get from New York to Toledo, which is the right way to go? A westerly course, of course. As you can tell, I'm being trickier than usual in this section. I'm challenging some popular assumptions people have about methods and how to choose them. Is west really a "right" direction and east a "wrong" one? Of course not.

As methods go, "right" and "wrong" are just opinions. The only valid criterion of a method is whether or not it is *workable*. In the New York–Toledo journey, both east and west are workable methods and, therefore, acceptable. North and south are not workable; therefore, not acceptable. North and south are not wrong; they just won't *work* for a journey from New York to Toledo.

Methods can sometimes *indicate* intentions. If you were driving west from New York, for example, we could reasonably assume that your immediate intention was not to visit New England. The operative words are *sometimes* and *indicate*, because it's not until you land in Toledo and say, "Yes! Eureka! This is it!" that we'll know your intention was truly Toledo.

Let's say someone has an intention to hide. He (let's make him a he) discovered at an early age that to be spontaneous, outgoing, sensitive, and expressive got him into trouble with some of the authority figures. ("Be quiet! Can't you see we're watching television?" "Settle down." "Be a good little boy and sit still.") He decided to hide the expressive parts of

Bring me my bow of burning gold,
Bring me my arrows of desire,
Bring me my spear O clouds, unfold!
Bring me my chariot of fire!

WILLIAM BLAKE

himself.

If he intended to hide his sensitivity and enthusiasm, what methods might he use? Being withdrawn, not going out, being shy, not participating. He might even start creating some physical methods: stammering, putting on weight, or even developing an illness—such as asthma or a heart problem: perfectly reasonable reasons not to participate. He might generate a need for glasses—which can be great to hide behind. In later years, he may let his hair cover part of his face or grow a beard.

And what if life at certain times became too intolerable? What if he decided, time and again, "I can't take it anymore. I don't want to live." If he formed an intention to die, what are some of the methods he might use to fulfill that intention?

Gunshot, car accident, poison, tuberculosis, leukemia, cancer, drowning, carbon monoxide, knife wound, slit wrist, heart attack, stroke, diphtheria, decapitation, a too-meaningful relationship with Blue Beard, bubonic plague, earthquake, flood, volcano, anorexia, falling, syphilis, wild beasts, cholera, guillotine, hanging, shark, piranha, electric chair, polio, gas chamber, hepatitis, lethal injection, flu, meningitis, or the relative newcomer, AIDS.

A life-threatening illness is just one of many methods to fulfill an intention to die. It might be that somewhere inside, the person with a life-threatening illness has or did have an intention to die.

Maybe.

It's worth a look. Intentions are often unconscious. Once discovered, however, intentions can be changed.

The strangest
and most fantastic fact
about negative emotions
is that people actually
worship them.

P. D. Ouspensky

Where Does Negative Thinking Come From? Or Why Are We Doing This to Ourselves?

Why do we use the power of our mind to create a negative reality? If our mind can generate health, wealth, and happiness as easily as illness, poverty, and despair, why aren't we healthy, wealthy, and happy all the time?

If a genie appeared and offered you a choice—health, wealth, and happiness or illness, poverty, and despair—which would you choose? If the former is the obvious choice, why do we sometimes choose the negative? There must be something else—something deeper—generating the impulse to think negatively.

Although you may have another word to describe the phenomenon, allow me to call this spring of negative thinking *unworthiness*. It's more than just a feeling or a passing thought; it's a ground of being, a deep-seated belief that "I'm just not good enough." Other words for it are insecurity, undeservingness, and low self-esteem.

Unworthiness undermines all our positive ideas and validates all our negative thoughts.

When we think something good about ourselves, unworthiness pops up and says, "No, you're

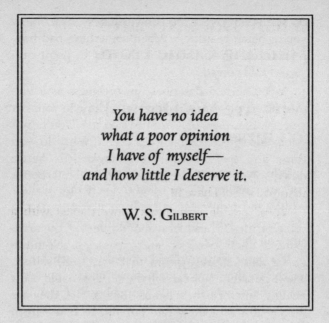

You have no idea
what a poor opinion
I have of myself—
and how little I deserve it.

W. S. GILBERT

not." When we desire something positive for ourselves, unworthiness says, "You don't deserve it." When something good happens to us, unworthiness says (often with our own lips), "This is too good to be true!"*

When we think something bad about ourselves, unworthiness agrees, "Yes, that's true, and furthermore . . . ." When we tell ourselves we can't have or

*The one I seem to use most often is "Whoa!"—an equestrian term meaning, "Hold it! Too much! Stop all this goodness; I can't take it!"

do something we want, unworthiness says, "Now you're being realistic." When something bad happens to us, unworthiness is the first to point out, "See? I told you so."

Jack Canfield describes unworthiness as a vulture sitting on your shoulder, squawking in your ear an endless stream of "You can't do it!" "You're not good enough!" "Don't even try!" "Who do you think you are?" "You'll never make it!" "Settle down!" "You don't deserve it!" "Somebody better than you should have it!"

Some people cover their unworthiness with a self-confidence and bravado bordering on arrogance.* Their cover-up encompasses a self-indulgence and self-absorption that are, well, selfish. These people (it appears on the surface) could use a healthy dose of unworthiness. But, in fact, they are merely lost in a desperate attempt to hide—from themselves as much as from anyone else—the fact that they just don't feel worth it. They think the unworthiness is *real*, not just an illusion, and they respond by concealing it rather than laughing at it. (Did you ever try to conceal a vulture? It can be pretty funny to everyone but the person trying to conceal it.)

If unworthiness is so fundamental, does this mean we're born with it? I believe humans were born to have joy and to have it more abundantly; that the birthright of everyone is loving, caring,

*"Some people" like *me*.

The childhood
shows the man,
As morning
shows the day.

JOHN MILTON

sharing, and abundance. All the negative stuff has just been layered on top of our essential core of goodness. (Not that there isn't strong genetic predispositioning—but that's another book.)

Where does unworthiness come from? A look at how children are raised might offer a clue.

Imagine a child—two, three, or four years old—playing alone in a room. An adult, usually a parent, is nearby. What for? To praise the child every five minutes? No. For "supervision." (Did your parents have super-vision? Mine did.) The adult is on hand "in case there's any trouble."

The child is playing and having a wonderful

time. Two hours go by. The child is "behaving" wonderfully. The interaction with the adult world is minimal.

Suddenly, the child knocks a lamp off a table. *CRASH!* What happens next? *Lots* of interaction with the adult, almost all of it negative. Yelling, screaming ("This was my favorite lamp," "How many times have I told you?" "Bad, bad, bad") and probably some form of physical punishment (spanking, no more playing, "go to your room"). Almost the only interaction in two hours from the adult community was: "You are bad. Shame on you."

As an infant, we get unconditional, almost never-ending praise. Goo-goo ga-ga. Once we grow a little and begin exploring our world, much of our interaction with adults—the symbols of power, love, authority, and life itself—consists of being corrected. *Don't* do this. *Don't* do that.

If we draw a picture, we get praise. If we draw the same picture again, we get less praise. If we draw the same picture five times in a row, we are told to try something new.

If we pour jam on the cat, we are scolded. If we pour jam on the cat a second time, we are scolded more severely. If we pour jam on the cat five times, we may begin wishing that, like the cat, we had nine lives.

The more we do something good, the less praise we get for it. The more we do something bad, the more punishment we receive. Some children learn to do negative things just to get attention

Few parents nowadays
pay any regard
to what their children
say to them.
The old-fashioned respect
for the young
is fast dying out.

Oscar Wilde

because they figure (using child-logic) that negative attention is better than no attention at all. To a child, being ignored can seem like abandonment.

Inside, a part of us begins to add up all the times we're called "wonderful" and all the times we're called "bad." The bad seems to outnumber the wonderful.

We may begin to believe we *are* bad; that unless we do something new and remarkable and tremendous, we're not going to be thought of as good; that we must strive, work hard, and never disobey if we hope to get even a little appreciation; that our goodness must be *earned* because we are, after all, essentially bad.

Bad, unlovable, not good enough, undeserving, unworthy.

From this fertile ground spring our negative thoughts. Sure, we have a lot of positive thoughts, but we tend to believe the negative ones more. A positive thought, checked against this belief of unworthiness, is labeled "False." A negative thought feels at home. The unworthiness proclaims it true, accurate, *right*.

Another reason we don't feel quite as magnificent as we might is technology—the mass communication of sounds and images is a relatively new phenomenon.

A hundred years ago or so, if you played a musical instrument or sang with any degree of competence, you would be among the best any of your acquaintances had ever heard. (The phonograph wasn't invented until 1877.) If you danced, juggled, or "play acted," you were in demand for socials and other gatherings. (The first motion pictures weren't shown publicly until 1894.) If you read books or could write more than your name, you were considered a local scholar and called upon to read or write for those who could not—which was the majority of the population, by the way. (In 1880, only 2.5 percent of high-school aged children went to high school.)

Today, all our achievements are compared with the best of the best. We have become *accustomed* to the highest form of excellence as our standard to judge everything from intelligence ("Did you read about that three-year-old who memorized the en-

You mean you can actually spend $70,000 at Woolworth's?

BOB KRASNOW

After seeing Ike and Tina Turner's house

tire *Encyclopedia Britannica?"*) to brute force ("So you can lift car. Big deal. I saw this guy on TV who could pull a jumbo jet—with his *teeth!"*) to absurdity ("You think that's big? I heard about a girl who could blow a bubble bigger than her whole body!")

One wonders, for example, if Beethoven would have been encouraged to follow his musical bent if, as a child, he had been constantly compared to Mozart (who was twenty-six at the time of Beethoven's birth). Mozart made a living composing and performing at age five. Beethoven didn't become a professional musician until the ripe old age of eleven. If Mozart's childhood performances had been shown again and again on TV, one can imagine a seven-year-old Beethoven, struggling with a composition, being told, "Mozart did better than this when he was *four!*"

With the best-of-the-best as the standard, it's little wonder that our initial inklings of uniqueness, brilliance, and perhaps even genius can be trampled under the crushing hooves of "You think that's good? Well, I saw on TV . . . ."

In fact, we don't even need the critical "help" of others. We make *our own* comparisons (in which we lose) long before we dare to share our accomplishments or desires with others. With larger-than-life achievements and achievers on all media fronts, it's little wonder we might think our meager initial offerings—and, perhaps, we ourselves—don't make the grade.

No matter how good we may be, we just aren't good enough.

The highest possible stage
in moral culture
is when we recognize
that we ought to
control our thoughts.

Charles Darwin

Negative Thinking and Life-Threatening Illness

There are as many examples of how negative thinking helps bring about life-threatening illnesses as there are people who have them. We each have our own personal list of disasters—those things that push us "over the edge," that make us decide life isn't worth living.

For some, it's one or two tragedies, the depth and intensity of which created a desire to die. For others, it's the daily dose of "slings and arrows"—the situations to which we respond: "What's the use?" "Why bother?" "Who cares?" The accumulation of these over the years forms the desire: "Why should I bother anymore?"

The latest example of a *method* that many are using in response to the *intention* "not to bother anymore" is AIDS. Yes, more people are using the "tried and true" methods of cancer, heart disease, and others—but AIDS is a perfect example of how we let negative thinking "win" in the "never-ending struggle for truth, justice, and the American Way." (That's the opening to *Superman*—a standard no one I've ever met lived up to.)

I'm not saying negative thinking causes AIDS—or any other life-threatening illness. I am suggesting that negative thinking promotes conditions in the mind, body, and emotions that make it *possible* for the AIDS virus (or whatever *does* cause AIDS—there seems to be some controversy on this point)

Attachment is the great
fabricator of illusions;
reality can be attained
only by someone
who is detached.

Simone Weil

to take root.

Negative thinking helps provide the *opportunity*. The illness takes it from there. Once it takes root, how quickly the illness progresses and grows depends a lot on how much fertilizer we give it from that great manure generator—negative thinking.

Probably the most common negative thought surrounding AIDS is fear. Anyone in the so-called "high-risk group" is a candidate for the epidemic of fear that's spread far faster than AIDS itself. (Actually, the only people in the high-risk group are those who practice high-risk activities.) If you've had a test that indicated the presence of HIV antibodies in your system, you probably are even more susceptible to the dis-ease of fear.

The epidemic of fear (a subset of the epidemic of negative thinking) is one of the most easily spread. Unlike any viral or bacterial illness, fear can be caught over the telephone, from reading newspapers, or from watching television.

For those afraid of catching AIDS—especially people who have the antibodies to the HIV virus in their system—every symptom of *every* disease generates the terror of imminent death.

A cold? "Oh my God, pneumocystis!" A bruise? "Kaposi's sarcoma!" A sore in the mouth? "Thrush!" A little perspiration because the bedroom is too warm? "Night sweats!" It's hypochondriac heaven: fear enlarges every minor symptom into a fatal illness.

This fear is the same for every life-threatening illness. There is a certain "high-risk group" for every illness, and the people within that group often torture themselves. For cancer, it's smokers. Thirty percent of all cancer deaths are smoking-related. Smokers may worry so much about cancer that they need another cigarette.

People with possible genetic predispositions to illness tend to worry. "My father died at sixty-five of a heart attack, my grandfather died at sixty-five of a heart attack, and I'm almost sixty."

Fear, fear, fear.

The tragic results of the epidemic are many:

1. From a medical point of view, negative thinking suppresses the immune system, raises the blood pressure, and creates a general level of stress and

He was a poor
weak human being
like themselves,
a human soul,
weak and helpless
in suffering,
shivering in the toils
of the eternal struggle
of the human soul
with pain.

LIAM O'FLAHERTY

fatigue in the body. In short, infections, cardiovascular irregularities, the degeneration of muscles, and the random growth of unwanted cells get more opportunity.

2. From a thoughts-are-creative point of view, our worry about a particular disease tends to create that disease. There's an old saying: "What you fear may come upon you." It's old because there's a certain degree of truth in it. Medical students and psychology students will often take on the symptoms of the disease or disorder they are currently studying. In some cases, they produce the disease itself. The thought, "Oh my God, it's cancer!" every time you cough might be misinterpreted by your body as an invitation—or even a directive.

3. If you're thinking an illness might be AIDS or lung cancer, and it turns out to be just the flu, you might say, "Thank God, it's the flu!" Such enthusiasm and gratitude for the flu may create more flu.

4. The more people believe they are going to die "within a few years, at best," the less they tend to start long-term projects—career goals, relationships, moving—which, in turn, tends to make life less fulfilling and enjoyable, therefore less livable. After a while, the question, "What have I got to live for?" might not have a satisfactory answer. The desire to die takes root.

5. It's a miserable way to live. If we had a bomb strapped to our chest and were told it could go off at any time, that might be something, over time, we could learn to live with. (We all live with a similar situation in that we know we're going to die, but we don't know when.) If, however, we were told the bomb would tick precisely 1,243 times before exploding, every time the bomb started ticking we'd stop everything we might be doing and start counting. Some days it might only tick ten times, other days it might get up to 287, but while it ticked—panic. And, after a while, the fear that it *might* start ticking begins. So, even when it's not ticking, we're scared. It's a miserable way to live.

Once negative thinking has given the life-threatening illness the opportunity to enter the body, is it too late? Is the progression of a life-threatening ill-

If we could read
the secret history
of our enemies,
we should find
in each man's life
sorrow and suffering enough
to disarm all hostility.

LONGFELLOW

ness irreversible? I don't think so. I'm not being hopelessly optimistic about this, however; some things *are* irreversible.

Let's say, for example, that negative thinking had you throw yourself from the top of a thirty-story building. Once you were in the air, I would probably say it's too late for a change in thinking to greatly affect the physical outcome.

But for anything short of the law of gravity, there's a chance. (That's why it's called the law of gravity—levity has no effect upon it.)

Life-threatening illnesses tend to be either active or dormant. When dormant, they do us no further harm; they just sleep quietly.

The vital question is: What puts the illness to sleep and what keeps it sleeping? I like to think the gentle lapping of positive thoughts on the shoreline of the mind acts as a virtual Sominex (or Demerol or chloroform or nitrous oxide, as you prefer) to life-threatening illness.

Cardiovascular illnesses are directly related to the general mental-emotional-physical state of ease in the body. The more often the body is at ease, the less the heart must work and the less pressure is exerted on the entire cardiovascular system. (A primary goal of exercise, in fact, is letting the heart work less by becoming stronger.)

When the pressures caused by negative thinking are released and a natural state of ease returns, the cardiovascular system can heal itself and function as it was designed to.

Degenerative muscle diseases may be hastened along their course by degenerative thinking. Generating generative (positive) thoughts may help slow the degeneration and, perhaps, even regenerate muscles.

Cancer is, by definition, cells that are growing out of control. This pattern can be swift, or it can be slow. Cancer can take over a vital organ in a matter of weeks, or it can take decades. The cells can stop growing altogether for indefinite periods of time. When discussing "incurable" cancer (and more than fifty percent of all cancers are now considered curable), the medical establishment doesn't quite know why a cancer would slow, stop, or, more

The fear of death
is more to be dreaded
than death itself.

Publilius Syrus
FIRST CENTURY B.C.

mysteriously still, get smaller.

It's known as "remission." When it happens because of medical treatment, it is understood. "Your cancer is in remission." When it happens for "no good reason" (the patient's rediscovered desire to live and related changes in lifestyle not being a good enough "reason"), it's called "spontaneous remission." Doctors explain: "It's spontaneous, like lightning or earthquakes. It just happens sometimes. We don't know why."

Tens of thousands of cancer patients, whose cancers have been in "spontaneous remission" for years, know why. They changed their thinking, and the thinking changed the course of the cancer.

The same is true of any infection or life-threatening illness you can name. Some of the "miracle cures" were not miracles to the people who experienced them. These people discovered why they desired death, changed that to a desire for life, and got busy changing everything in their lives that was contributing to their physical demise.

Consider the remainder of this book a lullaby for any infection; a road map on ways to ease your cardiovascular system; lessons in how to heal the hurts of the heart; instruction in generating generative thinking to counteract degenerative illness; a guidebook on creating spontaneity in your commissions and your remissions; and a wake-up call to the worthiness, well-being, and wellness within you.

MACBETH: *Canst thou not minister*
to a mind diseased,
Pluck from the memory
a rooted sorrow,
Raze out the written
troubles of the brain,
And with some sweet oblivious antidote
Cleanse the stuffed bosom
of that perilous stuff
Which weighs upon the heart?

DOCTOR: *Therein the patient*
Must minister to himself.

SHAKESPEARE

PART II

THE CURE

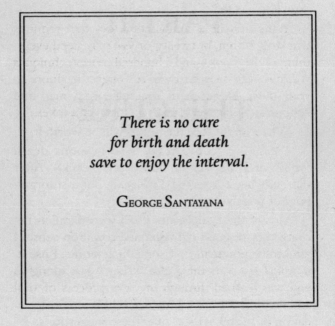

There is no cure
for birth and death
save to enjoy the interval.

George Santayana

The Cure

Yes, Virginia, there is a cure for the disease of negative thinking—dozens of cures, in fact. Any one of the techniques, suggestions, or ideas in this section may do it for you. Any one may be the key that opens whole new worlds of aliveness, enthusiasm, and health.

Yours may be a combination lock that requires five keys, or ten, or twenty, or you may need everything in this book—and a hundred more techniques you discover on your own—to open the doors to your inner kingdom of joy, self-confidence, and happiness. Whatever it takes is whatever it takes.

Whatever it takes, the results will be worth it.

I'm going to begin by talking about death (eeek!) and the fear of death (eeek! eeek!). After that, luncheon is served. I'm laying out a smorgasbord of positivity.

Mostly, these suggestions will seem familiar because they're good old-fashioned common sense. I tend to be pragmatic—if something works, I use it; if not, I try something else. What I pass along to you was learned through my own process of trial and error. It is from a firm—and substantial—foundation of mistakes that I offer these suggestions.

There's no particular order to this gathering of ideas. No "Do this first, then this, then this." You are the architect of your cure. Naturally, like all good architects, you'll be consulting with other professionals—but the Master Plan is in your hands.

Choosing the pathway to your cure is easy—just

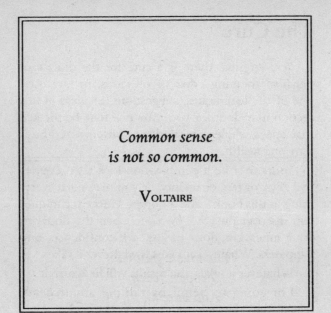

Common sense
is not so common.

VOLTAIRE

follow your heart.

Please don't just *read* this book; *use* it. *Do* some things. *Try* them. *Find out* if a technique works for you—if it produces uplifting results. If so, *do* it some more. If not, *throw* it away. Try something else. This book contains a lot of things to try.

And now, ***The Cure.***

The music that can
deepest reach,
And cure all ill,
is cordial speech.

EMERSON

One who longs for death
is miserable,
but more miserable
is he who fears it.

JULIUS WILHELM ZINCGREF
1628

If I could drop dead right now,
I'd be the happiest man alive!

SAMUEL GOLDWYN

Death 101 (Part One)

This is a crash course in death. Why death? Shouldn't we be focusing on *positive stuff*? Yes, but first we have to explore the motivation *behind* doing all the positive stuff.

If you're going to think more positively because you fear death, then whatever you do—no matter how positive—will be an affirmation of that fear.

As long as fear is looming large, you will probably continue with the process of improvement. As soon as fear no longer threatens, you may revert to old habits. When, for example, the medical cure for your illness is discovered, there's no need to fear dying of it; therefore, you may feel you can return to your former habits of negative thinking. That will, of course, recreate the intention to die, and another method of death is likely to appear.

If you use the techniques given in this book because you want to live a fuller, happier, more joyful, and productive life, then you have a foundation that will hold firm. If you undertake these methods as a frantic attempt to outmaneuver the Grim Reaper, the whole venture is, to paraphrase Henry Higgins, "doomed before you even take the vow."

Not that you must be perfectly calm in the face of your own mortality before any of these suggestions will work. Not at all. Fear can be a good motivator to *start* something. But fear must gradually be replaced with the desire for a positive result if long-term progress is to be made.

It also feels better—running *from* something you

Once you accept
your own death,
all of a sudden
you're free to live.
You no longer care
about your reputation.
You no longer care
except so far as your life
can be used tactically
to promote a cause
you believe in.

SAUL ALINSKY

fear is far less enjoyable than running *toward* something you desire.

Running from fear only strengthens fear—you are demonstrating that fear has power over you. Fear must be faced and gone through. The procedure of "getting over" fear is succinctly stated in the title of the book *Feel the Fear and Do It Anyway.* (A book I haven't read, so I can't recommend it, but it does have a great title.) Only then do we learn the truth of fear—that fear is merely an illusion, not a real thing.

Before I continue with my short course on death, let's stroll over to the next classroom and overhear a few pointers on fear.

The late F. W. H. Myers
used to tell
how he asked a man at a dinner table
what he thought would happen to him
when he died.
The man tried to ignore the question,
but, on being pressed, replied:
"Oh well, I suppose
I shall inherit eternal bliss,
but I wish you wouldn't talk about
such unpleasant subjects."

BERTRAND RUSSELL

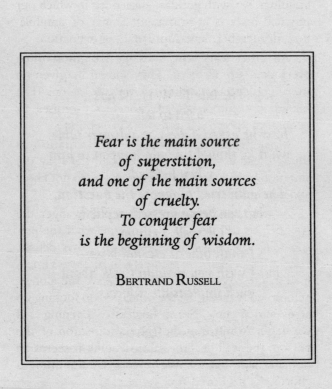

Fear is the main source
of superstition,
and one of the main sources
of cruelty.
To conquer fear
is the beginning of wisdom.

BERTRAND RUSSELL

Fear 101

There are some things it's good to have a healthy fear of—drinking poisons, leaping off tall buildings, sex with gorillas—situations in which our physical body is in imminent danger of annihilation, dismemberment, mutilation, or extinction.

All other fears—the ones we face most often every day—are illusions. They should be given no more credence or authority over our actions than television commercials, election-year promises, or people who try to sell us flowers in airports.

Most people approach a fearful situation as though fear were some sort of wall. Let's say the situation is walking up to someone we do not know and saying, "Hello."

As we think about approaching the stranger, the wall begins to form. As we imagine what the person may say in response, the wall grows denser. (The other person's response is almost always imagined in the negative: "Would you leave me alone!" Seldom do we imagine the other person looking up at us and singing "Some Enchanted Evening.") If we begin to move in the general direction of the person, the wall becomes almost solid. It seems an impenetrable barrier. We turn away, humming a chorus of "If I Loved You."

But the wall of fear *is not real.*

Fear as a barrier is an illusion. We have, however, been trained to treat this illusion as though it were real. This belief served us well in our childhood years. Our parents taught us to be afraid of

I'm not afraid to die.
I just don't want to be there
when it happens.
It is impossible
to experience
one's death objectively
and still carry a tune.

WOODY ALLEN

Life does not cease to be funny
when people die
any more than it ceases to be serious
when people laugh.

GEORGE BERNARD SHAW

everything new. This was—at that time—good advice. We were too young to know the difference between the legitimately dangerous and the merely exciting.

When we grew old enough to know the difference, however, no one ever taught us to take risks, explore new territories, and treat fear as energy for doing and learning new things. Fear as a reason *not* to do should be tucked away with all those other cozy childhood myths—Santa Claus, the Easter Bunny, and the Tooth Fairy. (The Tooth Fairy was particularly hard to let go of.)

If fear is not a wall, what is it? It's a feeling, that's all. It will not (cannot) keep you from physically moving toward something *unless you let it.* It may act up and it may kick and scream. It may make your stomach feel like the butterfly cage at the zoo. But it cannot stop you. You stop you.

The fear of meeting people, for example, is a particularly silly fear. Given that it's in a place where they're not going to slug you (Hell's Angels bars are not recommended), the worst that can happen is that someone will reject you. You are left with rejection. If you don't try, however, you have rejected yourself, and are left with exactly the same thing as if you had tried and failed—nothing.

If you do try, however, you may get what you want.

Even if you get rejected, you'll learn more from the experience than if you had never tried. You may learn, for example, that certain ways of approaching certain people in certain situations work better than others. We can learn as much (sometimes more) by what doesn't work as by what does. If we don't explore all the ways that *really* do and don't work, we are left with only the untested techniques from our imagination and what seems to work in the movies.

As Dr. Melba Colgrove once said: "Anything that's worth having is worth asking for. Some say yes and some say no."

To overcome a fear, here's all you have to do: realize the fear is there, and do the action you fear anyway. Move—physically—in the direction of what you want. Expect the fear to get worse. It will. After you do several times the thing you fear, the

You gain strength,
courage and confidence
by every experience
in which you really stop
to look fear in the face.
You are able to say to yourself,
"I lived through this horror.
I can take the next thing
that comes along."
You must do the thing
you think you cannot do.

ELEANOR ROOSEVELT

fear will be less. Eventually, it goes away.

Fear is something to be moved through, not something to be turned from. In fact, if you feel carefully, you'll discover that the only difference between fear (a supposedly negative emotion) and excitement (a reputedly positive emotion) is what we choose to call it. The sensation is exactly the same. We just add a little "Oh, no!" to fear and a little "Oh, boy!" to excitement, that's all.

Fear, then, can be seen for what it truly is—the energy to do your best in a new situation.

So, with that in mind, let's return to death.

("Oh, no!" "Oh, boy!")

People living deeply
have no fear of death.

Anais Nin

For certain is death
for the born
And certain is birth
for the dead;
Therefore over the inevitable
Thou shouldst not grieve.

BHAGAVAD GITA
2:27

Death and taxes
and childbirth!
There's never
any convenient time
for any of them.

SCARLETT O'HARA

Death 101 (Part Two)

If you think about it, the fear of death is one of the most useless fears we have. Dying is one of the few things that all of us will, sooner or later, do.

If we're going to be afraid of death, we might as well be afraid of breathing or gravity or *I Love Lucy* reruns or any of the other inevitabilities of life.

Unless we fully accept the inevitability of death, it's hard to enjoy this interval called life. ("This strange interlude," as Eugene O'Neill called it.) In other words, unless we get over our fear of death, we'll never really appreciate life. Unless it's okay to die, we'll never really live.

Someone I know was captured during a war and sentenced to death. He was put in a cell with a window facing the execution ground. Day after day, hour after hour, he watched his comrades marched before a wall and shot. He had no idea when his turn would come. It went on for six weeks. The war ended and he was released. Although he's one of the busiest people I know, he's also one of the calmest. He knows that, no matter what, the worst thing that can happen to him is that he'll die, and he's already faced that fear and come to terms with it.

Take a good look at your fear of death. Let yourself experience the fear. Find out what the fear's all about. Explore the many beliefs humans have about what happens after death. Are these really so terrible? There are, in fact, only three primary beliefs in our culture about what happens to

Death is nothing to us,
since when we are,
death has not come,
and when death has come,
we are not.

EPICURUS
341–270 B.C.

O death,
where is thy sting?
O grave,
where is thy victory?

I CORINTHIANS
15:55

us after death. Let's explore each of them.

> ***DEATH IS IT, THE END, FINITO.*** As soon as the blood stops flowing to the brain, we have no more experience. Our time here on Earth—which is wholly biological and nothing else—is over.

If this is what happens after death, we have nothing to worry about. Everything we experience is bioelectrical-chemical reactions, and when it stops, it stops. Our fear of death makes no more sense than the glow in a light bulb worrying about when the power is switched off. When the light is out, the light is out. Period. The end. Nothing.

IT'S HEAVEN OR HELL (OR MAYBE PURGATORY) FOREVER. When we die, we are judged by God and placed in one of three places: heaven (good), hell (bad), or (in at least one popular belief) purgatory (certainly not as good as heaven, but not as bed as hell).

If this is your belief, then you might consider life-threatening illness as a loving message from God: "Prepare yourself for Paradise." You may prepare yourself so well, in fact, and become so close to God, that God might ask, "Do me a favor?" and you'll say, "Sure. What?" and God may say, "Stick around another eighty years and continue to share the joy of Spirit with everyone."

WE KEEP COMING BACK UNTIL WE LEARN WHAT WE NEED TO KNOW. The Soul (who we really are) never dies; only the physical body dies. If the Soul has not learned all it needed to learn in one body, it picks up another (at birth) and continues with its education. This is generally known as "reincarnation" and is the most popular belief about life and death worldwide—although not so popular in the United States.

If this is the way things are, we have nothing to worry about. Death is like going from one room to another in a house, or taking off a suit and putting on a bathrobe (silk, with Alfred E. Newman's and my personal motto, "What? Me Worry?" embroidered on the pocket). Death is then a rest stop, a changing room, a summer vacation between semesters.

Either death is a state of nothingness
and utter unconsciousness, or,
as men say,
there is a change and
migration of the soul
from this world to another.
Now if death be
of such a nature,
I say that to die is to gain;
for eternity is then only
a single night.

PLATO

Nothing can happen
more beautiful than death.

WALT WHITMAN

Some say death is such a wonderful experience that the news must be kept from us or we'd all be killing ourselves just to get there. Of course, if we could fully perceive the joys of The Other Side, then we'd also know why we're here in the first place, so we wouldn't kill ourselves after all.

Take the time to conquer your fear of death. You can still live to be a hundred, and the years between now and then will be happier, healthier, and more exciting. And when it comes time to die, well, *bon voyage.*

Death is no more than passing
from one room into another.
But there's a difference for me, you know.
Because in that other room
I shall be able to see.

HELEN KELLER

To be, or not to be: that is the question:
Whether 'tis nobler in the mind to suffer
The slings and arrows of outrageous fortune,
Or to take arms against a sea of troubles,
And by opposing end them? To die: to sleep;
No more; and, by a sleep to say we end
The heartache and the thousand natural shocks
That flesh is heir to, 'tis a consummation
Devoutly to be wished. To die, to sleep;
To sleep: perchance to dream: ay, there's the rub;
For in that sleep of death what dreams may come,
When we have shuffled off this mortal coil,
Must give us pause. There's the respect
That makes calamity of so long life;
For who would bear the whips and scorns of time,
The oppressor's wrong, the proud man's contumely,
The pangs of disprized love, the law's delay,
The insolence of office, and the spurns
That patient merit of the unworthy takes,
When he himself might his quietus make
With a bare bodkin? who would fardels bear,
To grunt and sweat under a weary life,
But that the dread of something after death,
The undiscovered country from whose bourn
No traveler returns, puzzles the will,
And makes us rather bear those ills we have
Than fly to others that we know not of?

SHAKESPEARE
HAMLET

Suicide
(an optional chapter)

In time, life takes care of death; we don't need to help it along. That's why this is an optional chapter. Still, a discussion of suicide can be useful—as much to point out its life-affirming aspects as its death-hastening ones.

We can consciously end our life almost any time we choose. This ability is an endowment—like laughing and blushing—given to no other animal. Although suicide gives us the power of personal destruction, it also provides the power of personal life affirmation.

In any given moment, by *not* exercising the option of suicide, we are *choosing* to live.

Many people have put suicide in a forbidden-under-any-circumstances category because they were taught to, not because it was thought through. Blind obedience to custom robs these people of the option to *choose* life. (I am not referring, of course, to those who have made a religious, spiritual, or philosophical decision based on extensive soul-searching, but to those who thoughtlessly accept this cultural taboo.)

As this is an optional chapter, please allow me to state my personal views on suicide. In so doing, I do not wish to challenge your views on the subject. Something as precious as our life must be an individual, personal, and carefully considered choice. I'm just chatting with you here, friend to friend.

First, I think suicide should never be used to

I don't think suicide is so terrible.
Some rainy winter Sunday
when there's a little boredom,
you should always carry a gun.
Not to shoot yourself,
but to know exactly
that you're
always making a choice.

LINA WERTMULLER

escape the pain of loss. I have been through enough losses to know the feeling that life is no longer worth living; the anger, when I was certain only my death could adequately punish those who hurt me; and the hurt that made me believe: "I can't take this one moment longer!" And yet, I held in there—and I survived. Now I can't even remember the *names* of some of the people who had me contemplating suicide.

Since writing (with Drs. Colgrove and Bloomfield) *How to Survive the Loss of a Love* in 1976, I have received thousands of letters telling me of losses so tragic I cannot even comprehend the pain the people went through. Yet each of them survived, and each took the time to write a letter saying so, asking me to pass on the message that has been passed on from one survivor to another throughout history: you *will* survive.

I am reminded of the dialogue between Zorba and his young friend, a writer:

> ZORBA: Why do the young die? Why does anybody die?
>
> WRITER: I don't know.
>
> ZORBA: What is the use of all your damn books, then? If they don't tell you that, what the hell do they tell you?
>
> WRITER: They tell me of the agony of men who cannot answer questions like yours.

Often we don't know *why* a loss happens—especially when it happens to the young or innocent—but we can hold firm to the truth (often forgotten in times of loss) that we *will* survive.

Following a loss, *thoughts* of suicide are a *natural part* of the healing process. *Acting* on those thoughts, however, is never advisable, even when the losses cause inevitable and perhaps permanent changes in one's life—such as major financial loss or physical disability. Just because we won't have the *same* life as before is, in my estimation, no reason to end life.

When, then, would I consider suicide? When death is inevitable and the quality of life has become unbearable.

Please understand that, even at this point, I do not *recommend* suicide to others; I am simply saying

Human life consists in mutual service. ¶ No grief, pain, misfortune or "broken heart" is excuse for cutting off one's life while any power of service remains. ¶ But when all usefulness is over, when one is assured of an unavoidable and imminent death, it is the simplest of human rights to choose a quick and easy death in place of a slow and horrible one.

CHARLOTTE PERKINS GILMAN

this is the point at which I would *consider* it for myself. Whether I would do it or not I do not know.

Does considering suicide under these particular circumstances run counter to the message of this book? I think not. We all must die some time, and some of us will die from diseases. This is not a book promising (or even recommending) physical immortality. This is a book for those who may have found life painful at some point and created an intention to die, an intention that may now be manifesting in a life-threatening illness. Facing death in all its forms—including at one's own hand—can help us live more fully *now.* Living more fully now can help reverse an intention to die, and the method of death (the disease) can thus be reversed along with it.

Hearing that we have a life-threatening illness is a loss—even if we are quite certain we can overcome it. Overcoming takes work—work that we had not anticipated or planned for. Some of our best-laid *other* plans, then, will have to go *a-gley.** But merely *getting* the news of a life-threatening illness is no reason to go shopping for a tank of carbon monoxide.

In 1988, I was "spiritually diagnosed" by a charlatan named John-Roger as having not one but *two* life-threatening illnesses: tuberculosis *and* AIDS. Alas, at the time I believed John-Roger actually had some spiritual connection and could accurately predict such things. He gave me nine months to live. (Generous of him, huh?)

As it turns out, he was just manipulating me (using my belief in his spiritual sovereignty) into putting his name on books I was writing (such as an earlier edition of this book) and giving him all the money. He told me he would keep me alive and healthy as long as the books kept rolling out and the money kept rolling in (to him).**

*An old Scottish word taken from Robert Burns's 1785 phrase: "The best laid schemes o' mice and men / Gang aft a-gley." *A-gley* means, essentially, "down the toilet."

**My fifteen-year sojourn with John-Roger is detailed—with humor and photographs—in my book *LIFE 102: What to Do When Your Guru Sues You.* Available at bookstores or call 1-800-LIFE-101.

> *Beware!*
> *To touch these wires*
> *is instant death.*
> *Anyone found doing so*
> *will be prosecuted.*
>
> SIGN AT A RAILROAD STATION
>
> *Who knows?*
> *Maybe my life belongs to God.*
> *Maybe it belongs to me.*
> *But I do know one thing:*
> *I'm damned if it belongs*
> *to the government.*
>
> ARTHUR HOPPE

His diagnosis (thankfully false—I have neither tuberculosis nor AIDS) allowed me to see how I would react to hearing I had nine months to live. My reaction? I seriously considered committing suicide *that day.*

The diagnosis itself was a loss, and I was responding to the pain and fear of *that.* I had no symptoms, naturally, because I didn't even have the diseases. But I *thought* I did, and that thought produced a loss which I responded to with thoughts of suicide. I am glad I did not follow through on those thoughts. I see now it would have been a mistake.

Even if the diagnosis had come from a competent medical doctor—or series of them—I would still not consider that a reason to end my life. (Change it, certainly; end it, no.) As we'll explore later in the book, no diagnosis is foolproof, and predictions of "time remaining"—even from the most knowledgeable experts—are just "best guesses" based on statistical averages. They may or may not apply to you or me. Only time will tell.

Whatever *my* views on suicide are, however, I do not want to force them on someone else, nor do I want someone else's views enforced upon me—especially by law.

Laws that prohibit the terminally ill from obtaining a peaceful, painless death are barbaric. That early death, of course, must *always* be the patient's choice—or the choice of someone designated by the patient (in writing and witnessed) to make that choice for the patient should he or she become mentally incapacitated. To force people to die slow, agonizing deaths when they are ready to die, willing to die, and wanting to die—but cannot do it themselves due to physical incapacity—is inhuman. And yet, that's the law in almost every state in this country.

Many people do not so much fear death as the *pain* of dying. If we choose to consider suicide an option, we know that the length and degree of our suffering will be—as it always has been—our personal choice.

I must leave all that!
Farewell, dear paintings
that I have loved so much and
which have cost me so much.

CARDINAL JULES MAZARIN

1661

If you don't go
to other men's funerals
they won't go to yours.

CLARENCE DAY

How to Die

The final lesson in my crash course on dying is ten suggestions on how to die. You can file these away until you need them.

1. Get things in order. Things you don't want people to see? Destroy them. Things you want people to have? Give them away. ("Let the season of giving be yours and not that of your inheritors"—Gibran, *The Prophet.)* Pay debts. Make notes of what you've done. Make it easy for whomever you choose to take care of things after.

2. Make a will. Of things that weren't given away, decide who gets what. Put it in writing. Make it legal. Choose an executor. Do you want to be cremated or buried? Decide what kind of funeral—if any—you want. Bette Davis said, "I don't want donations made to any charities in my name. I want lots and lots of flowers!" If that's how you feel about it, say so. In writing. And don't forget to make out a "living will" if you don't want extraordinary medical measures used to prolong your life.

3. Say good-bye. Good-byes don't all have to take place on your deathbed. You can say good-bye to people, and then see them every day for the next fifty years. Tell people what you would want them to know if you never saw them again. Give them the opportunity to do the same. Usually, it boils down to simply, "I love you."

4. Don't spend time with people you don't want to spend time with. When people hear someone is dying, they all want to make a pilgrimage. Many of

On no subject are our ideas
more warped and pitiable than on death.
Let children walk with nature,
let them see the beautiful blendings
and communions of life and death,
their joyous inseparable unity,
as taught in woods and meadows,
plains and mountains
and streams of our blessed star,
and they will learn that
death is stingless indeed,
and as beautiful as life,
and that the grave has no victory,
for it never fights.
All is divine harmony.

JOHN MUIR

these people you haven't seen in years and, if you lived another hundred years, would probably never see again. Say good-bye on the phone. Tell them you're just not up to a visit. You don't owe anyone anything.

5. Spend time alone. Reflect on your life. Make peace with it. Come to terms with it. Forgive yourself for everything. Learn what you can from what's happened, and let the rest go. Mourn the loss of your life. Come to a place of understanding and acceptance. You may be surprised how quickly you get there.

6. Enjoy yourself. Make a list of all the movies you want to see or see again. Rent them. Watch them. Read the books you never got around to. Listen to your favorite music.

7. Relax. Sleep. Do nothing. Lie around. Recline. Goof off.

8. Pray. Listen. It is said people are closest to God at birth and at death. If you missed God the first time around, catch the diety on the return. Whatever inspirational or spiritual beliefs you hold dear, hold them even closer. You are being held close, too.

9. Enjoy each moment. Appreciate what is, here and now. That is where eternity is found. You may only have a few here-and-now moments, but it's a few more than most people will ever have.

10. When it's time to go, go. Let go. Say one last good-bye and mean it. Say good-bye so completely that you'll never want to come back, you'll never even look back. All the good you take with you. The rest is good-bye and moving on.

Do most of these sound more like suggestions for living than for dying? That's because they are. The best way to die is to live each moment fully. Then, when the time for death comes—be it next week or fifty years from now—it's just another event in an already eventful life.

Prayer indeed is good,
but while calling
on the gods
a man should himself
lend a hand.

HIPPOCRATES

Part II: THE CURE

ONE:

ACT-CENTUATE THE POSITIVE

I know *accentuate* is not spelled "act-centuate." I just wanted to stress the need for *act*-ion. Some say, "To do is to be." Others say, "To be is to do." I tend to agree with Francis Albert Sinatra: "Do, be, do, be, do." I'll even stoop to jokes stolen from coffee mugs to emphasize the need for *action.*

I'll pull out songs from the forties, too—such as "Ac-Cent-Tchu-Ate the Positive," a song written by Johnny Mercer (lyrics) and Harold Arlen (music) during the darkest days of World War II. It became a theme song for an entire country actively involved in *doing something*. (Winning a war.) They did it.

And so can you.

The apprehension
of the good
Gives but the greater
feeling to the worse.

SHAKESPEARE

The Case against "Positive Thinking" (Part One)

As you may have gathered from what you've read thus far, I am obviously against negative thinking. So, if I'm against negative thinking, I must therefore be in favor of positive thinking.

No.

No?!

No.

Positive thinking, as taught and practiced by many people, is not as dangerous as negative thinking, but it has its downside.

Thoughts are powerful, more powerful than most people give them credit for being. They are not, however, *all-powerful.* There is more to reality than just thoughts.

For example, try to turn a page in this book without doing anything physical. Don't touch it or move it; just hold the book still and try to turn a page with your thoughts. Or try to think a glass of water to your mouth, or pick up the phone and think-dial a number. You see what I mean? Thoughts are powerful, but not all-powerful. There's a lot of power in our physical abilities, too.

When some people first discover how powerful thoughts are, they begin worshiping the mind. They deny the truth of what's actually happening for a mental image they find more pleasant. This creates a separation between the positive thinker and reality. This separation can be the cause of dis-

I am not a pessimist;
to perceive evil
where it exists is,
in my opinion,
a form of optimism.

ROBERTO ROSSELLINI

orientation, confusion and, eventually, illness.

As an example, suppose you had a small cut on your forehead. The positive thinker might say, "Your head is fine. The cut is only an illusion. *Think* of your forehead as healed. *Imagine* your forehead perfect."

I would probably say, "Oh, you cut your forehead. Let's wipe the blood off, put on some antiseptic, and bandage it." While I was physically taking care of what needed to be done, I might suggest you hold a positive image of the cut healing quickly. But most likely I'd ask, "What happened?" because there's a certain therapeutic quality in talking about the incident. Also, I'd be curious to know.

And, there may be a lesson in the accident—if nothing else, the way to keep it from happening again.

If I'm not in favor of positive thinking, what am I in favor of? If I'm not in favor of negative thinking, I must be in favor of *something* positive.

I am.

I recommend *focusing on the positive.*

Why is it no one ever
sent me yet
One perfect limousine,
do you suppose?
Ah no, it's always
just my luck to get
One perfect rose.

Dorothy Parker

Focusing on the Positive

In any given moment, there is ample evidence to prove that life is a bed of thorns or a garden of roses. How we feel about life depends on where we place our attention, that is, what we focus upon.

Did you ever notice that every time you are given a rose, the stem is covered with thorns? (If you take the thorns off, the flower wilts more quickly. Florists know this, which is why they leave the thorns on.) Do you say, "Why are you giving me this stick with thorns on it?" Of course not. You admire the beauty of the rose. Even if you prick yourself in your enthusiasm, it never seems to hurt—you are too engrossed in appreciating the rose and the person who gave it to you.

Right now, in this moment, without moving from where you are, you can find ample evidence to prove your life is a miserable, depressing, terrible burden, or you can find evidence to prove your life is an abundant, joyful, exciting adventure.

Let's start with the negative. Look at all the imperfections around you. No matter how good anything is, it could be better, couldn't it? Look for dirt, disorder, and dust. See all the things that need cleaning, repairing, and replacing? An endless array of clutter, chaos, and catastrophe assaulting your senses. And all those *damn* alliterations in this paragraph. Dis-gusting.

Now, explore the same environment with an attitude of gratitude and appreciation.

Look around the same area you just surveyed

One should sympathize
with the joy, the beauty,
the color of life—
the less said about life's sores
the better.

OSCAR WILDE

and find the good. You can start with whatever you're sitting or lying on. It's probably softer than a concrete floor. Look at all the other objects you use but take for granted—glasses (both seeing and drinking), tables, windows, the walls and ceiling sheltering you from the elements. Consider the wonder of the electric light. A hundred years ago, you would have to have been very rich or very lucky to have had even one. And you probably have more than one—and a TV and a radio and many other electronic marvels.

What around you do you find aesthetically pleasing? A painting you haven't really looked at in years? The detail work on the clothes you're wearing? A flower? A vase? Wallpaper? Carpet? When was the last time you took a moment to appreciate *colors?*

Did you notice that you tended to feel better when you focused on the positive things in your surroundings? The process of focusing on the positive to produce more positive feelings works the same with things even more intimate than your surroundings—your body, for example.

If you look for all the things wrong with the body, boy, are you going to find them. Pains here, bumps there, rough spots here, too much fat there—the list goes on and on (and, as we get older, goes on and on and on and on).

But take a look at all that's right with your body. Even if you have a pain in your left foot, you can be thankful there's not one in your right. How about all those processes we take for granted? Digestion, circulation, respiration, assimilation, thinking—yes, we think without having to even think about it. And let's not forget the five senses. Some people take them so much for granted they can't name all five without thinking, "Let's see, what's the fifth one?"

It's as though there were two attorneys in your mind, one gathering evidence for "Life is Awful" and the other gathering evidence for "Life is Wonderful." You're the judge and can rule out any evidence you choose. Your decision is final. Which judicial ruling do you suppose would lead to more joy, happiness, peace, ease, and health?

To focus on the positive is not to disregard cer-

Try thinking of love
or something.

CHRISTOPHER FRY

tain warning signals of a negative nature that, if ignored, eventually lead to inconveniences at best and disaster at worst. (If we use these "negative" signals to avoid disaster, then they're not so negative after all. Some even call them guardian angels.)

Let's say you're driving down the freeway and the little light goes on, telling you you're running out of gas. I do not suggest ignoring that bit of "negativity" and focusing on how wonderful it is that none of the other warning lights is on. I suggest you get some gas.

Here, by the way, is where negative thinking comes in. The negative reality is that you're low on gas. Negative thinking begins the litany, "I wonder if I'm going to run out of gas before I reach the next station. What will I do if that happens? I'm in the middle of nowhere. What if some highway robbers get me? If I do get to a gas station, will it be the kind I have credit cards for? I bet it will be more expensive than in town. I bet it will be self-service and the pump will be dirty and my hands will smell funny after. I knew I should have filled up in town. Why am I so lazy and stupid?" Etc., etc., etc.

During this inner tirade (which, for accomplished negative thinkers, takes place in under five seconds) the driver, in his or her anxiety, usually speeds up, which only wastes gas.

What I suggest is this: take note of the negative information, decide what to do about it (whatever corrective action seems to be in order) and return to focusing on the positive (in this case the music, the scenery, the passengers) while working on eliminating the negative.

With medical conditions, it's good to keep track of symptoms, but it does no good to dwell on them. The positive thinker might deny the early symptoms of a disease, making a cure more difficult. The negative thinker might turn every mosquito bite into a killer bee sting.

Positive focusers take a middle road. They note symptoms accurately so they can be reported to their health-care provider. They make an appointment. Beyond that, there's no point in dwelling on the symptoms, so they turn their attention to things more positive.

While we're considering the idea that there is

We are wide-eyed
in contemplating the possibility
that life may exist elsewhere
in the universe,
but we wear blinders
when contemplating
the possibilities
of life on earth.

NORMAN COUSINS

sufficient evidence in any given moment to prove that life is wonderful or that life is terrible, let's take a look at how this works even closer to home: in our memories of the past and our anticipation of the future.

Here, too, we can muddle in the negative: "Tommy wouldn't play with me when I was six." "I have to go to the dentist next week, and I hate the dentist."

Or, we can do positive thinking: "I'm winning the Oscar this year," when we've never been in a movie. "I'm going hiking and camping next week," when we've just had major surgery. "I have so many wonderful friends," when the phone hasn't rung in two weeks.

Or, we could try focusing on the good memories that actually happened and on realistic plans we look forward to with pleasure. "That movie on TV last night was so good." "Helen's coming to visit tomorrow; that will be nice." "The book I ordered should be arriving any day."

Yes, it's good to "live in the moment," but who does that all the time? As long as you're living in memories of the past and projections of the future, you might as well make them *happy* memories and *joyful* projections.

I will be giving some techniques later in which you can let your imagination run positively wild. There can be great value in this. What I'm talking about here is day-to-day, ordinary thinking. In my view, negative thinkers need to get their minds out of the sewer and positive thinkers need to get their heads out of the clouds.

Have I made a clear distinction between positive thinking and focusing on the positive? It's a subtle but important difference. Positive thinking imagines any wonderful thing at all, no matter how unrelated it is to the actual events of one's life. Focusing on the positive starts with what's real, what's actually taking place, and moves from there in a joyful direction.

If you spend all your time in a positive future, when will you appreciate the present? The present is the future you dreamed of long ago. Enjoy it.

"Optimism," said Candide,
"is a mania for
maintaining that
all is well
when things
are going badly."

VOLTAIRE

The Case against "Positive Thinking" (Part Two)

There is a story told of a Master who saw a dead dog decaying in the road. His disciples tried to keep the unsightly animal from him, but the Master saw the unfortunate animal and said, "What pearly white teeth." Even amid stench and decay, there was still something beautiful to behold.

The Master did not—as some positive thinkers might—say the dog was "only sleeping." The Master did not throw a stick and say, "Here, Rover, fetch!" The Master first perceived the reality and then found something good about it.

Positive thinkers sometimes use positive thinking to justify their inability to accept the moment. They have a long list of "shoulds," and, unless reality measures up to their imagined state of perfection (which it almost never does), they retreat into positive thoughts, affirming that, thanks to their thoughts, the future conditions of the world will be better for everyone.

In other words, some people use positive thinking as a holier-than-thou-sounding form of denial.

A major problem with positive thinking and illness—especially life-threatening illness—is: what about the illness? If you are told to positively think yourself healthy and then get sicker, you may add personal blame to the worsening illness. "If I had only thought *more* positively, I would be well by now. Where did I fail?"

An optimist may see
a light where there is none,
but why must the pessimist
always run to blow it out?

MICHEL DE SAINT-PIERRE

This is especially true of positive thinkers who tell stories of miracle cures. "If only you think positively, and believe, you, too, can have a miracle cure." Well, maybe, or maybe not.

It took a lot of negative thinking—decades in some cases—to bring on a life-threatening illness. Why should a week or two of positive thinking get rid of it?

Now, I'm all for miracles, and I've seen my share, but miracles can't be counted on. If they could, by definition, they wouldn't be miracles. I tend to follow the Pragmatic Creed: "Hope for the best, prepare for the worst, and shoot down the middle."

If you have a miraculous healing, wonderful! Take all the credit for it. If you have a slow, progressive recovery, great! If you have the usual series of ups and downs that life-threatening illnesses often go through, find *something* to be grateful for every day, every hour, every minute. Each time you find something, it will make you smile in your heart.

Positive thinking only puts a gap between where you are physically and where you think you "should" be. There are no "shoulds" to a life-threatening illness. You'll be happier, and probably heal faster, if you let go of as many "shoulds" as you can. (More on this later.)

Now I'd like to explore an area in which I take fundamental issue with positive thinkers—how to respond to loss. Positive thinkers might say, "There is no loss, only the opportunity for new experiences. Rejoice!" I say: loss hurts. It also infuriates. That's natural. That's human. To deny the pain and anger with an attitude of platitudes may do more harm than good.

The sound of her
silk skirt has stopped.
On the marble pavement dust grows.
Her empty room is cold and still.
Fallen leaves are piled against the doors.
Longing for that lovely lady
How can I bring my
aching heart to rest?

Han Wu-Ti

187–57 B.C.

ON THE DEATH OF HIS MISTRESS

Learn to Mourn

This is a lifetime of good-byes. As the years go on, you'll say good-bye to both people (through moving, change, or death) and things (youth, that semi-tight body you once had, hair, prized possessions). Eventually, you'll say good-bye to it all with your own death.

Learning to mourn, to grieve, to say a good good-bye, is an invaluable tool.

When a loss takes place, the mind, body, and emotions go through a process of healing as natural as the healing of a physical injury. Know that feeling lost, sad, angry, hurt, fearful, and tearful at good-byes is a natural part of the healing process.

We recover from loss in three distinct but overlapping phases. The first phase of recovery is *shock/denial/numbness;* the second, *fear/anger/depression;* the third, *understanding/acceptance/moving on.*

No matter what the loss—from a missed phone call to the death of a loved one—the body goes through the same three phases of recovery. The only difference is the *time* it takes to go through each stage and the *intensity* of the feelings at each point along the way.

When we first hear of a loss, our initial reaction is **shock/denial/numbness.** Often we say, "Oh, no!" We can't believe what we've heard. We go numb.

This ability to deny and go numb is a blessing. Catastrophic losses are too hard to take all at once. It has been suggested that the reason some people

Warm summer sun,
shine kindly here;
Warm northern wind,
blow softly here;
Green sod above,
lie light, lie light
Good-night, dear heart,
good-night, good-night.

MARK TWAIN

EPITAPH FOR HIS DAUGHTER

have slow, terminal illnesses as their method of dying is because it's going to take them a long time to say good-bye, and they want to do it right.

The next phase, **fear/anger/depression,** is the one most commonly associated with loss. We think we'll never love or be loved again (fear). We wail against the situations, people, things, and unkind fates that "caused" the loss (anger). We cry, we feel sad, we hurt, we don't want to go on (depression).

One of the toughest feelings to accept is anger at the one who is dying (even if it's yourself). "Why are you leaving me?!" a voice inside wants to know. To feel angry at someone for dying, or angry at yourself over your own death, is perfectly normal.

It's a natural stage of recovery that one must pass through. (Pass through—not remain in.)

Finally we come to **understanding/acceptance/moving on.**

We understand that loss is part of life. We accept the loss we suffered, and begin to heal. When healing is well under way, we move on to our next experiences.*

I put this information on grieving in the section "Act-centuate the Positive" because mourning is a positive human ability. It allows us the flexibility to adapt to change. It is not "negative" to feel pain, fear, and anger at loss. It's a natural, human response. The negativity enters when the process of healing is suppressed, glossed over, and denied.

Accept the process. Accept the numbness, the fear, the pain, the anger, the sadness, the tears, and, eventually, accept the healing.

Accepting the healing can be difficult. People may expect you to mourn longer than you find necessary, or they may want your mourning to "hurry up." People often offer comfort to ease their own discomfort. "There, there," they say, "everything's all right," when, in fact, everything is *not* all right.

Grieving must be done in its own time.

*The book *How to Survive the Loss of a Love* by Melba Colgrove, Ph.D., Harold H. Bloomfield, M.D., and me explains the process of healing in detail. Available at bookstores or call 1-800-LIFE-101.

We are healed
of a suffering
only by experiencing it
to the full.

MARCEL PROUST

To deny the reality that pain hurts only delays the healing process. Take the time to grieve, to mourn, to say a good good-bye. At the point of genuine understanding and acceptance of your own death (not just a mentally constructed understanding and acceptance) lies the ability to understand and accept the magnificence of life.

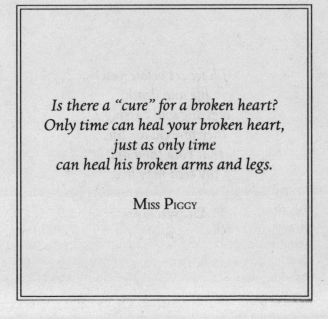

Is there a "cure" for a broken heart?
Only time can heal your broken heart,
just as only time
can heal his broken arms and legs.

Miss Piggy

I have set before you
life and death,
blessing and cursing:
therefore choose life,
that both thou and
thy seed may live.

DEUTERONOMY

30:19

Choose by Doing

It's time for you to make a choice. The choice I'm talking about is The Big Choice—to live or to die ("To be or not to be").

The problem is, there's a Catch-22 in making that kind of choice.

If deep down inside you no longer want to continue living—for whatever reasons—consciously knowing this can help you avoid a great deal of confusion, torment, and anguish. If you've put yourself on a plane headed for Cleveland, there's no point complaining to yourself and others, "I don't want to go to Cleveland."

If you have chosen to die, avoiding negative thinking is still important. Negative thinking contaminates "the moment," and between now and your death, you might as well enjoy every moment.

The irony is that when people finally "give up" and do appreciate the moment, they often realize that life can be a wonderful place. They see it wasn't life itself, but their *reaction* to life that was causing the dis-ease.

Then they sometimes begin a negative-thinking pattern of "I don't want to die after all," which, once again, pollutes the moment, which makes life less livable, so why live anyway, so I might as well die.

Other people, when asked, "Do you want to live or die?" say—at once and with great emotion—"I want to live!" These people may then spend so much time struggling against death that life be-

Destiny is not
a matter of chance,
it is a matter of choice;
it is not a thing
to be waited for,
it is a thing
to be achieved.

WILLIAM JENNINGS BRYAN

comes an agonizing battle, and some part of them again says, "Why bother?"

Can you see, then, the Catch-22 involved in a once-and-for-all decision to live or to die?

The decision to live or to die is not one that can be made once, and that's that. It is to be made in each moment. And that decision is demonstrated by *action.*

If you are taking part in life-destroying activities, wallowing in misery, and indulging in negative thinking, then—no matter what you *say*—I'd say you were, in that moment, choosing to die.

If you are actively involved in life-enhancing

activities and do them with a positive focus and enthusiasm,* I'd say in that moment you were choosing to live.

If you ask yourself in this moment, "Do I want to live or die?" I say, "Look at what you're doing, feeling, and thinking for the answer."

Are you doing all you can for your health, happiness, and positive focus? And are you doing it with an attitude of, "This *will* make me healthier, happier, and more positive," or are you moaning, "If I don't do all this damn healthy stuff I'm gonna die and I don't want to die so I'll do it"?

Take a frequent look at your thoughts, feelings, and activities. Set an alarm to go off at regular intervals—every hour, say. No matter what you're doing when the alarm goes off, stop and take an honest look at where you are and what you've been doing—mentally, emotionally, and physically—since the last alarm sounded.

If it's been life-supporting, joyful, and positive—congratulate yourself. If it hasn't you can "course-correct." Commercial aircraft, flying over water, are off course 95 percent of the time. Nevertheless, they still get to where they're going. The onboard navigational system is continually making infinitesimal course corrections. You can get to your goals this way, too—even if you're "off course" the vast

*The word *enthusiasm* comes from the Greek *en-theos,* which means "one *[en]* with God *[theos]*" or "inspired by God." I like to think of it as being "one with the energy of the Divine."

We should be careful
to get out of an experience
only the wisdom that is in it
and stop there;
lest we be like the cat
that sits down
on a hot stove lid.
She will never sit down
on a hot stove lid again
and that is well;
but also she will never
sit down on a cold one
any more.

MARK TWAIN

majority of the time.)

If your evaluation of the interval between alarms indicates some negativity—don't be surprised, don't get upset, just change it.

Being negative about being negative is one of the slickest traps negativity has. It seems as though you're agreeing that negative thinking is bad—so bad, in fact, that it's worth getting upset about it whenever it happens. Then when you discover you've been feeling bad about feeling bad, you feel bad about that. And on and on—or should I say down and down?

Let it go. Forgive yourself. Make whatever corrections seem necessary. Move on. (I'll be giving specific techniques for all of these later.)

As Woody Guthrie once said, "Take it easy, but take it."

*Until one is committed,
there is hesitancy,
the chance to draw back,
always ineffectiveness.
Concerning all acts of initiative
(and creation)
there is one elementary truth,
the ignorance of which
kills countless ideas and splendid plans:
That the moment one
definitely commits oneself,
then Providence moves too.
All sorts of things occur to help one
that would never otherwise have occurred.
A whole stream of events issues
from the decision,
raising in one's favor all manner
of unforeseen incidents
and meetings and material assistance,
which no man could have dreamed
would have come his way.
I have learned a deep respect
for one of Goethe's couplets:*

*"Whatever you can do,
or dream you can, begin it.
Boldness has genius,
power and magic in it."*

W. H. Murray

THE SCOTTISH HIMALAYAN EXPEDITION

Commit to Life

No matter what you *think* your decision about living or dying is, commit to life.

By committing to life, I don't mean committing to live another so many years. (How many years "should" we live anyway?) I mean, commit to living each moment fully, productively, joyfully. Commit to health, wealth, and happiness—not as a distant dream, but as a here-and-now reality.

You may not know fully *how* to do that yet, but "hows" are just methods. When the commitment is clear, an intention rises from that commitment, and the methods appear.

Rather than tell yourself, "I don't know how to fully live my life, so I can't commit," commit yourself to life and then set about discovering how to live.

All this can be summed up in one of my favorite phrases: "The willingness to do creates the ability to do." Be willing to live your life fully. The ability, methods, behaviors, and opportunities to do this will appear.

Then *do* them!

Never put off till
tomorrow what you can
do the day after tomorrow.

MARK TWAIN

Live Your Life *Now*

Don't put off living until you are "better." That's probably just the latest in a series of perfect reasons why you haven't fully lived up until now. ("I'll do it when I'm older." "I'll do it when I've learned more." "I'll do it when I have more money." "I'll do it when I find my soul mate." "I'll do it when I have the time." "I'll do it when . . .")

Start doing what you've always wanted to do *now*. Start enjoying each moment (by finding something enjoyable in it) *now*.

I'm not talking about executing every grand scheme your imagination has ever created. ("I've always wanted to be Ruler of the World.") I'm talking about overcoming the tendency to say, "When my life is better, then I'll be able to start focusing on positive things."

Start now.

We often form a habit of procrastination. Yes, we put off unpleasant activities, but we also tend to put off the enjoyable ones, too. We dole out pleasure, contentment, and happiness as though they were somehow rationed. The supply of these is limitless (as, by the way, is the supply of misery, pain, and suffering). We do the rationing ourselves.

If you look, you'll find all the perfect reasons why you shouldn't enjoy your life, why you should postpone enjoyment until certain things are different.

I say, the only thing that has to be different for you to enjoy your life is where you focus your at-

This is the true joy in life,
the being used for a purpose
recognized by yourself as a mighty one;
the being thoroughly
worn out before you are thrown
on the scrap heap;
the being a force of nature
instead of a feverish
selfish little clod
of ailments and grievances
complaining that the world
will not devote itself
to making you happy.

George Bernard Shaw

tention. Look for all the positive things taking place in and around you *right now*. As you find them, naturally you'll feel more joyful.

In life we have either reasons or results. If we don't have what we want (results), we usually have a long list of reasons why we don't have the results. We tend to rationalize (pronounced "rational lies"). All this is (a) a waste of energy and (b) a convincing argument that we can't have what we want, which becomes (c) another reason not to live.

I suggest that when you don't get what you want, rather than waste time and energy explaining why you don't have it, find another way to get it. If you can't find something positive about your environment, look again—with "fresh eyes." Try another point of view. Be creative. What good are you taking for granted? If you can't find anything, hold your breath. Within a few minutes, you'll *really* appreciate breathing.

Death is not
the greatest loss in life.
The greatest loss
is what dies inside us
while we live.

NORMAN COUSINS

Strengthen Your Intention to Live

The intention to live can be strengthened. You obviously have *some* intention to live, or you wouldn't be alive. (When people completely lose the intention to live, they fade very fast.)

Beyond that, you have gotten this far in a book that obviously affirms life. There is a self-selection process that takes place with personal-growth books: the people who aren't ready for them don't read them. Their intention *not* to grow is stronger than their intention to grow; therefore, the book is put down—literally and verbally—and not picked up again. So, since you've gotten this far in the book, I'd say your intention to live is rather strong.

The intention to live can be made stronger by a simple, but often uncomfortable, technique.

The technique is this—go to a mirror, look into your eyes, and say out loud, over and over: "I want to live."

What generally happens is that the many thoughts, feelings, and attitudes that created the intention *not* to live begin to surface. You may feel awkward, scared, unworthy, foolish, stupid, embarrassed, angry, tearful, enraged, or depressed. These are not easy to feel. The tendency is to avoid them, to stop the process.

I suggest you persevere. Behind all the fear, anger, unworthiness, and frustration is the natural intention to live—the love you feel for yourself and

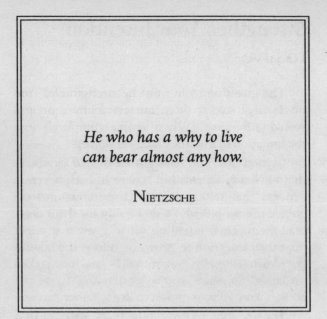

He who has a why to live
can bear almost any how.

NIETZSCHE

your life. When you connect with this love and affirm your intention to live, that intention becomes strengthened. Your will to live comes more alive.

You can do this process as often as you like, but start slowly. Set a timer and do it for, say, one minute. The next time, if one minute wasn't too bad, do it for two minutes. Then three. Then four.

Before you start, I suggest you ask a white light to surround, fill, and protect you, knowing only that which is for your highest good can take place while you do this process. (More on using the light later.)

Although uncomfortable at times, saying "I want

to live" will give you not only a strengthened intention to live, but also a diagram of your negativity. Is it mostly angry or mostly fearful? How do you convince yourself you're not worth it? What feelings and thoughts make you want to run from life? This process will answer those questions in a short period of time.

The goal of the process is to strengthen your intention to live—not necessarily to live for a certain numbers of years, but to live life fully in each moment.

If you take good care of the moment, the years will take care of themselves.

In spite of illness,
in spite even
of the archenemy sorrow,
one can remain alive
long past the usual
date of disintegration
if one is unafraid of change,
insatiable in intellectual curiosity,
interested in big things,
and happy in small ways.

Edith Wharton

The Willingness to Change

"The universe is change; our life is what our thoughts make it." Does that sound like some radical New Age thought to you? It wasn't even new when Marcus Aurelius Antoninus (121–180 A.D.) said it.

Conquering negative thinking may require some major changes, not just mental ones, but emotional and physical ones as well—what is generally known as your lifestyle. You may have to change your job, where you live, the city in which you live, friends, clothes, habits, all sorts of things. As the Koran (13:11) states, "God changes not what is in a people, until they change what is in themselves."

If you want to get better, be willing to change, be open to change, welcome and invite positive changes into your life. Remember, "There is nothing so permanent in life as change." More metaphysical psychobabble? Heraclitus said, "Nothing endures but change," around 500 B.C.

If you're in a rut, if you've grown accustomed to tolerating intolerable situations, change may not be comfortable and change may not be easy. It takes courage to take an honest look at one's life, discover what's no longer working, and then change it. Mark Twain reminds us, "Courage is mastery of fear—not absence of fear."

If you're faced with a life-threatening illness, you, frankly, have little choice. (I am assuming you have made the decision to live.)

Courage is the price
that life exacts
for granting peace.
The soul that knows it not,
knows no release
From little things;
Knows not the livid
loneliness of fear,
Nor mountain heights
where bitter joy can hear
The sound of wings.

AMELIA EARHART

What you have right now in life is the result of what you thought, felt, and did up to this time. If you want things to be different, to be better, you will have to change what you think, feel, and do.

It's as simple as that. Simple, but not necessarily easy. Not necessarily easy, but necessary. As Anais Nin noted, "Life shrinks or expands in proportion to one's courage."

Take a good, honest look at your life. Decide which things, situations, and people you tend to think most negatively about. Get rid of them. Yes, that one. The one about which you thought, "If I could only get rid of ______________, but I don't dare."

That one. Dare.
Throw it out, send them packing, walk away.
In other words, change.

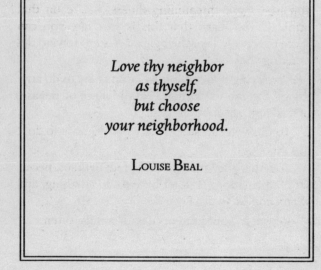

Love thy neighbor
as thyself,
but choose
your neighborhood.

LOUISE BEAL

You Don't *Have* to Do Anything

Whatever you do, do it because you choose to do it, not from any misguided sense of duty, or obligation.

Sometimes people need to be pushed to the brink before they realize that this life belongs to *them,* not to the demands and desires of others. If you have a life-threatening illness, you're on that brink. If you learn that this is *your* life, you can more effectively take the necessary steps toward de-brinking yourself.

Try saying this out loud: "I don't *have* to do anything." Say it a few times. Feel the sense of release, of freedom, of unburdening?

To this you can add: "And what I choose to do, I can do."

Together they make a nice (and, perhaps, necessary) affirmation: "I don't have to do anything, and what I choose to do, I can do."

Repeat it—out loud or in your mind—often.

I only have
"yes" men around me.
Who needs "no" men?

MAE WEST

Avoid People and Situations That Upset You

Those things, people, situations, and experiences you don't like—avoid them. Stay away. Walk away. Do something else.

Some might call this cowardly. I call it smart. The world is brimming with things, people, and experiences. We will never experience all of them if we live to be 10,000. So why not associate with the ones that naturally please you?

Yes, in some situations you will really want C, and in order to have C you must pass through A and B. In those cases, keep your eye on C. Keep reminding yourself *why* you're messing with A and B. Tell yourself that soon you'll be at C, and that C will be worth it.

Some examples of what to avoid: parties you don't want to go to, people you don't want to see, TV shows you don't want to watch (but think you should), movies everybody else has seen but hold no appeal for you, and so on.

This idea goes contrary to the "Confront It All" attitude of some self-help books. These books claim you grow through confrontation.

Yes, this is true. Tribulation and confrontation are great teachers. There is, however, quite enough tribulation presented to you *naturally*. You don't have to *seek* it. It will seek you, and some of it will be unavoidable. *That's* the time to practice acceptance, patience, and forbearance.

My father worked
for the same firm
for twelve years.
They fired him.
They replaced him
with a tiny gadget this big.
It does everything that my father does,
only it does it much better.
The depressing thing is
my mother ran out and bought one.

WOODY ALLEN

But if you can avoid the unpleasantness in the first place, by all means do so.

Style is knowing
who you are,
what you want to say,
and not giving a damn.

GORE VIDAL

Its name
is Public Opinion.
It is held in reverence.
It settles everything.
Some think it is
the voice of God.
Loyalty to petrified opinion never yet
broke a chain
or freed a human soul.

Mark Twain

Don't Worship the God of Other People's Opinion

Some people (let's face it: *most* people) do things they don't want to do (or don't do things they want to do) because they're afraid of what others might think or say about them.

I call this "worshiping the god of other people's opinion." The opinion of another becomes more important than our own wants, needs, and desires. As Charles Dudley Warner put it, "Public opinion is stronger than the legislature, and nearly as strong as the Ten Commandments."

We sacrifice much to the Great God of Opinion—happiness, self-worth, freedom. And that opinion is often inaccurate. "Truth is one forever absolute," wrote Wendell Phillips, "but opinion is truth filtered through the moods, the blood, the disposition of the spectator."

If your faith in yourself is strong, the opinion of others (which, often, they got from the opinion of others, who got it from the opinion of still others) is not so influential. As Thoreau said, "Public opinion is a weak tyrant compared with our own private opinion. What a man thinks of himself, that is what determines, or rather, indicates, his fate."

And Emerson:

> It is easy in the world to live after the world's opinion; it is easy in solitude to live after our own; but the great man is he who in the midst of the crowd keeps with perfect sweet-

You may talk of the tyranny
of Nero and Tiberius;
but the real tyranny
is the tyranny
of your next-door neighbor.
Public opinion is a permeating influence,
and it exacts obedience to itself;
it requires us
to think other men's thoughts,
to speak other men's words,
to follow other men's habits.

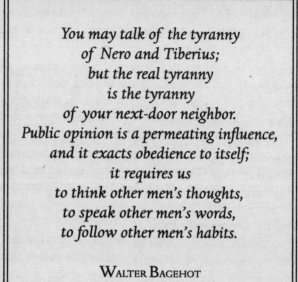

WALTER BAGEHOT

ness the independence of solitude.

Or, as George John Whyte-Melville stated more simply, "In the choice of a horse and a wife, a man must please himself, ignoring the opinion and advice of friends."

Of course, if you live in the freedom of your own thoughts and desires, you must also give the same freedom to others. Learn to accept the behavior of others that doesn't fit *your* opinions. (Such as the opinion that other people shouldn't have opinions about you.)

When you find yourself disapproving of someone, examine your opinions. Explore your list of "shoulds" and "shouldn'ts." See your opinion as merely opinion, not truth, and therefore not worth getting upset about.

Others' opinions of you and your opinions of others are the cause of a great deal of unnecessary negative thinking. (All negative thinking is unnecessary, but the guilt, fear, and resentment generated by opinions are particularly unnecessary.)

Learn, in fact, to relish the differences between people. Imagine how dull the world would be if we all thought, spoke, and acted the same. (Spend a summer in Maine sometime and see what I mean. On second thought, just take my word for it.)

"It were not best that we should all think alike," Mark Twain tells us. "It is difference of opinion that makes horse races."

Applaud freedom wherever it may appear. Learn to praise the idiosyncrasies, the eccentricities, the quirks, and the singularities of others.

It will help you to praise your own.

The return from your work
must be the satisfaction
which that work brings you
and the world's need of that work.
With this, life is heaven,
or as near heaven as you can get.
Without this
with work which you despise,
which bores you,
and which the world does not need
this life is hell.

William Edward Burghardt Du Bois

Do You Like Your Job?

Mr. Du Bois knew whereof he spoke: this message was given to his newly born great-grandson on the occasion of Mr. Du Bois's ninetieth birthday. He loved his work (he was, among other things, a founder of the NAACP) and didn't give up the ghost (or his work) until he was ninety-five.

Most people tend to think of the division between work and play the way Mark Twain saw it: "Work consists of whatever a body is obliged to do. Play consists of whatever a body is not obliged to do."

Some people, however, have discovered, as Shakespeare pointed out, "If all the year were playing holidays/To sport would be as tedious as to work." Or, as Jerome Klapka Jerome put it, "It is impossible to enjoy idling thoroughly unless one has plenty of work to do."

If you go to a job you despise, filled with things you hate to do, populated with people you don't like, find another job. "If you cannot work with love but only with distaste," Kahlil Gibran tells us, "it is better that you should leave your work."

Work takes up entirely too many of our waking hours for us to let it be a drudgery. "Every really able man, in whatever direction he work," wrote Emerson, "if you talk sincerely with him, considers his work, however much admired, as far short of what it should be."

I don't like work
—no man does—
but I like what is in work
the chance to find yourself.
Your own reality for yourself,
not for others;
what no other man
can ever know.

JOSEPH CONRAD

Get a job you enjoy. Before finding that job, you may have to find your career first—your calling, your avocation. "Blessed is he who has found his work," said Carlyle. "Let him ask no other blessedness."

"In order that people may be happy in their work," John Ruskin tells us, "these three things are needed: They must be fit for it. They must not do too much of it. And they must have a sense of success in it."

The idea of "work" implies there is something you do that you would not do without the reward. For most people, the reward is money. If you see the primary reward of work as money, I suggest you change the reward. Try loving, maybe. Or service—knowing you are providing people with something they really need. Or creative expression. ("That's entertainment!")

Sometimes you don't need to change your work—all you have to change is your *attitude* about work. Many good things have been said about work and working over the years: "Back of the job—the dreamer who's making the dream come true!" (Berton Bradley) "Work keeps us from three great evils: boredom, vice, and need" (Voltaire).

If you want to make your dreams come true, it will require work—doing something you're not necessarily thrilled about doing for the sake of a desired goal. Thomas Alva Edison told us, "There is no substitute for hard work."

Some people get religious about their work. The motto of the Benedictine order is, *"Orare est laborare, laborare est orare."* ("To pray is to work, to work is to pray.") Some, such as Carlyle, wax poetic: "All work is as seed sown; it grows and spreads, and sows itself anew." While others, such as Marcus Aurelius Antoninus, are downright gruff: "In the morning, when you are sluggish about getting up, let this thought be present: 'I am rising to a man's work.'"

I doubt if that thought would get me out of bed, but this one, from Gibran, might: "Work is love made visible."

If we think of work as a way of manifesting our love, then whatever job we do can be fulfilling.

> *I will work*
> *in my own way,*
> *according to the light*
> *that is in me.*
>
> LYDIA MARIA CHILD

If you're working at McDonald's, instead of thinking, "Oh god, not another busload of tourists with a Big Mac Attack!" you can think, "I'm helping provide food so that these people can enjoy their journey." Either way, you'll be wrapping the same number of burgers and boxing the same number of fries. With one attitude, however, you'll feel miserable; with the other, you'll feel useful.

So, if you hate your job, either change your job or change your attitude about the job. One or the other. Don't indulge in negative thinking about it.

You may say, "I can't afford to be without this job." If you're hopelessly mired in disliking the job, you can't afford to keep it.

If you have a life-threatening illness, regaining your health is Job #1. Until Job #1 is done, everything else is just filler.

The spirit of self-help is
the root of all genuine growth
in the individual;
and, exhibited in the lives of many,
it constitutes the true source
of national vigor and strength.
Help from without
is often enfeebling in its effects,
but help from within
invariably invigorates.

SAMUEL SMILES

1859

What You Do Strengthens You

A strong mental attitude is built the same way physical strength is gained—by repetition. Manipulating weights builds physical strength. Manipulating thoughts builds mental strength.

You may have a habit of negative thinking, built over years of repeating negative thoughts. This repetition has made the habit strong.

Focusing on the positive may not be as strong yet; it may, in fact, be a 97-pound weakling. The way to make it strong is to exercise it. Use it often. Unlike physical exercise, if you do too much positive focusing, you will seldom wake up sore the next morning.

Decide what you want to become stronger in. Become strong by doing it.

I am different
from Washington;
I have a higher, grander
standard of principle.
Washington could not lie.
I can lie, but I won't.

Mark Twain

Commitments

If you want to be happy, keep all of your commitments—and don't expect other people to keep any of theirs.

When we make a commitment, we "give our word." Giving something as valuable and as powerful as our word should not be taken lightly. When we don't fulfill our word, a part of us begins to mistrust ourselves. Over time, the effects of broken commitments build up. One begins to have serious self-doubts and uneasy feelings.

This self-doubt feeds the unworthiness, causing tiredness, confusion, lack of clarity, and a general sense of "I can't do it."

Parallel to this disintegration in our relationship with ourselves is the deterioration of our relationships with others. If you make a series of commitments and don't keep them, people—at best—don't trust you. At worst, it's a great deal of *Sturm und Drang*—hurt feelings, anger, betrayal, accusations, abandonment.

It's easy to see that if you've been, shall I say, *freewheeling* in your commitments—either with yourself or with others—you have plowed, irrigated, and fertilized the soil in which negative thinking thrives.

To reverse this—and encourage a crop failure—I have a few suggestions:

1. Don't make commitments you're not sure you can keep. If you're not sure, say you're not sure. If a definite maybe is not good enough, it's better to tell

There's one way
to find out
if a man is honest—
ask him.
If he says, "Yes,"
you know he's a crook.

GROUCHO MARX

the other person no.

2. Only make commitments that are important to you. If a commitment is important enough, you'll keep it. If it's not important enough to keep, don't make it.

3. Learn to say no. Don't make commitments that are important to others but not important to you just because you're afraid of "hurting their feelings." In doing this, you will either (a) break the commitment later, causing more hurt feelings, or (b) keep the agreement, hurting your own feelings. It's better to say, "No, thank you" up front.

4. Communicate. As soon as you think you

might not be able to keep a commitment, let the other person know. Don't just say, "Sorry, can't make it." Renegotiate. Changing a commitment is asking for a favor. Do it nicely.

5. Write down your commitments with others. Keep a calendar and note your appointments. This (a) helps you remember them and (b) avoids scheduling conflicts.

6. Write down commitments with yourself. Write this on the first page of your calendar: "All commitments with myself will be put in writing. Everything else is just a good idea." This keeps you from thinking the "good idea" to go jogging tomorrow at 6 a.m. is actually a commitment. If it *is* a commitment, write "Jogging, 6 a.m." in your calendar. And do it.

7. Declare things finished. If you have a half-dozen half-read books lying around open, gathering dust, declare your reading of them finished. Put book marks in them and put them away. Tell yourself, "I'm done with this for now." You can always go back and pick them up again, but for now, release yourself from any implied commitment you have with yourself to read them. The same works with commitments with others. When you know you're not going to be taking part in something people expect you to be taking part in, let them know that, until further notice, you won't be there. It's amazing how much energy declaring things finished can free up within you.

8. Forgive yourself. Forgive yourself for any broken agreements in the past. Forgive yourself for

> *We can secure*
> *other people's approval,*
> *if we do right*
> *and try hard;*
> *but our own is worth*
> *a hundred of it.*
>
> MARK TWAIN

judging yourself for having broken those agreements. While you're at it, forgive yourself for breaking any agreements you may make in the future. (More on the technique of forgiveness later.)

It may help you keep your agreements—and not make agreements you don't plan to keep—if you understand the four primary reasons people break agreements. They are

1. Approval. We say we'll do something we really don't want to do because we're afraid someone might disapprove of us—then we don't have time to keep all the conflicting agreements.

2. ***Comfort.*** It often seems more comfortable not to keep the commitment. This is actually a false sense of comfort. Usually greater discomfort is the result. We also tend to make agreements we don't want to make because we don't want the discomfort of saying no. Learn to say no.

3. ***Rebellion.*** Breaking agreements for rebels is a knee-jerk reaction to feeling hemmed in, limited, or tied down in any way. Rebels especially feel rebellion toward (a) authority figures and (b) ultimatums. Unfortunately, rebelling against the "doctor's orders" (ultimatums issued by an authority figure) can be fatal.

4. ***Unconsciousness.*** Unconsciousness is a reason people break agreements. There are other important things to say about this, but I forgot them. Maybe I'll remember later.

Keeping agreements (and not making agreements you don't plan to keep) is a good way to learn about your need for other people's approval and how to replace it with self-approval; how to expand your "comfort zone" so you'll have more freedom; and how to move from automatic, unthinking rebellion into conscious, voluntary cooperation.

The second part of this little "secret of happiness" is simple—whenever anyone breaks an agreement with you, let it go. In your mind, let the other person out of the agreement at once. Imagine that the person called with the best reason and apology in the world.

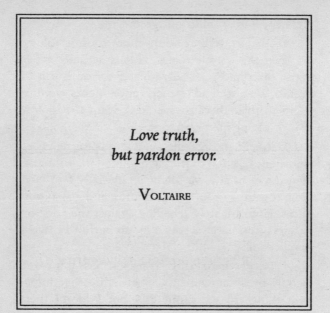

Love truth,
but pardon error.

VOLTAIRE

Let it go.

Expecting human beings to keep their agreements is (a) not realistic, and (b) an invitation to irritation.

When someone breaks an agreement—especially someone important to you—it may bring back earlier images and feelings of being let down, betrayed, and abandoned. Use the opportunity to heal these memories from the past, not to add further injury to yourself in the present. (More on the healing of memories later.)

INTERVIEWER:
You've been accused of vulgarity.

BROOKS:
Bullshit!

MEL BROOKS

Tom appeared on the sidewalk
with a bucket of whitewash
and a long-handled brush.
He surveyed the fence,
and all gladness left him
and a deep melancholy settled down
upon his spirit.
Thirty yards of board fence
nine feet high.
Life to him seemed hollow,
and existence but a burden.

MARK TWAIN

TOM SAWYER

The Thought-Feeling-Action Pyramid

In order to make progress, three things are necessary—a thought, a feeling, and an action. They form a pyramid:

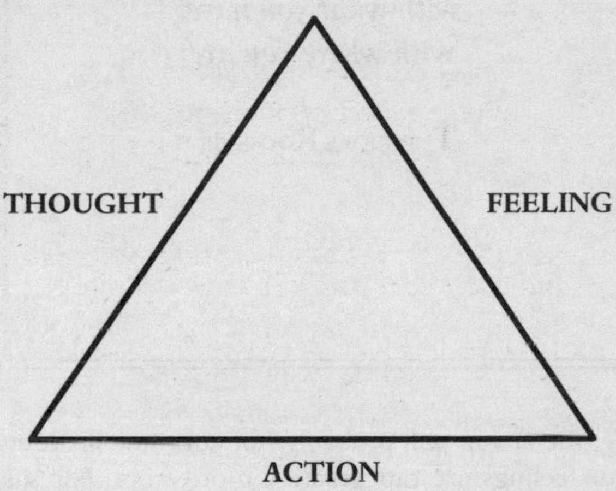

If we have a thought and a feeling, but no action, we're just spinning our wheels. If the thoughts and feelings are negative, this combination usually becomes worry, depression, and frustration. If the thoughts and feelings are positive, it's often just unproductive "positive thinking." (Meditation, contemplation, visualization, or spiritual exercises do not fall in the "unproductive" category. More on those later.) A *physical action* is required to make the thought and feeling tangible.

If we have a thought and an action but no feel-

Do what you can,
with what you have,
with where you are.

THEODORE ROOSEVELT

ing, the action will probably not continue for long. Our feelings are our greatest motivators. For sustained physical action, we need to *feel* something about what we're doing.

If we have a feeling and an action, but no directed thoughts, we're like a powerboat without a rudder. There's no logical, rational direction. This happens a lot with addictive behaviors—drug abuse, alcoholism, compulsive sex. The emotions say, "I want it." And the body says, "You got it," before the mind can even engage. Later, the mind may say, "You know you shouldn't have done that." We knew, but we "forgot." Temporary insanity.

If any one of the three sides of the pyramid is

missing, the structure collapses. We cannot do productive work. We cannot accomplish what we want to accomplish.

Knowing this, I offer the following advice: if you don't have a matching thought, feeling, and action all available at the same time, release yourself from whichever ones you do have.

For example, if you have the thought, "I'd like to go swimming," and the emotions say, "Swimming! Oh boy, swimming!" but there's no available water, let the thought and the feeling go.

If you're by a lake, in a bathing suit, and your mind says, "Swimming would be good for us," and the body says, "I'm ready," but the feelings say, "I am not at this moment emotionally equipped to deal with cold water," let go of the thought and the physical preparedness.

If the emotions want to go swimming and the body is ready to go swimming, but the mind says, "I think this water is polluted and may not be safe," let go of the feeling and the physical readiness.

You "let go" by refocusing on something the mind, emotions, and body are willing to do—and can do—*together. Now.*

Did you ever feel you were going in three directions at once? Maybe you were. Maybe your mind wanted one thing (let's clean the garage), the emotions wanted another (let's go dancing), and the body wanted another (let's take a nap). You cannot do all three things at the same time. Two of the three will have to go—or maybe all three will go, and the mind-body-emotions triumvirate will agree

God, give us grace
to accept with serenity
the things that cannot be changed,
courage to change
the things which should be changed,
and the wisdom to distinguish
the one from the other.

Reinhold Niebuhr

1943

to do something else.

It's as though the mind, body, and emotions have little "minds" of their own. Sometimes you have to ask the Inner Henry Kissinger to step in and negotiate for you. "First we'll take a nap, then we'll clean the garage, then we'll go dancing, okay?"

Sometimes you simply have to lay down the law (lovingly) and tell the body, "No nap"; the emotions, "No dancing"; or the mind, "The garage is clean enough."

However you work it, don't let yourself be caught in nonproductive thinking, feeling, or doing. The result is ineffectiveness, and ineffectiveness feeds a lack of self-esteem ("I knew I couldn't do it"), which leads to more negative thinking, which leads to a triggered Fight or Flight Response, which leads to—well, you already read that part of the book.

The greatest pleasure I know is
to do a good action
by stealth,
and to have it found out
by accident.

CHARLES LAMB

If You Want to Feel Good about Yourself, Do Good Things

One of the easiest ways to feel good about ourselves is to do good things. The operative word is *do*.

What's "good"? I'll let you decide. Whatever you think is good—as long as it doesn't hurt yourself or others—is fine with me.

It could be doing good things for yourself—mentally (learning something new, focusing on the positive, reading a good book—well, you're already doing that), physically (exercise, massage, eating well) or emotionally (practicing forgiveness, spending time with a loved one, seeing a good movie).

Or it could be doing something good for someone you know, or for someone you don't know, or for a group, or for nature, or for the whales, or for world peace, or for the planet as a whole.

Again, the key is *action, doing, involvement*. We are, as Madonna was kind enough to point out, living in a material world. As Madonna's spiritual teacher, Olivia Newton-John, once said, "Let's get physical." Sending people nice thoughts is, well, nice, but sending them notes saying how nice you think they are is even nicer.

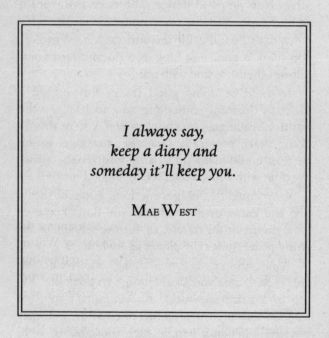

I always say,
keep a diary and
someday it'll keep you.

MAE WEST

Write Down the Good

Whenever something good happens, write it down. Buy a special notebook—perhaps one of those cloth-covered, fancy, hard-cover ones—and use it to list all the good in your life.

Include the good that happens to you and the good you do for yourself and for others. Spend ten minutes a day—or longer—remembering and writing the good.

The entries don't have to be long. They don't have to make sense to anyone but you. "Watched beautiful sunrise," "Talked to Grandma," "Saw great TV show," "Pain in left arm is less," "Got letter from Chris."

Begin your notebook with the entry, "Bought myself the most wonderful book," followed by, "Am writing the most wonderful book"—because you will be.

We tend to forget the good and remember the bad. We seem to be programmed that way. Writing down the good helps reprogram us. We retrain ourselves to focus on the positive and then to work with that positivity in a physical, material way (writing).

Use the book whenever you're feeling low. Read through it. Remember the good. It will lift your spirits and help reestablish your self-esteem.

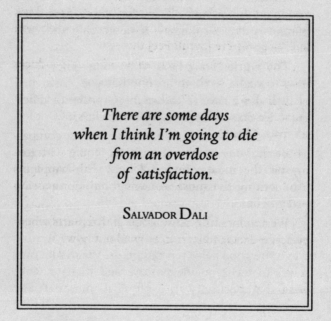

There are some days
when I think I'm going to die
from an overdose
of satisfaction.

Salvador Dali

Doing Things with Joy Will Create More Joy

If you want more joy in your life, do whatever you're doing with more joy.

How? Just *do it*. How do you behave when you're joyful? Behave that way. What do you think when you're joyful? Think that way. How do you feel when you're joyful? Feel that way.

The joy begins a cycle of joy, which produces more joy, which produces even more joy.

You don't have to do anything special or different—just do whatever you're doing with joy.

The same is true of loving, happiness, compassion—all the good attitudes of life. Doing with loving produces more loving. Doing with happiness produces more happiness. Doing with compassion produces more compassion.

It's a wonderful, upward spiral that starts whenever you decide to start it. How about now?

I cannot give you
the formula for success,
but I can give you the formula
for failure which is:
Try to please everybody.

Herbert Bayard Swope

You Can Have *Anything* You Want—You Just Can't Have *Everything* You Want

No matter how powerful we are, we have a few fairly significant limitations:

1. We can put our physical body in only one place at one time.
2. We have only twenty-four hours each day, 365 days each year. (Except every fourth year, when we get one more day.)
3. We have only so many years on this planet. (Somewhere between zero and one hundred fifty, tops.)

Given all this, it's obvious that we can't—contrary to the claims of some positive thinkers, self-help books, and TV commercials—"Have it all." There's just too much "all" and not enough time.

You can, however—contrary to the claims of negative thinkers, third-grade teachers, and those who *always* listen to reason—have *anything* you want. The only limitations on "anything" are, "Can it be gotten by anyone?" and "Is it available?" If the answer to those two questions is yes, it's there for you as well.

Don't get lost in "possible" or "impossible." If you have no money and say, "I want ten million dollars," some might think it's impossible. But it's not. Lots of people have started out with no money

One must not lose desires.
They are mighty
stimulants to creativeness,
to love and to long life.

ALEXANDER BOGOMOLETZ

and made ten million dollars.

Just concern yourself with "workable" and "not-workable." Not-workable might be, "I want to be the first man on the moon." That's not workable. It's already been done. But to be the first *woman* on the moon—that's workable. It hasn't been done yet.

To get what you want takes ten simple steps. Simple, but if your desire is gargantuan, not necessarily easy. These ten steps also work for less-than-gargantuan desires, in which case fulfillment will be easier.

If you keep in mind that you can't have *every-*

thing you want, here's how to get *anything* you want:

1. Focus all your attention on what you want. Be "obsessed" by it.

2. Visualize and imagine yourself doing or having whatever it is you desire.

3. Be enthusiastic about getting and having it.

4. Know exactly what you want. Write down a detailed description. Draw pictures. Make models.

5. Desire it above all else. Above everything else. Above all.

6. Have faith with involvement. *Know* you can have it, that it's already yours. Be involved with whatever you need to get it.

7. Do the work required. How do you know how much work is required? When you have it, that was enough. Until you've got it, it's not enough.

8. Give up all attitudes and activities opposing your goal.

9. Pretend you already have it.

10. Be thankful for what you already have.

There. That's it. How to get anything you want.

If you have a life-threatening illness, these steps can be the blueprint for your recovery. As long as *one other person* has survived the illness you currently have, you can be number two. And if no one

We lived for days
on nothing
but food and water.

W. C. Fields

has survived the illness, you can be number one.

Frankly, however, the stickler in there—"the fine print," if you will—is number five: *Desire it above all else.* Some people wonder if there is something beyond this physical world. They start to desire—above all else—an answer to the question, "What happens after death?"

If they believe in God, they often—above all else—want to know God, to feel God's presence more abundantly, to prepare, as they say, "to meet their maker."

Even W. C. Fields, shortly before his death (Christmas Day, 1945), was discovered by a friend propped up in bed reading a Bible. "Bill!" his friend said. "You don't believe in God. What are you doing reading the Bible?"

"Looking for loopholes," Fields replied. I like to think he found his loophole.

The struggle is not just between the habit of negative thinking and the positive focus required to heal your body; the struggle is also between staying here—in this body, on this planet—or going on to someplace many people have described as far greater than here.

As the king in *The King and I* said, "Is a puzzlement."

As the bumper sticker reads: "Everybody wants to go to Heaven, but nobody wants to die."

Or, as I say, "You can have anything you want; you just can't have everything you want."

(Lots more on choosing and obtaining what you want is in my book *DO IT! Let's Get Off Our Buts.* Available at bookstores, or call 1-800-LIFE-101.)

To every thing there is a season,
and a time to every purpose
under the heaven.
A time to be born, and a time to die;
a time to plant, and a time to
pluck up that which is planted;
A time to kill, and a time to heal;
a time to break down,
and a time to build up;
A time to weep, and a time to laugh;
a time to mourn, and a time to dance;
A time to cast away stones,
and a time to gather stones together;
A time to embrace,
and a time to refrain from embracing;
A time to get, and a time to lose;
a time to keep, and a time to cast away;
A time to rend, and a time to sew;
a time to keep silence,
and a time to speak;
A time to love, and a time to hate;
a time of war,
and a time of peace.

ECCLESIASTES
3:1–8

What Is Your Purpose?

Everyone has a purpose. Very few people know what theirs is. What's yours?

A purpose can be summed up in just a few words. It usually begins, "I am . . . ." It's a simple but powerful statement about why you're here and what you are here to do.

In fact, it's what you've already been doing all along. You have been fulfilling your purpose your whole life, even if you don't consciously know what your purpose is.

A purpose is not a goal. A purpose can never be obtained, reached, or checked off. A purpose is fulfilled, continuously, in every moment. Goals that can be defined, achieved, and noted are but way stations along life's purpose.

Some examples of purposes: "I am a joyful explorer," "I am a lover of life," "I am a servant of spirit," "I am a giver of happiness," "I am a willing student of life," "I am a scout," "I am a servant of humanity," "I am a joyful giver," "I learn and I teach," "I know and I grow," "I am a silent contributor," "I am a cheerful disciple," "I am an intense appreciator," "I am a lighthearted creator." Get the idea?

A purpose is general enough to fit many situations, but specific enough to fit you perfectly. "I am a student of life" might fit almost anyone. "I am a festive student of life" might be *you*.

You may *want* your life to go in a certain way. That's not necessarily your purpose. Statements

Nothing contributes so much
to tranquilize the mind
as a steady purpose—
a point on which the soul
may fix its intellectual eye.

Mary Wollstonecraft Shelley

about what you want are called affirmations. We'll talk about those later. Your purpose is what you are *already doing*. You can look back on your life and say, "Yes, I've been doing that all along," and you can look ahead and say, "Yes, that's what I'll be doing from now on."

The purpose also implies directed action and movement. "I'm here" or "I'm a human" or "I am a child of God" may be accurate, but they don't indicate movement. A purpose indicates both movement and direction.

To discover your purpose, begin by telling yourself, "I want to know my purpose." It may be immediately evident, or it may take a while to reveal itself.

Look back on your life. Write down the words (uplifting ones, please) that describe the activities and general thrust of your life thus far. As you write, a few may hit you as "right." You can also ask the people who know you well to suggest words (uplifting ones, please) that apply to you.

Write the words that seem right on another piece of paper. Experiment with them. Eventually the two or three that describe the thrust of your life will reveal themselves.

A purpose is not something you *create;* it's something you *discover.*

Once you know your purpose, it becomes a golden divining rod. When you're wondering, "Should I do this or should I do that?" look to your purpose. If one action is in line with your purpose and the other is not, the choice of which way to move becomes clear. If neither is in line with your purpose, look for more options. If both are in line with your purpose, it's dealer's choice.

It's a good idea to keep your purpose to yourself. This keeps it powerful and prevents comments such as, "You don't seem much like a joyful giver to *me!*" Keeping your purpose private also removes the temptation to choose a purpose that will impress others. ("Let's see, what would sound *real good?*")

Once you discover your purpose, you have answered the time-honored question, "Why am I here?"

If you know your purpose, but haven't been fulfilling it as completely as you might, this could be

The secret of success
is constancy to purpose.

BENJAMIN DISRAELI

contributing to your discontent.

If you know your purpose is "I am a joyful giver," but you've been more of a begrudging giver or a joyful hoarder, that can cause dis-ease: blockages of energy, a sense of not belonging here, a feeling "something's not right" (and all the negative thoughts that accompany that feeling).

When you bring yourself more in line with your purpose—in an involved, active way—you may notice your energy flows more freely, the blocks and the tensions in your body release, you become more active, vibrant, and alive—healthier.

A man needs
a purpose
for real health.

Sherwood Anderson

I want death to find me
planting my cabbages.

MICHEL EYQUEM DE MONTAIGNE

1533–92

What Do You Want?

Most people don't know what they want. They think they know, but they really don't. An interview might sound something like this:

"What do you want?"

"I want a million dollars."

"What would you do with it?"

"I'd quit my job."

"Then what?"

"I'd buy things."

"Like what?"

"A car. A house. Furniture."

"Then what?"

"I'd travel."

"Where?"

"Uh, Europe, Hawaii."

"Then what?"

"I'd lie back and enjoy my life."

"Doing what?"

"Driving my car. Living in my house. Swimming in my pool. Watching TV."

"All the time?"

"Well, no. I'd travel some more."

"Where?"

"Uh, I don't know. What does it matter where? *Would you get off my back!?*"

Most people could not make a list—one through ten, in order of importance—of what they

It is the chiefest point of happiness that a man is willing to be what he is.

ERASMUS

1465–1536

want to have, do, or be.

Having such a list is invaluable. It helps us sort the opportunities that come our way. (Contrary to the popular belief, opportunity doesn't knock just once—it will knock you down.) It helps us set goals. It assists us in making plans. It answers that burning question, "What am I going to *do* for the rest of my life?"

Avoid the inaccurate statement people in loss situations tend to make. Don't say, "If I only had my health (or whatever was recently lost), I wouldn't ask for anything ever again!" Don't kid yourself. If you had your health back, you'd soon want other things. So, find out what those other things are. Sometimes by finding out what those things are and by doing them, you can have your health "miraculously" return.

To make your list, get a few hundred 3 x 5 cards and begin by writing down everything you want to have, do, or be—one per card. Free-associate. The sky's the limit. Write down all your desires, goals, wants, and needs. Spend some time with it. Include material, mental, emotional, physical, and spiritual goals. Make a complete list.

Now review the list. How many of the things do *you* really want, and how many did you write down because you think you *should* want them? Do you really want, say, a Rolls Royce, or is that just a symbol of something else? (Have you ever driven a Rolls Royce?) Remove from the list the things you don't really want.

Go through the list again and, with the ten steps from the chapter "You Can Have Anything You Want—You Just Can't Have Everything You Want" in mind (page 191), ask yourself about each item, "Am I willing to do the work required?" "Am I willing to make a plan and follow all ten steps to get this?" If you've discovered your purpose, ask yourself, "Is this in line with my purpose?" If the answer to any of those questions is no, remove the card from the pile, say good-bye to that goal, and let it go. The next time you think about this goal, tell yourself, "I thought about this one and decided not to do it."

Now see if any items on your list are in conflict with any others. "I want to be a concert pianist"

> *We must cultivate our garden.*
>
> VOLTAIRE

may conflict with "I want to be an Olympic medalist." (Each requires a lot of daily practice.) "I want to party every night" and "I want a quiet home life" seem to conflict. (If you go out partying every night you might have a quiet home life—you won't be there, but your home will be quiet.) Between the two conflicting desires, choose the one you want more and cross the other off your list.

Then do a first-pass prioritization. Sort the cards into three piles: "A" (I want this very, very much), "B" (I want this a lot), or "C" (I want this).

When you're done, count the number of A's, B's, and C's. If you have more than ten A's, eliminate all the B's and C's. if you have ten A's and B's, eliminate all the C's. (people seldom get to the C's anyway, so why pretend?) Keep eliminating until you have ten.

Go through the cards and pick the *one* that's most important. Then go through the remaining nine and select the most important. Continue until all ten are prioritized.

On each card, answer one important question: "How will I know when I've reached this goal?" Be specific. Then you'll know when to cross it off your list to make room for another.

Behold—Your Life Plan.

Given that we only have twenty-four hours in the day, 365 (or 366) days in the year, and only so many more years on this planet, achieving this list may be all you'll have time for. Certain material items will be obtained and replaced by others, but some goals, such as being healthy and feeling happy, may take the rest of your life—even if that's another ninety-nine years.

When you get right down to the root of the meaning of the word "succeed," you find it simply means to follow through.

F. W. Nichol

Do It

Now that you know what you want, make a plan, put it in motion, and do what you choose to do.

Here are some thoughts on successful action:

1. Break each goal into do-able steps. If you want to be a lawyer but haven't gotten your high school diploma, your next do-able step might be "Call the board of education and find out where and when the next high-school equivalency test is being given." The next do-able step after that might be "Take the test." Based on the results of the test, the next do-able steps will follow. In the meantime, you can start pricing BMWs.

2. Make a plan. Once you have your next do-able step for each goal, schedule them. Get a calendar, date book, or appointment book (if you don't already have one) and fill it up.

3. Be flexible. As you make progress, you'll discover new information that may lead to changes in plans.

4. Be willing. Remember: "The willingness to do creates the ability to do."

5. Don't let how you feel about something stop you from doing what you know you need to do. Feel the feeling (fear, guilt, unworthiness, hurt, anger) and do it anyway. Move your body—physically—in the direction of your goals. The feelings may complain. Expect them to. Thank them for their "advice" and move ahead.

Even if you're
on the right track,
you'll get run over
if you just sit there.

WILL ROGERS

6. Turn fear into excitement. As I said before, if you feel carefully, you'll notice that the physiological feeling we call "fear" and the physiological feeling we call "excitement" are the same feeling. One we label "bad" and the other we label "good." If you feel "that feeling" and automatically call it "fear," stop and call it "excitement" instead. Whenever you hear yourself saying (to yourself or to someone else) "I'm afraid," change it to "I'm excited." Then it becomes *preparation energy*. It keeps your mind focused, your energy up, your attention clear—just what you need to help you do new and "exciting" things.

7. Turn stubbornness into determination. Like

fear and excitement, stubbornness and determination are the same energy. Both include steadfastness, constancy, power, and drive. For most people, it's a matter of turning "won't power" (stubbornness) into "will power" (determination). When you find yourself being stubborn (I *don't* want this), find out what you *do* want and, using the same energy, move toward it.

8. ***Do it as though you were teaching it to another.*** Set a good example, even if no one else is around. Follow through with the precision, dedication, courage, kindness, and persistence one would expect of a great educator teaching a beloved pupil. In a sense, that's exactly what you're doing—you are teaching various parts of you how to live more fully.

9. ***Be response-able.*** Be willing to respond to *whatever* happens along your path. Don't fall into the negative-thinking trap of labeling certain occurrences "setbacks," "disappointments," or "letdowns." Consider them, instead, challenges. *Respond* to them in such a way that you get what you want. That's response-ability.

10. Ask. Learn to ask for what you want. Ask for help, guidance, instruction—whatever you need. The worst people can do is not give you what you ask for—which is precisely where you were before you asked. As they used to say on TV, "You have everything to gain and nothing to lose." Also, don't expect people who've offered you help (especially ones close to you) to be mind readers. Let them know what you need as you need it. Don't assume they "should" know "if they really loved me." They

> *The destiny of mankind*
> *is not decided*
> *by material computation.*
> *We learn that we are spirits,*
> *not animals,*
> *and that something is going on*
> *in space and time,*
> *and beyond space and time,*
> *which, whether we like it or not,*
> *spells duty.*
>
> SIR WINSTON CHURCHILL

can love you very much and still not know. Ask.

11. Do it with love. Be gentle with yourself and others. Don't become so obsessed with the goal that the *process* is not enjoyable. Send the light of your own loving ahead of you. When you get there, the loving will have prepared a place for you. Be kind, gentle, and enjoy the journey.

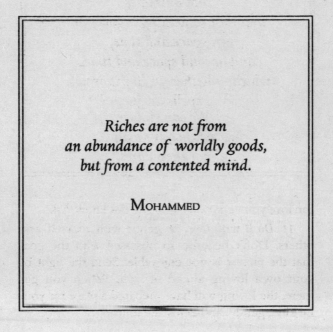

Riches are not from
an abundance of worldly goods,
but from a contented mind.

Mohammed

We can endure
neither our evils
nor their cures.

LIVY

59 B.C.–A.D. 17

If You're Not Actively Involved in Getting What You Want, You Don't Really Want It

Write that in big letters somewhere you can read it often. A lot of negative thinking, depression, frustration, and illness stems from people's *thinking* they want something they don't really want.

How do you know what you really want? Whatever you are *actively involved* in getting, that's what you really want. Everything else is just what you *think* you want. If you think you want something and you're not actively involved in getting it, you're probably just kidding yourself.

It's true that, in every moment, you can't be actively involved in doing something about *everything* you want. How, then, can you tell what you're actively involved in?

Here's where your calendar can prove useful. Have you scheduled activities that support each of your goals in, say, the next two weeks? If not, ask yourself: "Is this goal becoming another one of my 'laters'?" ("I'll do it later, later, later," and it never gets done.)

I'm pragmatic. If someone tells me, "I'm dependable! You can count on me," I say, "Great," and watch carefully. If she (in the last example I used *he;* this time I'll use *she*) is late three times in a row, but continues to say she's dependable, I tend to base my

There is no failure
except in no longer trying.

Elbert Hubbard

opinion of her dependability more on her actions than on her words. Not that she means to deceive. She may, however, be deceiving herself.

If people say they want health, I look to see what they are *doing* about it. Are they actively involved in healing? Are they doing everything they can to promote healthy ideas, healthy feelings, and healthy actions? Are they exploring options for greater health? If so, I'd say they really want health.

If, however, they're involved in life-damaging activities, I'd say they have a desire for lesser health.

We are more than our minds, more than our thinking process. We are also more than our feelings and more than our body. Most people have spent so much time in either thinking or feeling, they *think* that a thought or *feel* that a feeling *is* them. To *think* you want something or to *feel* you want something doesn't necessarily mean that's what *you* want.

What you want—what you *really* want—is what you are making real through action.

If you think you want something but you're not doing much to get it, you have three choices:

1. You can go on the way you've been: kidding yourself and pretending you really want this thing that you don't really want—or aren't willing to do the necessary work to get. This causes frustration ("Why can't I have what I want?), hurt ("I never get what I want"), resentment ("Other people get what they want; why not me?"), and unworthiness ("I guess I don't really deserve it").

2. Give up the goal. Realize it's a nice idea, and if it were in the next room, you'd probably go to the next room and partake of it. It is, however, not something you really want *more* than *other things* you are actively seeking.

3. Do whatever is necessary to reach the goal. Eliminate from your schedule activities that support goals with lower priorities than the one in question. As you move toward your goal, certain mental, emotional, and physical objections will be raised. No matter what

I believe that
anyone can conquer fear
by doing the things
he fears to do,
provided he keeps doing them
until he gets a record
of successful experiences
behind him.

ELEANOR ROOSEVELT

complaints your mind, emotions, and body fling at you, *if you know you need to do it, do it anyway.* Gently, lovingly—but firmly—teach the objecting parts of you that you have a new goal, a new priority, and that your actions will now be in alignment with achieving that goal.

Those are your choices. Most people choose by default—they "choose" #1 by not choosing, and things go on as they have in the past. I suggest you choose from options 2 or 3. Either will put you more actively in charge of your thoughts, feelings, and actions.

I will not steep
my speech in lies;
the test of any man
lies in action.

PINDAR

522–433 B.C.

He that lives upon hope,
dies fasting. *

BENJAMIN FRANKLIN

* My favorite typo of all time comes from the dignified and most-proper *Harper Book of American Quotations*. By inadvertantly altering only one letter, this Franklin quote became: "He that lives upon hope, dies farting." Maybe it's not a typo after all.

The Two Sides of Hope

Remember the story of Pandora's Box?

Pandora was sort of the Eve of Greek mythology—the First Woman, told not to do something by God (by Zeus, in this case), but she did it anyway.

Pandora was given a box (a jar, actually) and told not to open it because it contained all the evils of the world. She took the jar/box with her on her honeymoon. Alas, it was a dull honeymoon, so she opened the jar/box.

Just as in *Raiders of the Lost Ark* when the Nazis opened the Ark and all the ghosts came whooshing out with Industrial Light and Magic visuals and Dolby SurroundSound, when Pandora opened the jar/box, all the evils of the world escaped. The last evil in the jar/box was hope. What happened to hope is not clear. Some stories say it remained inside; others say it got out. But all agree that hope was the last item in the jar/box.

Most people interpret this as good news—yes, evil has been added to the world, *but* we've been given hope so that we can take care of all that evil.

Did you ever consider that hope might be one of the evils of the world?

If it weren't for hope, perhaps we would have cleaned up all the other evils long ago. We would have gotten sick and tired of being tired and sick and sent them packing—"Back to the jar/box!"

What we sometimes do instead is tolerate evil

Hope is a good breakfast,
but it is a bad supper.

FRANCIS BACON
1624

A gentleman
who had been
very unhappy in marriage,
married immediately
after his wife died:
Johnson said,
it was the triumph
of hope over experience.

BOSWELL

and *hope* it's going to go away. "Oh, I hope it will be better tomorrow," we sigh, never doing anything productive to get rid of "it" today. ("It" being whatever evil we happen to be currently sighing about.)

The hope I'm talking about is the kind of hope that inspires passivity, resignation, and stagnation.

If there's a situation in your life—be it a life-threatening illness or any other "evil"—and you're using hope to stimulate you to greater and greater depths of inaction, lethargy, and torpor, the dark side of hope has gotten hold of you.

Shake it off. Become active. Do something to replace the evil with what you really want. Move toward a positive condition in which the evil cannot exist. (Don't "get rid" of evil—replace it with what you prefer and focus on the goodness of that.) Turn the evil around. *Evil* spelled backwards ("turned around") is *live*.

You can hope things will get better, but if you're not taking specific, energetic, and frequent actions to make things better, you've got the wrong kind of hope working for you. (Or, more accurately, working against you.)

That the limiting kind of hope is almost epidemic in our culture is reflected by the frequent misuse of the word *hopefully*. As you may recall from Grammar 101, *hopefully* is an adverb (it ends in *ly*); therefore, it should be used to modify (describe) a verb.

Verbs are, of course, action words—run, jump, skip, look, walk, duck—words that describe movement. You can run hopefully, jump hopefully, skip hopefully, look hopefully, walk hopefully, and duck hopefully—which means you are running, jumping, skipping, looking, walking, and ducking *with hope*.

As the song goes, "Walk on, walk on, with hope in your heart." You are *walking*, and you're doing it with an attitude of *hope*.

All this is fine. It is correct English, and it is—to my way of thinking—correct living. You hope as you *do something*. You *take an action* while anticipating (hoping) the action will have a positive outcome. Well and good.

Most people, however, use the word *hopefully* as

There is nothing
so well known as that we
should not expect
something for nothing—
but we all do
and call it Hope.

Edgar Watson Howe

a replacement for the phrase "I hope."

"We will hopefully be going to the store" means, "We will, I hope, be going to the store." "This problem will go away, hopefully" means, "This problem will go away, I hope." "Hopefully I'll be able to do it" means, "I hope I'll be able to do it."

Traditionally, this use of the word *hopefully* is incorrect—but so many people use it in this way that many grammarians are (reluctantly) conceding a second usage. I'm not here to debate grammar. I'm more interested in how the word went from the active "being hopeful while taking an action" to the passive "I hope." Does that, I wonder, reflect a trend in our culture?

I look hopefully toward the day when people won't let hope stop them from doing what needs to be done. The combination of hope (anticipating a positive outcome) and action is a powerful way to get what one is hoping for.

Please use this information about hope for your upliftment and not as ammunition against others (or yourself). If someone says, "Hopefully you'll get better," don't say, "Yeah? Well, what are you *doing* about it?" Go to the essence of their communication—they are wishing you well—and thank them for it.

Do, however, listen to yourself. When you use the word *hope,* ask yourself, "Am I using it as a *replacement* for action or as an *adjunct* to action?" If it's a replacement, get moving. If it's an adjunct, keep moving.

But how shall we expect
charity towards others,
when we are
uncharitable to ourselves?
Charity begins at home,
is the voice of the world;
yet is every man
his greatest enemy, and,
as it were,
his own executioner.

Sir Thomas Browne

1642

Poor Charity

Charity began as a wonderful word. To quote from *The Dictionary of Word Origins:* "Charity was first an inner love; then a sign of this feeling; then an action or an act." The roots of charity include the Greek *chayrs,* meaning "thanks, grace," and the Latin *caritas,* "love, regard, affection," and *carus,* "to hold dear." *(Carus* is also the root of such words as *caress* and *cherish.)*

And what does *charity* mean today? The first three definitions in *The American Heritage Dictionary* read "1. The provision of help or relief to the poor; almsgiving. 2. Something that is given to help the needy; alms. 3. An institution, organization, or fund established to help the needy."

To give charity under this definition produces an immediate rift between giver and receiver. Although the material needs of the recipient may be met, both giver and receiver suffer separation. "I—superior and blessed among people—give proudly to you, poor, needy person." "I—poor, needy person—accept humbly this gift from you—magnificent, benevolent, rich person."

I am certainly not knocking charities or charitable feelings. It's just that a word that started out meaning love, regard, and affection has, for many people, come to mean pity.

This stigma on the word affects people who are, as the phrase goes, "forced to take charity." (Note the implied destitution and helplessness in that.)

The onus of having to go to a charity, because

Charity degrades
those who receive it
and hardens
those who dispense it.

George Sand
1842

Charity creates
a multitude of sins.

Oscar Wilde

of the popular misdefinition of the word, can strike deeply at one's sense of self-worth—precisely what one does not need when in need.

Ironically, most charities are happy to help people who can truly use it. That's why the charity was formed in the first place. And the people who work for most charities were drawn there by a genuine desire to help others.

I'm afraid charity is a word that will forever be associated with the sort of human condition described in Emma Lazarus's inscription on the Statue of Liberty:

Give me your tired, your poor
Your huddled masses yearning to breathe free,
The wretched refuse of your teeming shore,
Send these, the homeless,
tempest-tossed to me:
I lift my lamp beside the golden door.

This, of course, hasn't been the policy of the Immigration Service for years. It is, however, the way in which any number of charities portray their beneficiaries when asking for donations. It's a successful tactic. It works. It will no doubt continue.

Rather than rehabilitate the word *charity,* let me introduce an alternate word—*service.*

Do all the good you can,
By all the means you can,
In all the ways you can,
In all the places you can,
At all the times you can,
To all the people you can,
As long as ever you can.

JOHN WESLEY

The Joy of Service

Ironically, *service*—which has the same roots as the words *serf, servile, servitude,* and *slave*—seems today to indicate an exchange between equals. "May I be of service to you?" has a very different slant to it than "Would you accept my charity?"

It's one of the great open secrets of the world that by serving others you serve yourself. As Emerson said, "It is one of the beautiful compensations of this life that no one can sincerely try to help another without helping himself." Those who have given to others for the joy of giving know the reward is just that—joy.

Service is a self-ish thing—in the truest sense of *self* ish. We do it because it feels good. And because it *feels good,* we want to do more. As a poet once wrote, "The greatest gift is to fill a need unnoticed." The gift is given, simultaneously, to both the giver and the receiver. "The love I give you is secondhand: I feel it first."

In service, the person serving and the person being served are one. By allowing others to serve you, you serve them. By serving others, you are serving yourself. It's the cycle of giving and receiving. Soon it's hard to tell who's giving and who's receiving. It just flows.

Besides making you feel good because you know that you have done good for others, service is physiologically good for you.

A study in Tecumseh, Michigan, for example, showed that regular volunteer work—more than

Lord, make me an instrument
of Your peace.
Where there is hatred
let me sow love;
where there is injury, pardon;
where there is doubt, faith;
where there is despair, hope;
where there is darkness, light;
and where there is sadness,
joy.

St. Francis of Assisi

any other factor—dramatically increased life expectancy. "Men who did no volunteer work were two and a half times as likely to die during the study as men who volunteered at least once a week."

Doing good for others enhances the immune system, lowers cholesterol, strengthens the heart, decreases chest pains, and reduces stress. A study at Harvard showed that even *thinking* about doing service produced positive psychological results.

Service can be done even from bed. The phone is a great tool of service with which you can—to quote Ma Bell—reach out and touch someone.

Give to live.

Kindness can become
its own motive.
We are made kind
by being kind.

Eric Hoffer

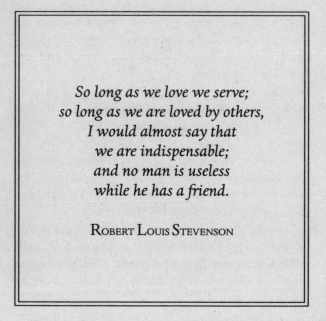

So long as we love we serve;
so long as we are loved by others,
I would almost say that
we are indispensable;
and no man is useless
while he has a friend.

ROBERT LOUIS STEVENSON

Let Others Serve You

One of the greatest forms of service is allowing others to serve you. Their giving might be of the "charitable" sort at first, but gradually they may learn the joy of giving. In allowing them to give, you have been part of their learning.

Giving to others feels good; it strengthens the physiology and enhances self-worth. When you let others give to you, you are giving them the gift of good feelings, strengthened physiology, and enhanced self-worth.

Each time someone does something for you, remind yourself, "I am worthy of this." If you weren't worthy, it wouldn't be taking place. (Pragmatism 101.) You *are* worthy. Accept the service.

When, through your service to others, you see how much there is to be gained, you will gladly let others serve you. Or you can learn this by watching the faces of the people as they serve you.

One of the greatest myths of our culture is that of the "rugged individualist"—independent, self-sufficient, "I can do it all myself." Hardly. Imagine what your life would be like if you had to meet *all* your needs yourself.

Did you make your own clothes? Did you weave the cloth? Did you grow the cotton? Did you chop the trees to make the loom and mine the ore to make the needles? Did you make the tools to chop the trees and mine the ore? Did you invent these?

If we look beneath the surface of almost anything we rely on, the myth of "independence" falls

Independence?
That's middle-class blasphemy.
We are all dependent
on one another,
every soul of us on earth.

George Bernard Shaw

apart. We are, in fact, *interdependent*. We depend on something someone has done—or is doing—for almost everything in our lives. And other people are depending on what we do and have done.

If you can assist others, without overtaxing or overextending yourself, do so. If you want assistance from others, ask for it. It's all part of the flow, the interaction, the interdependence, the interconnectedness of life.

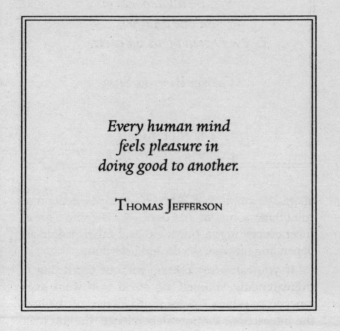

Every human mind
feels pleasure in
doing good to another.

THOMAS JEFFERSON

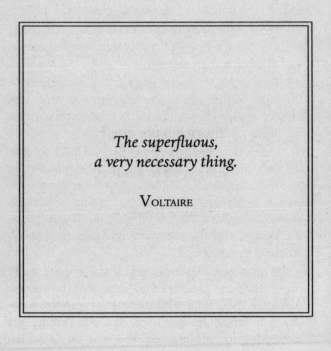

The superfluous,
a very necessary thing.

Voltaire

Get Off the Excitement Treadmill

Some people become addicted to excitement, to mental-emotional-physical intensity of any kind. Some of it is "positive," some of it is "negative," but all of it is thrilling, demanding, *exciting.*

Excitement addiction, like any other addiction, requires future levels of excitement to be greater, and greater, and greater still.

The results of this are graphically illustrated in a film that features an unfortunate mouse. (No, not one of those Disney antidrug films—this was a movie about a real mouse.)

The mouse had been surgically wired so that the pleasure center of the brain was stimulated by an electric current each time the mouse touched a switch in its cage. The mouse would touch the switch, an electric current would stimulate its pleasure center, and the mouse would fall on its back writhing in ecstasy.

At first, one "hit" was sufficient for quite some time. After the pleasure had subsided, the mouse would lie there for a while, smoke a cigarette, wonder if it would respect itself in the morning, get something to eat, and see who was on "The Tonight Show."

As time went on, however, the interval between lever hits grew shorter, and the amount of time the mouse could hold down the lever grew longer. Eventually, the mouse abandoned all nourishment

In Rome
you long for the country;
in the country
—oh inconstant!—
you praise the distant city to the stars.

HORACE
65–8 B.C.

In the valleys you look for the mountains
In the mountains you've
searched for the rivers
There is no where to go
You are where you belong
You can live the life you dreamed.

JUDY COLLINS

and sat, spasmodically pushing the switch several hundred times per minute.

Humans who become addicted to excitement do approximately the same thing—they need more and more but enjoy it less and less.

If you find yourself on this treadmill, get off. Slow down. Take it easy. Learn to appreciate the quieter, subtler, simpler pleasures of life.

The process is the one we discussed before—focusing on the positive. The positive is not necessarily what will get you excited. The positive is sometimes contemplating the wonder of a plant or reflecting on the amount of time and attention that went into making even the most common of objects—say, a drinking glass.*

Replace the idea of "excitement" with that of "enjoyment." When you feel the need for excitement, see if you can find something *enjoyable* instead. Too much excitement strains the body. Enjoyment, in its own quiet way, strengthens.

*An excellent book on getting off the excitement treadmill—and the physiological importance of doing so—is *Treating Type A Behavior and Your Heart* by Meyer Friedman, M.D., and Diane Ulmer, R.N., M.S. Available in paperback from Fawcett Books, New York.

Do not take life
too seriously.
You will never
get out of it alive.

Elbert Hubbard

Take It Easier

Be easier on yourself, on everyone, on everything. Suspend your judgments of the way things should be, must be, and ought to be. Suspending judgments gives you greater ease.

Consider ease the antidote for disease.

Do things that bring you ease—quiet walks, resting, hot baths, being with friends, meditating, contemplating, reading, writing.

Approach life with acceptance, patience, flowing, giving, grace, effortlessness, simplicity, allowing, acquiescing, permitting, forgiving.

Write these words—and others like them—on separate cards and put them in places you will see them. Pick one of these attitudes each day and no matter what happens, meet it with that attitude.

It often happens
that I wake at night
and begin to think about
a serious problem
and decide I must tell
the Pope about it.
Then I wake up completely
and remember that I ***am*** *the Pope.*

Pope John XXIII

What Would a Master Do?

When challenged by a situation you're not quite sure how to respond to, ask yourself, "How would a Master handle this?" or "How would the perfect ___________ respond to this?" (Fill in the blank with whatever "role" you happen to be playing—the perfect *friend*, the perfect *boss*, the perfect *employee*, the perfect *lover*, the perfect *patient*.)

If you have religious or spiritual beliefs, ask yourself how the One you worship would respond to the situation. If you admire certain leaders—masters—in their chosen fields, ask yourself what they would do.

You'll probably get an answer. You're not obliged to *follow* that answer, of course, but, you will at least have another option.

For the most part, Masters don't get upset—at least not for long. They have, as the sayings go, "the wisdom of Solomon," "the patience of Job," and "the love of Christ." If you have this kind of wisdom, patience, and love, what is there to be upset about?

Within us we *all* have that kind of wisdom, patience, and love. It's just a matter of calling on it.

Life is too short to waste
In critical peep
or cynic bark,
Quarrel or reprimand:
'Twill soon be dark;
Up! Mind thine own aim,
and God speed the mark!

Ralph Waldo Emerson

Complaining

Some people are remarkably good at knowing not only what's wrong, but also whom to tell about it, and how. These are the effective complainers. Their complaints often result in improvement.

Most people, however, are ineffective complainers. They moan, groan, kvetch, and complain to anyone who will listen.

This phenomenon can be seen from 4 p.m. until 7 p.m. every working day. It's the daily National Convention of the "Ain't It Awful?" Club. The Club Motto is *Miseria Libere Companio* ("Misery Loves Company"). Bars and cocktail lounges all over the country serve drinks at half-price, and, for the price of a drink, people tell each other their troubles. For some unknown reason, this segment of time is known as The Happy Hour.

Conversations between some people consist of a litany of how unfair it all is. When these people ask their friends, "What's new?" what they mean is, "Any news of fresh disasters?"

If your learning to focus on the positive, the habit of complaining is, to mix metaphors, not flowing with the river in the direction the horse is riding. If you're looking for things to complain about, you'll find them—and you'll find the consequences of negative thinking as well.

To reverse this habit, here are two suggestions:

1. ***Only complain to someone who can do something about it.*** If your water bill seems too high, there's no point in telling anyone but the water

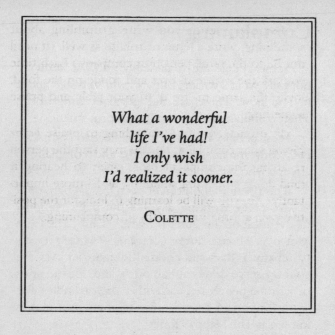

What a wonderful
life I've had!
I only wish
I'd realized it sooner.

COLETTE

company or someone who's had experience dealing with the water company. If your reception on cable TV is not up to par, telling a friend will do no good unless that friend has solved a similar problem or happens to work for the cable company. Effective complaining helps keep your conversations positive. You may find some people, if they can't complain, have nothing to talk about.

2. Compliment at least as often as you complain. If you're a complainer who knows how to get things done through effective complaining, well and good. I suggest, however, you add a step to each negative communication—compliment at least as often as you complain.

For every letter you write grumbling about something, write a letter of tribute as well. (It need not be to the same person or company.) Each time you ask the maitre d' over and condemn the food, invite the same maitre d' to your table and praise something.

If, in fact, you find something to praise *before* giving your complaint, (a) you may find the person receiving the complaint more open to hearing it (and doing something about it), and—more importantly—(b) you will be learning to look for the positive even in situations worthy of complaining.

You grow up the day
you have the first real laugh
—at yourself.

Ethel Barrymore

If It'll Be Funny Later, It's Funny Now

Probably some of the best anecdotes in your personal repertoire are stories of how disaster befell you. With the passage of time, most tragedies have a way of becoming comedies.

Start looking at "bad" situations in life as raw material for your opening monologue. Ever notice how much humor is based on misfortune? What's the difference between laughing about something and crying about it? Attitude. Which would you rather do?

Yes, sometimes crying is appropriate. But laughter—as long as it doesn't become a form of denial—is often the best response to those slings and arrows of outrageous fortune. As the tribulations mount, tell yourself, "This is great! I can't wait to tell so-and-so!"

The people you know who laugh easily, talk to them often. As Evelyn Waugh said, "We cherish our friends not for their ability to amuse us, but for ours to amuse them."

The growth
of the human mind
is still high adventure,
in many ways
the highest adventure on earth.

NORMAN COUSINS

Laugh

Many years ago, Norman Cousins was diagnosed as "terminally ill." He was given six months to live. His chance for recovery was one in five hundred.

He could see that the worry, depression, and anger in his life contributed to, and perhaps helped cause, his disease. He wondered, "If illness can be caused by negativity, can wellness be created by positivity?"

He decided to make an experiment of himself. Laughter was one of the most positive activities he knew. He rented all the funny movies he could find—Keaton, Chaplin, Fields, the Marx Bros. (This was before VCRs, so he had to rent the actual films.) He read funny stories. His friends were asked to call him whenever they said, heard, or did something funny.

He was in pain so great he could not sleep. Laughing for five solid minutes, he found, relieved the pain for several hours so he could sleep.

He fully recovered from his illness; and lived another twenty happy, healthy, and productive years. (His journey is detailed in his book, *Anatomy of an Illness*.) He credits visualization, the love of his family and friends, and laughter for his recovery.

Some people think laughter is "a waste of time." It's a luxury, they say, a frivolity, something to be indulged in only every so often.

Nothing could be further from the truth. Laughter is essential to our equilibrium, to our

I have never made
but one prayer to God,
a very short one:
"O Lord,
make my enemies ridiculous."
And God granted it.

VOLTAIRE

well-being, to our aliveness. If we're not well, laughter helps us get well. If we are well, laughter helps us stay that way.

Since Cousins's ground-breaking subjective work, scientific studies have shown that laughter has a curative effect on the body, the mind, and the emotions.

So, if you like laughter, consider it *sound medical advice* to indulge in it as often as you can. If you don't like laughter, then take your medicine—laugh anyway.

Use whatever makes you laugh—movies, sitcoms, *Monty Python*, records, books, *New Yorker* cartoons, jokes, friends.

Give yourself permission to laugh—long and loud and out loud—whenever anything strikes you as funny. The people around you may think you're strange, but sooner or later they'll join in—even if they don't know what you're laughing about.

Some diseases may be contagious, but none is as contagious as the cure—laughter.

No man is a failure
who is enjoying life.

WILLIAM FEATHER

Do Things That Make You Happy

Whatever makes you happy—as long as it doesn't hurt you or hurt someone else—do it.

Schedule pleasurable activities into your life with the same dedication, precision, and priority you give less-than-pleasurable ones.

Some people think that happiness just happens, and, yes, to a degree that's true. But happiness has a better chance of happening in situations you find enjoyable. Experienced positive focusers can find happiness in a garbage pile, but even experienced positive focusers find it easier to find happiness at a museum (or reading a good book, or watching a good TV show, or at the beach, or with friends).

Make a list of the things you enjoy doing. Do them often. Actively pursuing happiness is pursuing health.

Know you what it is to be a child?
It is to be something very different
from the man of today.
It is to have a spirit yet streaming
from the waters of baptism;
it is to believe in love,
to believe in loveliness,
to believe in belief;
it is to be so little
that the elves can reach to whisper in your ear;
it is to turn pumpkins into coaches,
and mice into horses,
lowness into loftiness,
and nothing into everything,
for each child has
its fairy godmother in its soul.

FRANCIS THOMPSON SHELLEY

Learn to Play Again

Children at play can create enormous amounts of fun, enthusiasm, and joy with whatever is at hand. A stick becomes a scepter. A stone, a throne. Two minutes later, the stick is a magic wand and the stone a pet dragon.

Somewhere along the way, we "serious adults" forgot how to play. Recapture that sense of being in the moment with whatever the moment has to offer.

One way is to play with young children—five, six, seven years old. They'll stretch your imagination while rekindling in you the sense of wonder you, too, once had.

You might get yourself some toys you played with—or wanted to play with—as a child: finger paints, Erector sets, crayons, dolls. Take a trip to a toy store and buy yourself whatever seems like fun.

Be your own nurturing parent. Give yourself permission to play.

If I had to define
life in a word,
it would be:
Life is creation.

CLAUDE BERNARD

FROM THE BULLETIN OF
NEW YORK ACADEMY OF MEDICINE

Be Creative

One of the great joys of life is creativity. Information goes in, gets shuffled about, and comes out in new and interesting ways.

Whatever creative activity you've always wanted to do—do it now. Writing, painting, sculpting, cooking, gardening, sewing, knitting, singing, playing an instrument, composing, dancing, choreographing, designing, photographing, acting, directing, video making—the list is endless.

It doesn't matter that you don't know how to do it "perfectly." (How many people who make a *living* at it do?) It doesn't matter how "good" you are. What matters is the creativity. Does it give you joy? Does it give you satisfaction? Is it fun? Does it make you feel more in touch with the creative flow of life? If the answer is yes to any of these, then do it.

Letting creativity flow through you can be therapeutic. "Energy flowing through a system acts to organize that system," as the *Whole Earth Catalog* reminds us.

Give yourself plenty of creative time and plenty of opportunities to create.

A noble person
attracts noble people,
and knows how to
hold on to them.

GOETHE

Choose Well Your Companions

If you know people who have a positive direction to their lives—or who are working on one—you may find them rewarding to be around.

Conversely, people who are addicted to their negative thinking—and refuse to recognize it—can be a drag. They feed you negativity and criticize every positive move you make.

Negative thinkers are a great challenge. If possible, avoid that challenge.

Fill your life with people who applaud your positive thoughts, feelings, and actions; who encourage you toward more and better; who know how to praise the good and the beautiful.

As I said before, you don't *have* to spend time with people you don't want to. If you choose to spend time with them, you're entitled to set the rules. "I don't want to discuss negative things." If they don't like it (and they probably won't), they're entitled to go elsewhere and spend time with people who do.

If there are people you feel you *must* spend time with (usually relatives), (a) try to do it on the phone, and (b) use the time with them to learn something about yourself. Watching how other people negate and sabotage themselves can provide you with a blueprint of how you may be doing it to yourself.

You don't have to get negative about their negativity.

I love tranquil solitude
And such society
As is quiet, wise, and good.

PERCY BYSSHE SHELLEY

The idea that it's better to spend time with uplifting people is also true of books, movies, TV shows, CDs—everything. Not that you have to watch *The Sound of Music* three times a day—it's just that certain sources of information reinforce the notion that "life is terrible," while other sources of information uphold the idea that "life is wonderful." (Try watching *Field of Dreams.*)

It's your life. Live it with people who are alive. It tends to be contagious.

My heart leaps up when I behold
A rainbow in the sky:
So was it
when my life began;
So is it now I am a man;
So be it
when I shall grow old,
Or let me die!
The child is
father of the man;
And I could wish my days to be
Bound each to each
by natural piety.

WORDSWORTH

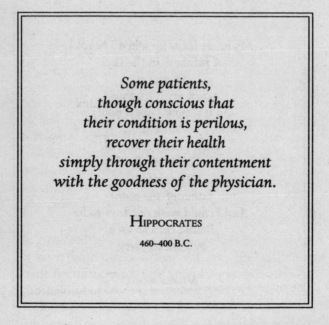

Some patients,
though conscious that
their condition is perilous,
recover their health
simply through their contentment
with the goodness of the physician.

HIPPOCRATES

460–400 B.C.

The Miracle of Modern Medicine

That sounds like an article from *Reader's Digest,* doesn't it? The fact is, modern medicine routinely does things that would have been considered miraculous only a century ago.

In some cases, far less than a century ago: Before the discovery of stable penicillin in 1941 and its widespread manufacture after World War II, pneumonia killed more people than any other complication. People would have a simple disease or accident, develop pneumonia, and die. Alexander the Great, the most powerful man of his day, died of pneumonia. King Henry VIII, the most powerful man of his day, died of syphilis. Since penicillin, deaths in the Western world from pneumonia have dropped significantly, and syphilis deaths are almost not measurable (according to *The World Almanac,* 0.0 percent).

Although the remarkably expanded life span of human beings over the past two hundred years is more thanks to plumbing and transportation than medicine (carrying away refuse and adding fresh fruits and vegetables to the daily diet have done more to lengthen the life span than anything else), any number of formerly "incurable" diseases and maladies are now routinely cured.

It's interesting to sit with a group of people and ask, "Would you be alive today if medicine were only as advanced as it was one hundred years ago?"

Honor a physician
with the honor
due unto him
for the uses which ye may have of him:
for the Lord hath
created him.

Ecclesiasticus
38:1

Most people who had had syphilis, pneumonia, any other formerly fatal bacterial disease, a severe accident, or almost any operation—including appendectomy and Caesarean section—would have to say they'd be dead.

The discovery of just the Big Three—anesthesia, antiseptics, and antibiotics—directly accounts for the saving of tens of millions of lives each year.

There are miracles happening every day in medicine. You—or someone you know well—is still alive because of them.

When you think of medicine, don't just think of sterile science, lab coats, and test tubes. Ponder the wonder of medicine, the marvel of how far it has come—and how quickly. Consider the magic of it.

The history of modern medicine is less the story of predictable, plodding advances than it is a chronicle of miracles.

And the miracles continue.

The man who is
tenacious of purpose
in a rightful cause
is not shaken
from his firm resolve
by the frenzy of his fellow citizens
clamoring for what is wrong,
or by the tyrant's
threatening countenance.

HORACE

65–8 B.C.

Explore Every Medical Option

As I mentioned at the start of this book, nothing in this book is designed to replace proper medical treatment. The ideas in this book are designed to augment whatever treatment program you're on.

If you have a life-threatening illness, explore every possibility of treatment, of cure, or—at the very least—of delaying the progress of the disease.

All interest
in disease and death
is only another expression
of interest in life.

THOMAS MANN

Know the Disease

Your doctor has hundreds of diseases to learn and keep current on—you have just one. Know it. It is, after all, a visitor. Even an unwelcome visitor you'd probably spend some time getting to know. And the better you know it, the more ways you'll have of getting it to leave.

Ask your doctor about the disease, its treatment, its cure. When you've reached the limits of your doctor's knowledge (or patience), do some research. Read about the disease. Talk to other people who have it—or, better still, who no longer have it.

Become a co-creator of your own cure. Work with your doctor on the best course of treatment for you. Don't be the passive patient, taking pills and paying bills. Become involved.

As any good doctor will tell you, the treatment of many illnesses is as much an art as a science.

Become an artist.

The race is not always
to the swift,
nor the battle to the strong,
but that's the way to bet.

Damon Runyon

Focus on the Cure

The reason for knowing your disease is so that you can cure it. Keep that always in mind as you do your studying.

No matter how clever, powerful, or tenacious a disease may be (and some of them are remarkable), keep reminding yourself, "I'm smarter than that," "I'm more powerful than that," "I'm more persistent than that."

Because you are.

MARTIANS BUILD TWO IMMENSE CANALS IN TWO YEARS

Vast Engineering Works Accomplished in an Incredibly Short Time by Our Planetary Neighbors

NEW YORK TIMES

FRONT-PAGE HEADLINE
AUGUST 27, 1911

Don't Believe Everything You Read in the Papers (Magazines, TV, etc.)

Knowing the disease can not only help you work toward the cure; it can also keep you from getting worse due to fear. Once you know the disease, media accounts that once might have caused you to panic now only produce a smile and a sigh. (Although the temptation will be enormous, don't let your reaction get more negative than a sigh.)

The news media are, for the most part, the bringers of bad news. That statement, of course, is no longer news. And it's not entirely the media's fault—bad news gets higher ratings and sells more papers than good news. ("Three Americans Shot by Mad Gunman!" sells papers. "258,829,439 Americans Not Shot by Mad Gunman!" doesn't.)

When your disease is reported in the media, remember that the reporting is apt to (a) focus on the negative, and (b) be superficial enough to appeal to everyone. Because you have a vested interest in knowing about the disease, you may know more about it than the reporter who reported it. (The reporter probably has to cover every other known disease and Space Shuttle launchings, too.)

The media often fall into the "Is the glass half-full or half-empty?" trap. If a disease has a fifty-fifty survivability rate, the media tend to say, "Fifty percent of all people with this disease die," rather than, "Half the people diagnosed with this illness are

The French army
is still the best all-around
fighting machine
in Europe.

TIME

JUNE 12, 1939

cured." Same information, different slant.

Sometimes the reporting is so general it blurs the issue. Because the media only report that so-and-so "died of cancer," many people don't know, for example, that cancer is not one always-fatal illness, but a term describing a whole collection of illnesses, the majority of which are now considered curable.

Also, diseases in the media tend to follow a trend—they have their day in the spotlight and fade into obscurity. In the early eighties, herpes had its day. Now, although people still get and have herpes, you don't hear much about it. Now AIDS has the spotlight.

The problem with this kind of "fad reporting" is three-fold:

First, it tends to report rumors, speculations, and projections as facts. These tend to be more *sensational*. How does the media do this? By quoting some "expert." Experts seldom agree, especially at the early stages of studying a disease, and you can always find some expert who will say something hopelessly hopeless about anything.

Second, the most curative work on a disease is achieved after it has fallen out of media favor. When a cure—which usually happens in gradual stages of treatment and prevention—is found, the disease is by then in media exile, and the report of the cure is often relegated to a small article next to the used car ads—if reported at all.

Third, if the horrifying projections turn out to be exaggerated, no one bothers to report, "Five years ago we made a big mistake. Hope we didn't frighten you folks too much." (Remember during the herpes scare when experts were predicting that the virus would eventually attack the spinal column and people would die horrible deaths? How many retractions of this misinformation have you read?)

In the media, good news must, alas, also be taken with a grain of salt. If going against the popular grain and reporting the opinion of an overly optimistic "expert" will make a good headline, so be it.

As any reporter will tell you, when writing for the mass media on a complicated subject such as disease, the instructions are, "Generalize, simplify,

Comet Kohoutek
promises to be
the celestial extravaganza
of the century.

NEWSWEEK

NOVEMBER 5, 1973

and don't take up too much space (or time)." "All the news that's fit to print" often becomes "All the news that fits."

On the brighter side, the scare tactics of the media often make available more time, money, and resources for treatment and curc than might otherwise have been available. I just wish there were a way to do it without instilling all that fear—especially for the people who have to deal with not only the disease and their own fear of the disease, but everyone else's fear as well.

Everything you read
in the newspaper
is absolutely true
except for the rare
story of which
you happen to have
first-hand knowledge.

Erwin Knoll

The principles
of Washington's farewell address
are still sources of wisdom
when cures for social ills are sought.
The methods
of Washington's physicians,
however,
are no longer studied.

Thurman Arnold

Learn to Separate Opinion and Projection from Fact

Any time someone tells you that you only have so long to live, how much pain you will go through, or what you'll be able to do between now and your demise—it's a *prediction,* an *opinion* based upon a statistical norm. Nothing more.

The Experts Speak (by Christopher Cerf and Victor Navasky, Pantheon Books, New York) is 392 pages of small type featuring noted experts being wrong about almost every major event, discovery, and human endeavor of the past seven thousand years. According to the "experts," all of Beethoven's symphonies were trash, World Wars I and II could not possibly happen, and *Gone with the Wind* wouldn't make a nickel.

The Experts Speak is must-reading for anyone who must listen to "experts" make predictions about his or her life.

A general sampling. Edison: "The talking picture will not supplant the regular silent motion picture." Aristotle: "Women may be said to be an inferior man." Edison: "The phonograph is not of any commercial value." *Business Week,* 1968: "With over 50 foreign cars already on sale here, the Japanese auto industry isn't likely to carve out a big slice of the U.S. market for itself." Edison: "The radio craze will soon die out."

Here are a few of the quotes that concern us most directly, from the chapter, "The Annals of Medicine: Man's War Against Disease."

For the majority of people, smoking has a beneficial effect.

DR. IAN G. MACDONALD

(LOS ANGELES SURGEON)
QUOTED IN *NEWSWEEK*,
NOVEMBER 18, 1963

The abolishment of pain in surgery is a chimera. It is absurd to go on seeking it. . . . Knife and pain are two words in surgery that must forever be associated in the consciousness of the patient. To this compulsory combination we shall have to adjust ourselves.

—Dr. Alfred Velpeau
(French surgeon, professor at the Paris Faculty of Medicine)
1839

The abdomen, the chest, and the brain will be forever shut from the intrusion of the wise and humane surgeon.

—Sir John Eric Erichsen
(British surgeon,
later appointed Surgeon-Extraordinary to Queen Victoria)
1873

Louis Pasteur's theory of germs is ridiculous fiction.

—Pierre Pachet
(Professor of Psychology at Toulouse)
1872

One-half of the children born die before their eighth year. This is nature's law; why try to contradict it?

—Jean-Jacques Rousseau
(Author of the most widely read child-rearing manual of its day.)
1762

Every man who has sexual relations with two women at the same time risks syphilis, even if the two women are faithful to him, for all libertine behavior spontaneously incites this disease.

—Alexandre Weill
The Laws and Mysteries of Love
1891

A genuine kiss generates so much heat it destroys germs.

—Dr. S. L. Katzoff
(faculty member, San Francisco Institute of Human Relations)
1940

If excessive smoking actually plays a role in the production of lung cancer, it seems to be a minor one.

—Dr. W. C. Heuper
(National Cancer Institute)
quoted in *The New York Times*, April 14, 1954

My doctor
is wonderful.
Once, in 1955,
when I couldn't
afford an operation,
he touched up
the X-rays.

JOEY BISHOP

I quote these (and there are many, many more) to show that experts—even doctor experts—are human, and humans make mistakes. There are certain medical *facts,* but predictions about how long someone will live are just that—predictions, opinions, best guesses.

Unfortunately, when some people are told by a doctor—Authority Figure Extraordinary—"Your disease is incurable; you only have six months to live," they may believe it so faithfully they—with their own thoughts, feelings, and actions—sentence themselves to die within six months.

And they do.

If they had been given years, perhaps they would have lived years; and if the doctor had said, "There's a condition here, and if you work with me, together we can beat this," perhaps they could have—given a fully cooperative patient ready to do "whatever it takes"—beaten it.

Deeming a disease officially "incurable" often becomes a self-fulfilling prophesy. When people don't allow that to happen and cure themselves, they are usually told, "Ah, we made a mistake in diagnosis."

"How do you know you made a mistake in diagnosis?"

"Because the disease we first diagnosed is incurable, and since you no longer have any signs of it, it must not have been that disease, because that disease is incurable."

Some doctors don't like to admit that they misdiagnosed. They just call the healing a "spontaneous remission" and leave it at that. There's no rhyme or reason to the cure, they claim. It was "spontaneous." Besides, you're not "cured." The disease is just "in remission." It could flare up at any time. You were lucky, nothing more. Go home.

Other doctors, however, ask, "What did you do? How did you do it? Let's see what it was, and maybe it will help others." I loudly applaud this ever-growing group of medical practitioners.

AIDS, for example, is currently thought to be "incurable" and "always fatal" by most experts. The problem is, some people who have had AIDS before AIDS even had a name are still alive. Until *everyone*

The art of medicine consists of amusing the patient while nature cures the disease.

VOLTAIRE

who has AIDS dies, I don't understand how it can be called "*always* fatal."

Also reported as fact by most of the media is that ninety-nine percent of all people who currently test positive for the HIV antibody will die of AIDS complications. (One doesn't die of AIDS; one dies of the complications from opportunistic infections the AIDS-suppressed immune system can't fight off.)

This is devastating information for anyone who's ever taken an "AIDS test" and had a positive result. (There is no "AIDS test." The test is for the *antibody* to the HIV virus, the virus many experts believe causes AIDS. All the test shows is that the *antibody* to the virus is in the bloodstream. It does not show the *presence* of the HIV virus or of the disease AIDS, nor does it mean one will develop AIDS.)

Before taking this ninety-nine percent figure too much to heart (or head, and thinking negatively about it), consider the facts.

I'll go into detail on this as an example of how important it is to look beneath the well-circulated doomsday predictions about *any* disease so you can find information closer to the truth.

In 1978, at a sexually transmitted disease clinic in San Francisco, blood was taken from thousands of patients and stored as part of a study on hepatitis. When, in 1984, the test for the HIV antibody was discovered, an experiment was begun on 5,000 primarily gay men whose 1978 stored blood showed the presence of the HIV antibody.

By 1988, forty-eight percent of the people who had the HIV antibody in their blood in 1978 had developed AIDS.

These are tragic figures, but *this was all that was known in 1988*. Scientific fact stopped here. Expert projection and opinion, journalistic hysteria, and no small amount of homophobia took over.

Some experts looked at the graph and projected the rise of AIDS cases in the future based on what had happened in the past. Based on *this* assumption, they predicted that, by the year 2000, nearly everyone in the study would have AIDS. Based on *this* projection, they further projected that ninty-nine percent of *all people* who are HIV antibody–positive

*We have not lost faith,
but we have transferred it from God
to the medical profession.*

George Bernard Shaw

will die of complications arising from AIDS.

This 1988 series of assumptions and projections on projections failed to take into account the following:

1. A disease tends to affect the weakest and/or most susceptible portions of a population first. If these same experts had graphed the bubonic plague (which wiped out half of Europe from 1348 to 1350), they would have predicted Europe devoid of all human life by 1352. If they had charted the flu epidemic of 1918 (which killed more than twice as many people as World War I—20,000,000 worldwide, 548,000 in the United States), they would have projected the end of human life by 1925.

This, of course, is not what happened. The diseases ran their course and eventually died out without a "cure" ever being found. It would have been just as reasonable to predict that the same thing would happen to the people in the HIV test group as it was to predict that they were all doomed.

2. The people in the study were coming to a public clinic for sexually transmitted diseases. The majority of them had a history of syphilis, gonorrhea, parasites, herpes, and/or hepatitis. This brings up certain questions: (a) Were these people more susceptible to diseases than an "average" group of gay males? (b) Was the immune system, before being exposed to AIDS, already suppressed by repeated exposure to other diseases, and, if so, did that give AIDS a stronger foothold? (c) Was the health care they were given at a public clinic as good as the care other gay males received in private treatment?

3. The chances are very high that many of the men in this population would have had, through multiple sexual contacts, repeated exposure to AIDS. Multiple exposure to most viruses tends to produce a more severe case of the disease and to bring it on more quickly. The people in the study were already HIV positive by 1978, and the guide lines for "safe sex" were not announced for another six years.

4. Recreational drug use was higher than average among this population.

5. The number and frequency of sexual partners in this population were higher than average.

Public opinion
is compounded of folly,
weakness, prejudice,
wrong feeling,
right feeling, obstinacy,
and newspaper paragraphs.

SIR ROBERT PEEL

1788–1850

6. Many of the gay males in San Francisco in the late 1970s sometimes practiced sex that was not just "unsafe" (in terms of AIDS transmission) but *acrobatic*. Some of the activities, from a transmission-of-AIDS point of view, could be considered *ostentatiously* unsafe.

7. The study only goes as far back as 1978. There is no way of telling for how many years *before* 1978 these people were infected.

8. The people in the study have known since 1984 that they've had antibodies to HIV in their blood since 1978, and probably before. They've read reports about the study, as well as heard experts "predict" the grim state of their life expectancy.

They may have watched friends who were in the study die from AIDS, or even friends infected *after* 1978. Can you imagine the kind of negative thinking this can induce among this dwindling population of volunteers?

From what we now know about the transmission of AIDS, we can see that these people may have had more contributing AIDS factors than the general population—even more than the general population of people who currently test HIV antibody–positive.

Taking these eight factors into account, I don't see how the experts could have made the "ninety-nine percent prediction" for even the remaining members of the test group, much less the entire HIV antibody–positive population. (And why ninty-nine percent? Why not ninty-eight percent? Or one hundred percent? Or $99\frac{44}{100}$ percent?)

From the comfortable vantage point of 1995, we can see that the alarmists were wrong once again. The statistics from the San Francisco study—far from getting increasingly grave and horrifying—have gotten no worse. The percentage of people in that study who developed AIDS has stayed virtually the same since 1988, at around forty-eight percent. Did this make the front page of any newspaper? Did an evening television newscast open its broadcast with this wonderful information?

I saw an article about a year ago. The headline read: "AIDS INFECTION RATE LESS THAN ORIGINALLY THOUGHT." The article went on to say that the number of people "infected with AIDS" (as the press likes to misrepresent HIV antibody–

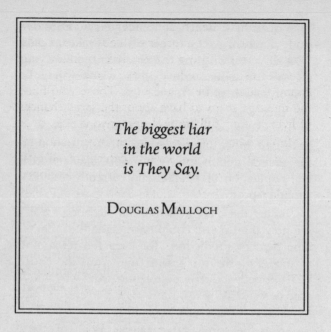

The biggest liar
in the world
is They Say.

DOUGLAS MALLOCH

positive) in the United States is not 1.5 million, as originally thought, but closer to one million. The article was three paragraphs long. The original scare projections were off by *one-third.* More than *500,000* fewer people were HIV antibody–positive than the blaring front-page headlines had first proclaimed. Where did I find this corrected information? Page 22, next to an ad for office supplies and FAX machines.

The studies of otherwise healthy people who happen to have HIV antibodies in their systems have been—uniformly and universally—encouraging. In other words, the news about being HIV antibody–positive is positive.

Far from a death sentence, HIV antibody–positive status is yet another of life's wake-up calls. "Watch your diet; do what you love; monitor your attitude; exercise; reduce stress; don't worry, be happy," seems to be its message. Those who heed the message seem to have about the same chances of living a long, full life as almost anyone else.

In late 1994, the World Health Organization reported that only about twenty percent of all HIV antibody–positive people *worldwide* had developed AIDS. When you consider that most of these people live in underdeveloped countries where life is hard, epidemics are rampant, drinking water is often contaminated, and medical treatment almost nonexistent, the prognosis is, in fact, good for those in a country with wholesome food, uncontaminated water, nutritional supplements, emotional support, access to information (if you dig for it), and two-movies-for-ninety-nine-cents video rental days.

It's been fun—in a Kafkaesque way—to watch the media adapt to the new, more optimistic information: each year they simply change the boilerplate statement in their reports. Currently, "The AIDS virus can remain dormant in the body for as long as fifteen years." Ten years ago it was five years. Next year it will be sixteen years. Why don't they just admit *they don't know*?

The "HIV-POSITIVE equals AIDS equals DEATH in a few years" falsehood will, I trust, be looked on as one of the most inaccurate—and cruelest—myths of the latter part of the twentieth century.

Do not put your faith
in what statistics say
until you have carefully considered
what they do not say.

William W. Watt

Before believing what you read, or even what you are told by a professional, you'd do well to find out (a) if the information is *fact* or *projection,* (b) where the study was done and under what conditions, and (c) who took part in the study and what's the difference between your life and theirs.

And remember, according to the experts, humans can't fly, the sun goes around the earth, and the *Titanic* is unsinkable.

We should always
presume the disease
to be curable,
until its own nature
prove it otherwise.

Peter Mere Latham

The more serious
the illness,
the more important
it is for you
to fight back,
mobilizing all your
resources—spiritual,
emotional,
intellectual,
physical.

NORMAN COUSINS

If One Has Done It, You Can Be Two. If None Has Done It, You Can Be One.

Whatever your disease, there are statistical tables telling you your odds of surviving the illness. Remember, however, you are a human being, not a statistic. The tables give statistical averages, not facts about your life.

The insurance industry's life-expectancy tables are an example of this. No matter what your age, they will tell you—to the month—when you will die. Of course, they can do nothing of the kind. But *statistically,* they're accurate.

The absurdity of relying on statistics is reflected in the insurance salesperson who was looking up the life expectancy of an elderly client. The salesperson looked and looked and finally said, "I'm sorry. I can't sell you insurance. You're already dead."

Let's say you have a disease with a very low rate of survivability—ninety-five percent of all people who have your disease die within a certain length of time. Don't look at the percentage and say, "Oh, ninety-five percent of the people who have this die. Of course, I'm one of the ninety-five percent." Ninety-five percent of the people hearing that information would say just that. It's probably what makes them part of the ninety-five percent.

There are
three kinds of lies:
lies, damn lies,
and statistics.

BENJAMIN DISRAELI

Tell yourself instead, "Five percent make it. Great. I'm in that five percent."

Five percent may seem like a small number, but when you multiply it times the number of people who have ever had that particular disease, it's usually a large number of people.

If the disease affects, say, 10,000 people each year, that means, statistically, 500 people will make it. You might find it hard to think of yourself as being part of five percent, but being one of 500—that's easier. After all, you only have to be *one* of those 500. And there's room for 499 others as well.

Even if only *one* other person survived the life-threatening illness currently visiting you, you can be number two. And if no one else survived it, you can be the first. You've probably always wanted to be first at something. Here's your chance.

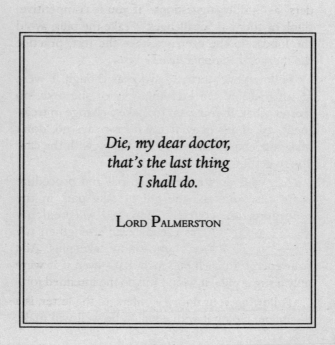

Die, my dear doctor,
that's the last thing
I shall do.

Lord Palmerston

Be the Perfect Patient

What your doctors want is your recovery. Give your doctors what they want. Get well.

While doing that, follow your doctors' orders to the letter. (If you're rebellious, just think of "orders" as "kindly suggestions." If you're competitive, think of them as "challenges.") Take the pills, avoid the foods, do the exercises, take the rest, practice the therapy, be cooperative.

Follow your doctors' advice as though it were an affirmation. Do everything he or she asks, no matter what. If you want to make a change in treatment, ask if it's okay. If the doctor says no, don't make the change. If you're not happy with the care you're getting, change doctors.

Ask your doctor what each pill and procedure is for. As you take the pill or take part in the procedure, tell yourself, "This pill *will* heal my ____________." "This exercise *will* strengthen my ____________." Don't just blindly take pills. Add your energy to each pill, such that—even if it were only a sugar pill—it would still do the intended job.

Following your doctor's orders, to the letter, is a discipline. Doing it with a will to be well will make you well.

To whom
can I speak today?
I am heavy-laden
with trouble
Through lack of
an intimate friend.

THE MAN WHO WAS TIRED OF LIFE

1990 B.C.

Consider Therapy

A book popular about twenty-five years ago was called *Psychotherapy: The Purchase of Friendship.* That's about the best definition of therapy I've heard.

Consider all the things you classically think a friend to be. (Coleridge: "Flowers are lovely; love is flower-like; Friendship is a sheltering tree.") As with all things rare, true friendship can be hard to find.

However, the qualities of a willing ear, enduring patience, sound advice, and the knowledge that "someone's in your corner" can be found in a good therapist.

If you have a life-threatening illness, you may find it invaluable to have someone you can just be yourself with, someone with whom you can openly discuss your fears and concerns (especially the ones you're afraid might frighten and concern your friends and loved ones), someone you can trust.

Such a relationship can be a lifesaver.

Whether you have a life-threatening illness or not, the goal of conquering a habit of negative thinking (or any other bad habit) can use the support, compassion, and guidance of a qualified therapist.

Select a therapist with care. Shop around. Just because a person is "a therapist" doesn't necessarily mean he or she can help you. Not all therapists are right for all people. Have initial sessions with several. Choose the one you feel most comfortable with, a natural empathy for, and, above all, one you can trust.

A faithful friend
is the medicine of life.

Ecclesiasticus

6:16

In working with a therapist, be honest about everything—including how you feel about the therapist. You can con and make nice and play games and spare the feelings and try to win the approval of everyone else in your life, but with your therapist, just be *you*. Don't pretend, cover up, or conceal. Give yourself the freedom to feel, think, and express whatever happens to be there.

Therapy is a place to explore yourself, express yourself, and experiment with new behaviors as well as to gain the comfort, support, love, caring, and experience of another.

It's a special relationship, one you're worthy of.

I was much further out
than you thought
And not waving but drowning.

STEVIE SMITH

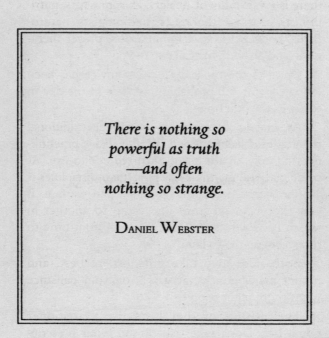

There is nothing so powerful as truth —and often nothing so strange.

Daniel Webster

Consider Alternative Therapies

In addition to the cornucopia of treatments offered by the "established" medical community, there is a vast body of healers, chiropractors, nutritionists, massage therapists, herbologists, naturopaths, body workers, acupuncturists, prayer therapists (and on and on) available to you.

Once all the medical doctors' advice has been followed, you will probably find time in the day to explore "the other side."

As you do, keep this in mind: the traditional medical establishment and the alternative practitioners do not, for the most part, see eye to eye. At some places along the borders of their disciplines is an uneasy truce; at other points, open warfare. If you choose to go from one camp to another in search of health, know that you will from time to time be in no-man's-land.

Both sides may take potshots, at best, and mount major attacks, at worst, on your dalliance with "those other people."

The attitude of the alternative practitioner might be, "Don't take that poison [your prescription medications] your doctor gives you. *That's* what's killing you. Stop it at once!"

The attitude of the established medical doctor is sometimes more benign—he or she has, after all, won the battle of who's best with the vast majority of the public and can afford to be magnanimous.

The only medicine
for suffering, crime,
and all the other woes
of mankind,
is wisdom.

THOMAS HENRY HUXLEY

The established doctor may dismiss the entire field of alternative healing with a comment such as, "It's a complete waste of your time and money."

I have found enormous value in each camp. When ill, I wouldn't dream of being without lavish attention from both. Some illnesses, traditional medical science can cure with a bottle of pills. I take the pills. Other illnesses have traditional medical science stumped, but for the natural healer, they are no problem. In those cases, I visit the alternative practitioner.

In some treatments the lines between traditional and alternative begin to blur. Traditional medicine begins incorporating alternative medicine, and alternative medicine begins including the traditional. Acupuncture, for example, once pooh-poohed by the traditionalists, is now used and accepted by more and more doctors. Dietary changes—once thought to have no significant effect on one's health as long as one was getting the daily minimum allotment of nutrients—are now, with many illnesses, standard medical advice.

More and more M.D.s are using alternative medicine in their practices, and more and more natural healers are saying, "A good shot of penicillin will clear this up faster than anything else," or "Have you tried aspirin?"

I applaud this "meeting of the minds." It may be some time before there is One Medicine. The day, frankly, may never come. Even if it never comes, use what works for you from either world and incorporate it all in your plan for wellness.

Don't be duplicitous: let each health-care provider—traditional or alternative—know what you're doing with the others. Some may throw up their hands and shriek, others may shake their heads in disapproval, but let each know you plan to continue. "What can you do for me *in addition* to this?" is what you want to know. If they say, "Nothing," move on. There are plenty of healers on both sides who are flexible enough to augment.

What you want is a cure. Where it comes from doesn't matter. Maybe it will be from this, maybe it will be from that, maybe it will be from everything together, and maybe your attitude and enthusiasm alone will heal you.

The philosophies of one age
have become
the absurdities of the next,
and the foolishness of yesterday
will become
the wisdom of tomorrow.

SIR WILLIAM OSLER

MONTREAL MEDICAL JOURNAL
1902

It doesn't matter. Be healed. Be well. That's what all healers worth their salt want.

MEANINGLESS PROVERBS

One does not
moisten a stamp
with the Niagara Falls.

P. W. R. Foot

No leg's too short
to reach the ground.

Lyndon Irving

She that knows why
knows wherefore.

Jim Snell

He digs deepest
who deepest digs.

Roger Woddis

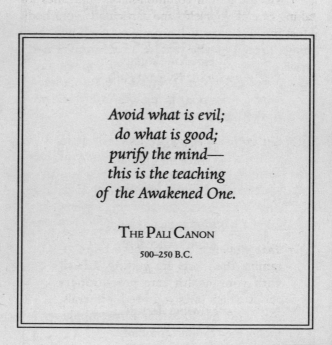

Avoid what is evil;
do what is good;
purify the mind—
this is the teaching
of the Awakened One.

THE PALI CANON

500–250 B.C.

Take Good Care of Yourself

This may seem redundant—not of what was in the book before, but of what you were taught as a child.

I will list certain common-sense guidelines for taking care of yourself—and particularly your body. Most medical types will assume you're doing these things already. Maybe you are; maybe you're not. I won't go into much detail. A part of you will say, "I know what you mean." Compare that inner knowledge with what you are doing and, if necessary, change your lifestyle.

- ***Get sufficient rest.*** How much sleep do you need? Go to sleep. When you wake up, that was enough. When you get tired again, go back to sleep. Use earplugs if noises bother you, a sleeping mask if light is troublesome.

- ***Take vitamins.*** You may need more vitamins than you are getting. Check with your health care practitioners about which ones you need. Minerals, too. And maybe other nifty supplements they can recommend.

- ***Eat sensibly.*** Remember the Four Basic Food Groups? Eat some of each every day. Especially fruits and raw vegetables, the food group most Americans omit from their diet. But eating only raw vegetables is not the answer, either.

> *I have had a good many*
> *more uplifting thoughts,*
> *creative and expansive visions*
> *while soaking*
> *in comfortable baths*
> *in well-equipped*
> *American bathrooms*
> *than I have ever had*
> *in any cathedral.*
>
> Edmund Wilson

Take the time to enjoy eating your food so that (a) it's fun, and (b) it's properly assimilated.

- ***Avoid fad diets.*** What's wonderful in Asia may not work here. Listen to your body. It will tell you what it needs. Learn to distinguish between wants and needs.

- ***Get some exercise.*** Because this book will find its way to people in all sorts of conditions, I'm not going to give any specifics. Check with your doctor.

- ***Get massaged.*** Okay, so maybe you didn't learn this as a child, but it's one that may awaken the child within you. Massage releases tensions, frees energy, removes physical blocks, and—perhaps most important of all—feels good. Indulge yourself. Often. You deserve it.

- ***Take hot baths.*** In this rush-rush, stand-up world, most people take showers. They're faster. More efficient. Some people haven't been in a hot bath for years. Too bad. They don't know what they're missing. Soaking in hot water, even for a few minutes, relaxes the body and soothes the mind faster than almost anything I know. So take a hot bath every day—whether you need it or not. And more often if you do.

How many cares
one loses
when one decides
not to be something
but to be someone.

Coco Gabrielle Chanel

Part II: THE CURE

TWO:

E-LIM-I-NATE THE NEGATIVE

I sandwiched this section on eliminating negativity between two sections on adding positivity. I did this for a reason. I firmly believe that the way to more health, wealth, and happiness is to *focus on health, wealth, and happiness*. This may sound simplistic, but many people try to obtain health, wealth, and happiness only by trying to eliminate disease, poverty, and unhappiness.

But the lack of disease is not necessarily health, the lack of poverty is not necessarily wealth, and the lack of unhappiness is not necessarily happiness. Sometimes we successfully eliminate a negative and discover we still don't have what we want. "After all that work!" we sigh. And, discouraged, sometimes we return to the negative.

Another problem with trying to get rid of something negative is that we must pay attention to the negative we're trying to eliminate. This attention gives it more energy—*our* energy—and some-

Give me chastity
and continence,
but not just now.

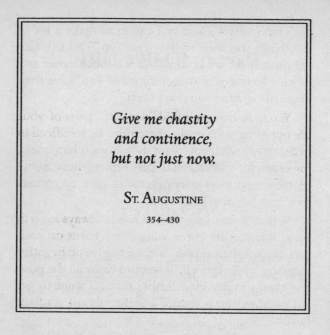

St. Augustine

354–430

times makes the negativity seem too great to overcome.

Doing nothing besides eliminating negatives to get what you really want can be the long way 'round. If there were one hundred objects on a table, and I wanted you to pick up object 27, I could tell you, as you randomly selected items, "No, don't pick up object 34. No, don't pick up object 29. No, don't pick up object 63."

Eventually, you would get to object 27, and I wouldn't say anything. You might, however, after twenty or thirty "Don'ts," give up. I could hardly blame you. It would have been much easier if I had simply said, "Pick up object 27."

That's why I asked you earlier to make a list of the things you *want* in life (your Top-Ten List). Going directly for what you want is a much easier and more effective way of getting what you want than eliminating what you don't want.

You may, however, find "negative" parts of your life opposing your goal—these must be sacrificed in order to get what you want. If you want happiness, for example, you must sacrifice unhappiness. Some of these opposites may be easy to give up; others may have become bad habits.

When eliminating the bad habits, always keep in mind *why* you are eliminating them. Focus on your *goal*. Rather than saying, "I want to give up negative thinking," tell yourself, "I want to enjoy all the positive things in my life." Rather than, "I want to get rid of this illness," say, "I want vibrant, radiant health."

Breaking bad habits can be difficult, but it's easier if you remember that what you're adding to your life (the goal) is more valuable than what you're eliminating (the habit).

In releasing yourself from the bondage of bad habits, don't try to eliminate all of them at once. That's just inviting failure. Take them one or two at a time, starting with the ones that will be easier for you to change. When these are under control, take on a few others that may be a bit more challenging. Build on the strength of each victory.

Over the piano
was printed a notice:
Please do not shoot
the pianist.
He is doing his best.

Oscar Wilde

Separate "Noticing the Negative" from "Negative Thinking"

We're not responsible for every thought that wanders through our brain, only the ones we hold there. The thought, "What an inconsiderate person," may float through our mind and probably do little harm. It's when we *add* to that thought ("And furthermore . . .") that we get into trouble.

Maybe the person *was* being inconsiderate. That might be an accurate observation. We start the cycle of negative thinking when we add "and I don't like that" to what we observe.

It's important to keep this distinction in mind when breaking the habit of negative thinking. Merely noticing that something is a certain way, and that that way might fall on the negative side of life, is not a "negative thought."

To notice a houseplant is withering is an observation, and not a positive one. From that observation, we have options.

One, the negative-thinking route: "Oh, the plant is dying. How many times have I told so-and-so to water the plants? Plants always die on me. I must have some plant-killing energy."

Two, the positive-action route: "I'd better water the plant. Apparently I'm not doing enough to impress upon so-and-so the importance of watering the plant; I'll write a note now. Plants don't seem to

The first idea
that the child must acquire,
in order to be actively disciplined,
is that of the difference
between good and evil;
and the task of the educator
lies in seeing that the child
does not confound good
with immobility,
and evil with activity.

MARIA MONTESSORI

do well in that location. Maybe I should get a hardier plant."

Every time we see something and think it might be better another way, we are not necessarily having negative thoughts. We get into trouble when we *get negative* and demand that things and people be different than they are.

If you're not willing to invest the time, activity, and money in making something the way you want it (assuming it's even possible), then you might as well accept it. Acceptance takes less than a second, consumes almost no energy, and costs absolutely nothing.

We live in a negative-feedback world. Often, the signal that tells us something needs attention is a negative one. *Noticing* these signals is not negative thinking. *Doing* something corrective about them is positive action. *Getting upset* about them is negative thinking.

The latter is what I'm suggesting you keep to a minimum.

If the essential
core of the person
is denied or suppressed,
he gets sick
sometimes in obvious ways,
sometimes in subtle ways,
sometimes immediately,
sometimes later.

Abraham Maslow

Depression

Does all this negative thinking produce depression; or are we depressed, and the depression causes negative thinking? Which became depressed first: the chicken or the egg?

Here I'm discussing *medical* depression, *biological* depression, not the sort of depression we feel when we say, "The popcorn at the snack bar has too much cholesterol. I'm depressed."

Many negative thinkers *can't help it.* They have a *physical illness* known as depression. It's an imbalance in the chemical functioning of the brain. A depressed brain *cannot hold* a positive focus for any meaningful length of time. Negative thoughts, on the other hand, flourish.

I know whereof I speak: I was depressed from at least the age of three, but I didn't discover it until I was forty-three. (That must be some sort of record for *non* self-awareness. Or denial. Probably both.) All those wonderful techniques and ideas I taught others in books, tapes, seminars, and PR appearances didn't work for me. Yes, they helped a little, but considering the time I had put in, I should have been happier than Mary Poppins. (Come to think of it, maybe Mary Poppins was a little depressed herself.) People would bump up against my anger or pain and exclaim, "I thought you wrote a book about not having negative thoughts!"

Shortly after I started treatment for depression (in 1993), the depression lifted like the proverbial veil. I felt good just being alive. I felt worthy for the

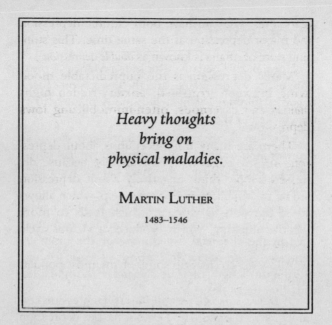

> *Heavy thoughts*
> *bring on*
> *physical maladies.*
>
> MARTIN LUTHER
>
> 1483–1546

first time in my adult life. Further, all the self-help stuff actually started helping. Not that life is now suddenly perfect. When I think and do negative things, I feel negative. When I think and do good things, however, I *finally* feel good.

There are three primary kinds of depression: *major depression, chronic depression,* and *manic depression.*

Major depression has a beginning, a middle, and an end—like the flu. Unlike the flu, however, major depressions often last for months.

Chronic depression (also called *dysthymia)* is a long-term, low-grade depression that can go on for years. (Yes, you can have both chronic depression and major depression at the same time. This stunning state of affairs is known as *double depression.)*

Manic depression is the unpredictable mood swing between irrational, anxiety-ridden highs *(mania)* and cavernous, often-immobilizing lows (depression).

There are many misconceptions about depression—mostly negative. Unfortunately, because depressed people think negatively about depression and its treatment, they don't get help, which allows the depression to worsen, which leads to more negative thinking, which produces a vicious cycle of suffering.

Allow me to clear up some of the most popular myths.

1. Depression is a mental illness. Depression certainly *affects* the mind and emotions, but depression is a *physical* illness—like diabetes, high blood pressure, or low thyroid. Specifically, depression is the body's failure to maintain the proper level of *neurotransmitters* in the brain. Neurotransmitters are the fluid through which the brain communicates with its many cells. When the level of neurotransmitters is too low, communication falters, brain functioning becomes inharmonious, and depression results. It is thought the *manic* (hyper) phase of manic depression occurs when the level of neurotransmitters is too high.

2. Depression cannot be easily treated. That was true just a few years ago, but medical breakthroughs since 1987 make depression among the

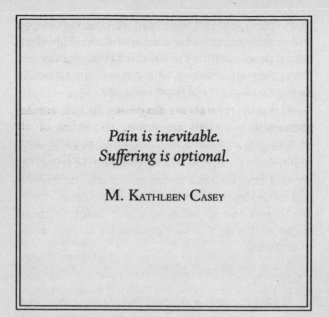

Pain is inevitable.
Suffering is optional.

M. Kathleen Casey

most easily and successfully treated of all major illnesses. The two major forms of treatment are antidepressant medication and short-term therapy (usually just fifteen to twenty sessions).

3. Antidepressants are "happy pills" that change your personality. Think of depression as a headache. If you've had a headache for months, years, or as long as you could remember, taking an aspirin and alleviating the headache will certainly make you feel better. It is, however, the same *you* feeling better. *Antidepressants only remove depression.* If you take an aspirin and don't have a headache, you won't feel much of anything. If you take an antidepressant and you don't have depression, you won't feel much of anything, either. Unlike, say, tranquilizers or pep pills, antidepressants have no mood-altering effect. When people say they're happier taking antidepressants, they are referring to the relief one naturally feels when the pain of depression lifts.

*4. **Antidepressants are dangerous.*** In fact, antidepressant medications are among the safest of all prescription drugs. Prozac, the most popular antidepressant, has had unparalleled negative press (more people know the side-effects of Prozac than know the symptoms of depression). This is because the Church of Scientology, for whatever reason, decided to attack Prozac with a great pile of falsehoods. More than ten million people regularly take Prozac worldwide; five million in the United States. Naturally, a handful of these people have displayed some aberrant behavior. A handful of *any* group of five million people will, at one time or another, display aberrant behavior. (Statistically, I'm sure it can be shown that a high percentage of mass murderers drank milk when they were growing up.) *All* medications have *potential* side effects, of course, and antidepressants are no exception. A relatively small percentage of people taking the new generation of antidepressants, however, experience any side-effects at all.

*5. **Antidepressants are unnatural and unhealthy.*** Not so. Antidepressants simply *balance* the level of neurotransmitters *already in the brain*. The positive effect of antidepressants comes from allowing naturally produced neurotransmitters to return to natural levels. That's all. Further, the misery of enduring depression is far more unhealthy—on all levels—than any known antidepressant side-effect.

The problems of alcoholism
and drug addiction
have strong links to depression.
The search for highs
may often begin
as a flight from lows.

NATHAN S. KLINE, M.D.

6. Healing depression means years of psychotherapy. The two forms of therapy shown to work best in healing depression (Cognitive Therapy and Interpersonal Therapy) are both short-term, closed-ended therapies—usually lasting just fifteen to twenty sessions. Both are more "retraining" and educational than they are lying on a couch and rhapsodizing on a therapist's traditional opening line: "Tell me about your childhood." The reason some people perceive, think about, and do depressing things is that *no one ever taught them a better way.* These therapies are about learning a better way.

7. If I have depression, I'm unusual. Hardly. More than fifteen million Americans currently suffer from depression. The sad fact is that *ten million of them don't know it.* These ten million go about blaming this and overreacting to that, but the *true* cause of their suffering, poor relationships, failure, and ill health is a biochemical imbalance in the brain (depression). The chances are one-in-five that you will have a depression at some time or another in your life.

A few additional thoughts on depression:

- People are more likely to be depressed the older they get. Those over sixty-five are four times more likely to have a depression than the general population.

- Depression is usually inherited, although the stress of life or chronic illness can cause depression, too. When I looked around my family tree and saw all the nuts growing on it, I realized I was *not* the product of the passion fruit bush (as I had always supposed).

- Many people with depression don't "feel depressed." One can suffer from depression and not feel sad, blue, or emotionally down.

- Untreated depression is the #1 cause of alcoholism, drug abuse, and other addictions.

- Depression is often an underlying cause of overeating, chronic fatigue, insomnia, headaches, bulimia, digestive disorders, aches and pains, and other physical disorders.

> *Physical and social functioning*
> *are impaired by depression*
> *to a greater degree*
> *than by hypertension,*
> *diabetes, angina,*
> *arthritis, gastrointestinal diseases,*
> *lung problems, or back ailments.*
>
> JOSÉ M. SANTIAGO, M.D.
>
> *JOURNAL OF CLINICAL PSYCHOLOGY*
>
> November, 1993

- Some people think they're depressed because they have difficult relationships. Perhaps they have difficult relationships because they are depressed.
- Depression inhibits the functioning of the immune system, increasing the incidence of illness and shortening life.

How to Tell if You Have Depression

According to the National Institutes of Health, if you have four or more of these symptoms for two weeks or longer, you may have depression. A diagnosis from a psychiatrist or other physician who specializes in depression is in order.

Symptoms of Depression Can Include:

- ❑ Persistent sad or "empty" mood
- ❑ Loss of interest or pleasure in ordinary activities, including sex
- ❑ Decreased energy, fatigue, being "slowed down"
- ❑ Sleep disturbances (insomnia, early-morning waking, or oversleeping)
- ❑ Eating disturbances (loss of appetite and weight, or weight gain)
- ❑ Difficulty concentrating, remembering, making decisions
- ❑ Feelings of guilt, worthlessness, helplessness
- ❑ Thoughts of death or suicide, suicide attempts
- ❑ Irritability
- ❑ Excessive crying
- ❑ Chronic aches and pains that don't respond to treatment

In the Workplace, Symptoms of Depression Often May Be Recognized by

- ❑ Decreased productivity
- ❑ Morale problems
- ❑ Lack of cooperation
- ❑ Safety problems, accidents
- ❑ Absenteeism
- ❑ Frequent complaints of being tired all the time
- ❑ Complaints of unexplained aches and pains
- ❑ Alcohol and drug abuse

Mysteriously and in ways
that are totally remote
from natural experience,
the gray drizzle of horror
induced by depression
takes on the quality
of physical pain.

WILLIAM STYRON

Symptoms of Mania Can Include

- ❑ Excessively "high" mood
- ❑ Irritability
- ❑ Decreased need for sleep
- ❑ Increased talking, moving, and sexual activity
- ❑ Racing thoughts
- ❑ Disturbed ability to make decisions
- ❑ Grandiose notions
- ❑ Being easily distracted

To find out more, please read a book I wrote with Harold H. Bloomfield, M.D., *How to Heal Depression*. Available at your local bookstore, library, or by calling 1-800-LIFE-101.

It's been troubling me.
Now, why is it that most of us
can talk openly about
the illnesses of our bodies,
but when it comes to our brain
and illnesses of the mind
we clam up
and because we clam up,
people with emotional disorders
feel ashamed,
stigmatized
and don't seek the help
that can make the difference.

KIRK DOUGLAS

He who has begun
has half done.
Dare to be wise;
begin!

HORACE

65–8 B.C.

Freedom from Addiction

Negative thinking is a bad habit. For many people it's an addiction. An addiction means some behavior is on automatic—it has control over you; you do not have control over it.

If you think you're not addicted to negative thinking, challenge yourself—put the book down, go about your life, and don't think a negative thought for the next hour. Starting now. Not one negative thought. Go.

ONE HOUR LATER . . .

How did you do? Now don't kid yourself by saying, "Oh, I only *noticed* the negative. You said that was okay." Is that *all* you did? Did you start to get upset about any of the negativity you noticed? If you did, you were doing more than noticing. You were adding to the noticing. What you were adding was negative thinking.

If you were unable to meet that challenge, you might want to take a good, honest look at how much control negative thinking has over your life.

Breaking addictions is not an easy process. If it were, they wouldn't be addictions. For the nonsmoker to give up cigarettes is easy; for the pack-a-day smoker, it's not. One is addicted; the other isn't.

For some, giving up negative thinking may be a snap. They're not addicted—they've been thinking negatively just because they thought they *should,*

If at first
you don't succeed
you're running
about average.

M. H. ALDERSON

that there was some *good* to be gotten from it. On learning they can get along marvelously without negative thoughts, these people just walk away from them. All they needed was permission.

For others, moving from automatic negative thinking to manual positive focusing is going to be a challenge—maybe the greatest challenge of their lives. And perhaps the challenge of lifc itself.

It's going to take time, perseverance, patience, forgiveness, determination, discipline, fortitude, enthusiasm, support, endurance and, above all, love. Love for yourself, love for the process, love for what you're creating in place of the addiction and, yes, even love for the addiction itself.

The past few years
have seen a steady increase
in the number of people
playing music in the streets.
The past few years
have also seen a steady increase
in the number of malignant diseases.
Are these two facts related?

FRAN LEBOWITZ

By perseverance
the snail reached the ark.

CHARLES HADDON SPURGEON

Take It Easy, but Take It

Going "cold turkey" on negative thoughts may be too much for some people. The nature of their thinking may be so negative that trying to stop all at once would leave them nothing to think about.

In such cases, replacing negative thoughts with a positive focus can be done more gradually, in two phases—first, taking the new steps and, second, maintaining the progress of the previously taken steps.

The following is not a definitive plan—it's more of a sample outline. You can modify the ideas here to suit your personal recovery program.

*1. **Start by simply noticing when you are thinking negatively.*** You don't have to do anything about it; just observe when it's going on. Rather than saying, "I'm *justifiably upset* over what's happening," say, "I'm really reacting negatively to this." Begin to notice that it's not *what's happening* but *how you're reacting* that's causing the problem.

*2. **Pause before thinking negatively.*** When you notice yourself starting to get agitated, tell yourself, "I'm going to wait two minutes before getting upset." Think about something else—something uplifting—for two minutes, *then* get flustered. Gradually work up to three minutes, then four, then five. Even if you start by putting just a few seconds between your automatic reaction and your postponed reaction, you are starting to take conscious control over the response. (It helps to have a prepared list of uplifting thoughts to focus on. Keep your "book of

Perseverance
is more prevailing than violence;
and many things
which cannot be overcome
when they are together,
yield themselves up
when taken little by little.

PLUTARCH

46–120 A.D.

good things" close at hand.)

3. Declare "negative-free zones" throughout the day. Plan two-minute segments throughout the day in which you entertain not a single negative thought. For these moments, focus so intently on the positive that negative thoughts have no place to exist. Increase the duration and frequency of these positive periods.

4. Pick minor areas you won't think negatively about anymore. Choose certain categories of thought you simply refuse to think negatively about. Start with areas that are not of critical importance to you. If you only occasionally get upset about, say, television commercials, tell yourself,

"No matter how dumb, stupid, boring, condescending, or misleading I find a television commercial, I will not get upset about it." Gradually expand your list until it includes all nonessential areas of your life. Make lists. If you find yourself thinking negatively about an area on your list, stop.

5. Increase the duration of "negative-free zones." Add a minute each day to your positive periods so that, eventually, you only have to think negatively a few times per day.

6. Save negative thoughts for certain times in the day. Set aside, say, four periods of fifteen minutes each in which you will think *only* negatively. Postpone all negative thinking until one of these times. Make a list of what you have to think negatively about so you won't forget. Do not add to the agenda items from areas you decided not to think negatively about anymore. Those are off limits, even during "the negative hour." If you don't get to everything on your list within one period, table it until your next meeting. Allow yourself one "emergency session" per day.

7. Add more central areas of your life to the "verboten" list. Decide you'll do no more negative thinking about, say, an important relationship; then extend the ban to all relationships. Gradually fold in business, money, health, death. Focus only on the positive aspects of these areas.

Plan so that everything winds up on the "think only positive" list at the same time as the scheduled "negative hours" are reduced to zero.

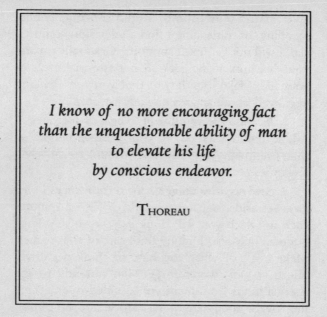

I know of no more encouraging fact than the unquestionable ability of man to elevate his life by conscious endeavor.

THOREAU

Congratulations. You are now free of the addiction of negative thinking.

Will you still have negative thoughts? Sure. But, as time goes on, you'll catch yourself sooner and the periods of negative thinking will be shorter. Also, positive focusing will lessen the intensity of the negative periods. A situation that would have had you fuming for days now has you percolating for only an hour. Something that would have had you terrified for several hours now has you worried for only a few minutes.

"I'm going to focus more and more on the positive aspects of life," is a life-long adventure.

Positive attitudes—
optimism,
high self-esteem,
an outgoing nature,
joyousness,
and the ability to cope with stress—
may be the most important bases
for continued good health.

Helen Hayes

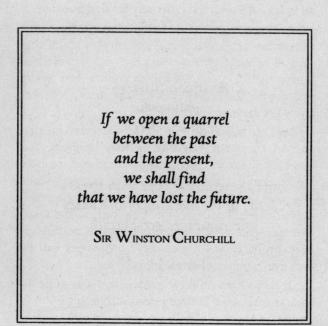

If we open a quarrel
between the past
and the present,
we shall find
that we have lost the future.

SIR WINSTON CHURCHILL

Keep Track of Negative Thoughts

If there's an area of negative thinking causing you trouble, keep track of it. Every time you have a negative thought in that area, make a tick mark on an index card reserved especially for that purpose.

At the end of the day you'll have a good idea how many times you thought negatively about that area. The number may surprise you. Sometimes seeing in black and white how much time we're wasting and harm we're doing to ourselves makes us realize enough is enough.

You can continue to keep a card a day on that area of thinking. It will chart your progress. You can look back over a month of cards and see how you're doing. It's a good feedback system. If the tick marks are increasing or staying about the same, maybe you need to do more to eliminate the negative thoughts. If the tick marks are decreasing (as they probably will be—simple awareness can be curative), congratulations are in order.

You can keep multiple cards if you like—one for each troublesome area of negative thinking.

Watching the number of tick marks decrease is a wonderful reminder that not only *can* you do it, but *you've already done it*. If you can do it in one area, you can do it in any area.

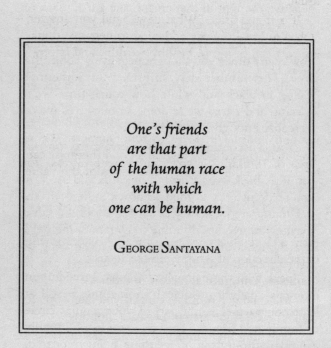

One's friends
are that part
of the human race
with which
one can be human.

George Santayana

The Power of Partnership

Let's face it—taking dominion over our thought process (the mind is a wonderful servant, but a terrible master) is not only challenging but, well, unusual.

If a friend asks, "What new?" and you answer, "Oh, I'm breaking my addiction to negative thinking so I can be more healthy, wealthy, and happy," you may be met by a blank stare and a "Huh?" (On the other hand, your friend may say, "It's about time!")

When starting something that's both challenging and unusual, it helps to have support. We've already discussed how helpful a good therapist can be. Later we'll be taking a closer look at the value of groups.

Now I'd like to explore the power of partnerships. Find one or two or three people you can form a close alliance with, people who are moving in the direction of a more positive focus.

Speak with these people at regular, agreed-upon intervals—daily, if possible. It's sometimes best if at least one partner is not part of your regular circle of family and friends. That way you can be totally candid without fear of anything being repeated, however unintentionally, and offending mutual acquaintances.

Don't gather too many positive-focusing partners—you're going for depth of relationship, not quantity. It is good, however, to have two or three just in case one decides to "drop out." (The road to

Each friend
represents a world in us,
a world possibly not born
until they arrive,
and it is only
by this meeting that
a new world is born.

ANAIS NIN

positivity is strewn with the abandoned vehicles of the faint-hearted.)

What do you talk about in your daily or thrice-weekly discussions? Why, the thrill of victory and the agony of defeat, of course. "I'm so proud about . . ." "I really blew it when . . ." "I can't find a way out of this . . ." "I found it helpful to . . ."

Chatter, laughter, swapping war stories, sharing secrets, giving and receiving support—all done in an atmosphere of nonjudgment, unconditional caring, and the knowledge that "we may not have come here on the same ship, but we're all in the same boat."

Two important points:

One, talk to each of your partners at least three times a week. This gives a sense of continuity, of flow. You can discuss the details of life that are often forgotten in less-frequent talks.

Two, keep your agreements with each other. If you say, "Tuesday at four," mean it. Keep it. Honoring your commitment creates a foundation of trust on which the partnership can build.

Necessary,
forever necessary,
to burn out false shames
and smelt the heaviest ore
of the body
into purity.

D. H. Lawrence

Burn 'Em

If one area of thought seems to be troubling you more than others, here's a good technique for lessening the power the thoughts have over you.

Get a clean sheet of paper and write down everything terrible about the situation. No one else will read it, not even you, so be as candid as you can. Don't worry about grammar or spelling or penmanship.

Include all the loaded words you can find. Get *really* negative. Add invectives, insults, profanity, abuses, railings, billingsgates, contumelies, obloquies, revilements, scurrilities, vituperations, curses, oaths, epithets, blasphemies, expletives, and swear-words. (Aren't thesauruses wonderful?) Get it *all* out of you and *onto* the paper.

Then burn it.

Don't reread it. Don't make a copy for your files (no matter how eloquently you expressed your wrath). Just burn it.

I hope I don't have to drag out Smokey the Bear or Sparkey the Fire Dog to tell you how to do this safely. Over the toilet bowl is a good place. You might want to hold the paper with a pair of tongs from the kitchen. ("Tina! Bring me my tongs!") After the ashes drop in the toilet, you have the extra satisfaction of flushing it.

If burning is not possible, tearing the paper into little pieces works just as well. If you can't write, dictate into a tape recorder whatever's bothering you and destroy or erase the tape.

Burn, burn,
burn like fabulous
yellow roman candles
exploding like spiders
across the stars
and in the middle you see
the blue centerlight pop
and everybody goes
"Awww!"

JACK KEROUAC

This process does two things—it gets the negative thoughts *outside of* and *away* from you. Then it destroys them.

A variation on this is to get a package of cigarette papers. Each time a negative thought appears from your "trouble area," write it on the cigarette paper and burn it over a large ash tray. It's a good idea to use tweezers or tongs to hold the paper—cigarette paper burns quickly, and you've already been burned enough by your negative thoughts.

To save matches, have a candle burning. Let the flame represent the light of who you are, eliminating the darkness of your addiction.

The fountain of content
must spring up in the mind;
and he who has so little knowledge
of human nature
as to see his happiness
by changing anything
but his own disposition,
will waste his life
in fruitless efforts,
and multiply the griefs
which he proposes to remove.

SAMUEL JOHNSON

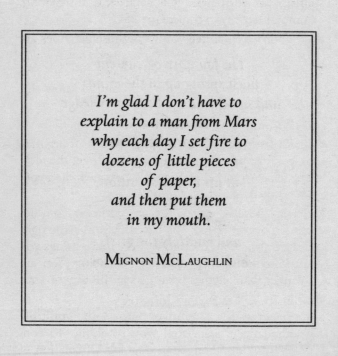

I'm glad I don't have to
explain to a man from Mars
why each day I set fire to
dozens of little pieces
of paper,
and then put them
in my mouth.

MIGNON MCLAUGHLIN

Activities That Contribute to Negative Thinking

Anything you abuse or overindulge in contributes to your negative thinking. Overindulgence reaffirms unworthiness. It is a physical affirmation: "I'm not worthy to control my life."

I don't have to tell you what those activities are for you. You know. They're the ones about which you've said, "I know this is a bad habit, but . . ." and "I wish I didn't do this, but . . ." and "I know this isn't good for me, but . . . ."

It's time to get off your buts.

I'll list some of the popular abuses. Yours may or may not be among them, but you'll get the idea. The idea? Stop it. Knock it off. It may be killing you. That's the negative way of putting it.

The positive way? You have authority and dominion over your life. You have the power, the right and, yes, the obligation to do only those things you know to be uplifting and life-enhancing. You are stronger than anything that gets in the way of your achieving this goal.

Smoking. Every smoker knows the multiple health dangers associated with smoking. To continue smoking, then, is an ongoing affirmation of illness. Every time smokers light up, the message they're giving themselves is, "I'm not worthy of health. I'm not able to control my hands, much less myself." By the very action of lighting up, smokers admit tobacco is a more powerful influence on their

Tell him to live
by yes and no—
yes to everything good,
no to everything bad.

WILLIAM JAMES

lives than they themselves are. This admission may do more harm than the physiological effects of the smoke. Stopping smoking is easy. You simply never put a lit cigarette in your mouth ever again. Period. It's getting to that point that's difficult.

Drug and alcohol abuse. If you automatically turn to drugs and/or alcohol in times of trouble, or if you find using them negatively affects your work, your relationships, or your general well-being, you're abusing them. The physiological effects of drug and alcohol abuse make it difficult for the abuser to hold positive thoughts. The residual toxicity of the chemicals in the body makes toxic thinking easy. This is why drug and alcohol dependence often needs dramatic, outside support—joining Alcoholics Anonymous or checking into a treatment hospital such as the Betty Ford Clinic. The cure, however, is easier than solving the primary problem—to admit that there's a problem in the first place.

Hanging out with negative people. Negative thinking is one of the most contagious diseases around. As George Herbert pointed out in 1651, "He that lies with the dogs, riseth with fleas." If you spend time with negative people, sooner or later you'll be thinking negative thoughts. To support their own weaknesses, people often gravitate toward similar people. "But everyone I know ____________." You can fill in the blank with the addictive behavior of your choice. "We can't *all* be wrong!" Every lemming thinks that about all the other lemmings as they head for the cliff. As you change your thinking, you may have to change some of your "friends." I put *friends* in quotes because the severe way some negative people criticize the positive movement of those around them I would hardly call friendly. And, by "changing friends" I mean finding new ones, not changing the thinking of the ones you have. If they want to change their thinking, they will. Give them a copy of this book. If they're ready, they'll act on it. If they're not, they probably won't even read it. So let it go. Changing your own thinking is a full-time occupation.

Compulsive sex. Some people seek sexual highs the same way drug and alcohol abusers seek chemical highs. Just because sex is "natural" (non-

> *A great many people have asked how I manage to get so much work done and still keep looking so dissipated.*
>
> ROBERT BENCHLEY

chemical) doesn't mean it can't be abused. It can. *What* you do sexually is not the issue. *Why* you do it is. Is it an expression of love for another, or is it a way of avoiding some inner feeling—loneliness, for example? Compulsive sex, like any lust, carries the message: "I'm not enough as I am. I need something or someone *out there* to make me happy. Without *that,* I'm worthless."

Workaholism. Is your work an expression of who you are, or is it the only place in your life you feel "in control"? People who work too much often do so from a desperate need to prove they are worthy. "I've done all this—see? I am worthy." The problem is, no accomplishment is ever good enough for these people. As one goal is about to be reached, a new, more difficult goal replaces it. The real problem, however, is that they never believe they are worthwhile *just as they are.* Worthiness is; it doesn't have to be earned or proven. If your work is your play and also your personal expression of life, then spending long hours at it is fine. So many people, however, hide from themselves in work that the term *workaholic* is now part of the language.

Complacency. Chronic inaction in areas you know need attention can be an addiction. Some people become habitually lethargic. Not taking an action becomes an automatic response. This stems from the belief, "I can't do it." Not doing anything "proves" the belief to be true, thereby strengthening the response that's there's no reason to respond. The habit of complacency is solved through action—physically moving and doing something. If the habit is strong, it may feel at first as though you're moving through Jell-O—every motion in every direction seems to have something pulling against it. That's the habit. You're stronger than it is. Keep moving. Set yourself a reasonable task and complete it. Then another. Then another. Show yourself you *can* do it, because you can.

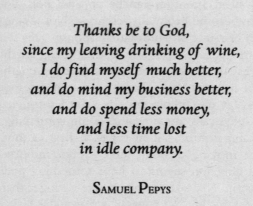

Thanks be to God,
since my leaving drinking of wine,
I do find myself much better,
and do mind my business better,
and do spend less money,
and less time lost
in idle company.

SAMUEL PEPYS

1660

The Twelve Steps

While exploring addictions, I would be remiss if I didn't discuss what is probably the most successful program for overcoming addiction—Alcoholics Anonymous.

For more than fifty years, through the AA program, millions of people have found freedom from their addiction to alcohol. The Twelve Steps—as the AA program is called—are so successful that more than one hundred fifty other organizations use them to overcome eating disorders, compulsive sex, drug abuse, and negative emotions.

The core of the AA program is described in the book *Alcoholics Anonymous* (also known as The Big Book). Here are the Twelve Steps, along with the three paragraphs preceding and the one paragraph following them. If you don't have a problem with alcohol, just substitute "negative thinking" (or whatever you feel your addiction to be) for "alcohol."

> Remember that we are dealing with alcohol—cunning, baffling, powerful! Without help it is too much for us. But there is One who has all power—that One is God. May you find Him now!
>
> Half measures availed us nothing. We stood at the turning point. We asked His protection and care with complete abandon.
>
> Here are the steps we took, which are suggested as a program of recovery:

Compassion for myself
is the most powerful
healer of them all.

THEODORE ISAAC RUBIN, M.D.

1. We admitted we were powerless over our addiction—that our lives had become unmanageable.
2. Came to believe that a Power greater than ourselves could restore us to sanity.
3. Made a decision to turn our will and our lives over to the care of this Higher Power, *as we understood Him, Her, or It.*
4. Made a searching and fearless moral inventory of ourselves.
5. Admitted to our Higher Power, to ourselves, and to another human being the exact nature of our wrongs.

6. Were entirely ready to have our Higher Power remove all these defects of character.
7. Humbly asked our Higher Power to remove our shortcomings.
8. Made a list of all persons we had harmed, and became willing to make amends to them all.
9. Made direct amends to such people wherever possible, except when to do so would injure them or others.
10. Continued to take personal inventory and when we were wrong, promptly admitted it.
11. Sought, through prayer and meditation, to improve our conscious contact with our Higher Power *as we understood Him, Her, or It*, praying only for knowledge of our Higher Power's will for us and the power to carry that out.
12. Having had a spiritual awakening as the result of these steps, we tried to carry this message to others and to practice these principles in all our affairs.

Many of us exclaimed, "What an order! I can't go through with it." Do not be discouraged. No one among us has been able to maintain anything like perfect adherence to these principles. We are not saints. The point is, that we are willing to grow along spiritual lines. The principles we have set down are guidelines to progress. We claim spiritual progress rather than spiritual perfection.

The best thing
about the future
is that it comes only
one day at a time.

ABRAHAM LINCOLN

No, *You Can't Afford the Luxury of a Negative Thought* is not an AA book, nor am I saying these twelve steps are the *only* way to break addictions. I just wanted to offer them as a way millions of people have found successful.

As far as I know, there is no Negaholics Anonymous (NA) for people who realize they are powerless over their negative thoughts. The closest I've found is Emotions Anonymous. If you consider that a negative thought is usually the step just before a negative emotion, then the goal of EA and the goal of overcoming negative thinking seem in alignment.

One of the advantages of AA, EA, and all the

other organizations that end with "Anonymous" is the meetings. These meetings provide support, camaraderie, and the knowledge, "I'm not alone in this."

For more information on AA or EA, telephone information and ask for the number in your area. Or, write for meeting times and places in your area. (Emotions Anonymous, P. O. Box 4245, St. Paul, Minnesota, 55104. Alcoholics Anonymous, P. O. Box 459, Grand Central Station, New York, New York, 10163.)

EA has a book entitled *EA: Emotions Anonymous*. AA has, in addition to *Alcoholics Anonymous*, a long list of publications. Write to the above addresses for information.

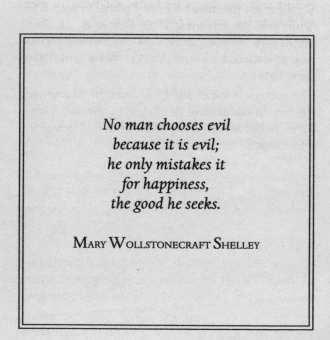

No man chooses evil
because it is evil;
he only mistakes it
for happiness,
the good he seeks.

MARY WOLLSTONECRAFT SHELLEY

What Are You Getting from This?

Pain hurts. We as human beings seem prepared to do almost anything to avoid pain. So why do we persist in doing things we know will bring us mental, emotional, and/or physical pain?

Return with me now to those thrilling days of yesteryear—childhood. Most children find that when something bad happens to them—an illness, an accident—they get an extra measure of care, understanding, sympathy, and love. "Oh, you hurt your finger! Let me kiss it and make it better." Injuries and illness seem to bring an outpouring of affection.

Given this scenario, it's not difficult for a child to conclude, "Injury and illness get me love." Some children then create accidents and sicknesses because they want the love, the cuddling, the pampering. The payoff.

It's not necessarily a conscious creation—although I'd bet just about everyone at one time or another faked an illness in order to stay home from school.

For the children unwilling to go through physical trauma to get attention, there are other ways.

Children who get their way by throwing tantrums sometimes grow up to be "rageaholics." When they don't get what they want, they get mad. Even in adulthood, getting angry sometimes gets them what they want. And probably quite a bit of

I always keep a supply of stimulant handy in case I see a snake— which I also keep handy.

W. C. Fields

what they don't want.

Some children misbehave to get attention, figuring even negative attention is better than no attention at all. These children can grow to be adults who go through life causing problems just to be noticed.

Actually, however, all of these payoffs are just *symbols* of loving, not the genuine article. But, when the real thing's not around—and people haven't yet learned how to give loving to themselves—a symbol will have to do.

Some of the popular payoffs people receive from indulging in negative behavior include attention, sympathy, avoidance, excuses, protection, acceptance, approval, martyrdom, deception, control, manipulation, and a sense of strength (albeit false), security, closeness, or accomplishment.

Other seeming benefits of negative behavior are avoiding responsibility, not having to risk, appearing to be right, self-justification, and appearing to prove worthiness. People even boast about their negativity: "I'm working out my problems," "I'm learning," "I'm getting a good emotional release," "Pain equals growth," and "I can handle pain."

You might want to take an honest look at what you're getting—or seem to be getting—from whatever negative thoughts, feelings, or physical manifestations you put yourself through. If you want attention, for example, that's a good thing to know. If you can find a way of getting all the attention you want without having to go through all the negativity, wouldn't that be easier? (Not to mention less painful.)

There's a simple way of getting payoffs directly—asking. "Would you please pay attention to me for a few minutes?" "Could I have some support?" "Tell me you love me." Yes, there's risk involved—you might not get the payoff. But—as you may have discovered—negative behavior doesn't always get it, either.

Make a list of what you're getting from your illness—the payoffs. Work on getting those things more directly. Once you're getting those things through other methods, you may be able to let the illness go.

There is luxury
in self-reproach.
When we blame ourselves
we feel no one else
has the right to blame us.

OSCAR WILDE

Making such a list requires unflinching honesty. The idea that we're doing something as drastic as creating a life-threatening illness just to get attention or sympathy or love is hard to accept. I'm not saying it's true in all cases. Yours may or may not be one. Only you really know.

Maybe you'll look at your list of payoffs and decide you don't need some of them after all. Then cross them off the list and tell yourself, "I don't need ______________ anymore. I can let that one go." The part of you that's creating the illness because it thinks you still want those things will listen and respond. This part of you *only wants you to have what you want!*

The remaining payoffs—the ones you really do want—give them to yourself. Love yourself. Pay attention to yourself. Nurture yourself. Cuddle yourself. Pamper yourself. Give to yourself so fully that whatever anyone else gives you will be just icing on the cake.

When you are filled by your own nurturing, there's no need to seek payoffs "out there." If there's no need to seek payoffs, maybe the illness that's seeking them for you will have no need to stick around.

*People are always
blaming their circumstances
for what they are.
I don't believe in circumstances.
The people who get on in this world
are the people who get up
and look for the circumstances they want,
and, if they can't find them,
make them.*

George Bernard Shaw

Accountability

If I even *hint* that people have more to do with creating, allowing, or promoting what happens to them than they ordinarily think, some people immediately take the defensive. "You mean this is *my fault?!* Is *that* what you're trying to tell me?"

No, that's not what I'm trying to tell anyone. That's the dark side of accountability—fault, blame, guilt. It's also the inaccurate side, a misuse of the concept. It's as though I gave someone a hammer and, instead of using it to hang pictures, the person used it to smash frames and then told me, "This hammer was a lousy thing to give me."

The light side of account-ability is realizing a simple fact—we are far more powerful than we generally like to admit. If we can see, for example, that we had a hand in creating, allowing, or promoting something we don't like in our life—even a life-threatening illness—we can also see how we have the power to get rid of it.

The word *accountability* comes from an ancient Roman term, which meant "to stand and be counted." I'm merely suggesting you might want to stand more and be counted (account-able).

Take a look at what you're happy with in your life—the people, the objects, what you've learned, all you've accomplished. The idea of accountability says you had a hand in all that—that you created, promoted, or allowed all of the good in your life. Let's take a look at creating, promoting, and allowing.

> *It is the commonest*
> *of mistakes to consider*
> *that the limit*
> *of our power of perception*
> *is also the limit*
> *of all there is to perceive.*
>
> C. W. LEADBEATER

Create. You saw it, you wanted it, you went out and got it. Simple creation. Maybe after you got it you didn't want it as much, but you got it nonetheless. It was your doing. If you saw, say, a Picasso reproduction and wanted it for your living room—you saw it, you bought it, you hung it in your living room. Creation.

Promote. Here you were a co-creator. Someone or something else was involved and together you created it, but it might not have happened if you did not have some outside influence. A friend has a Picasso hanging in her living room and offers to sell it to you. You think, "Not bad. Sure, I'll buy it." It ends up in your living room.

Allow. More subtle still. In these situations, you could have said, "Stop" or done something earlier on to avoid it, but you didn't. The same friend gives you the Picasso for your birthday. You think it's all right, but not what you would have chosen for the living room. You do, however, have that bare spot on the wall. It's been bare for months. You can't say you don't like it, because that's not entirely true. Besides, it might hurt your friend's feelings. And you can't say you have no place to hang it, because that's obviously not true either. So, accompanied by feigned squeals of delight, the Picasso ends up in your living room. And, over time, you've grown to like it there.

If you look at everything you like in your life, you'll find you had something to do with getting it—even if it was a passive act of allowing it to happen.

Now, apply these same concepts to *little* things in your life you *don't* like. Start small, now. Don't immediately stalk the great tragedies. That's one of the best ways of dismissing a new idea without having to fully explore it: apply it to the most challenging situation you can imagine and see if the concept holds up. It probably won't. It's as though we were newly introduced to math and an older relative suddenly gives us a problem in trigonometry: "Here. See if your math can solve *this.*" Eventually it can, but right now we're at nine minus six equals three.

So start with, say, the pictures on the walls you *don't* like. How did they get there? Why are they still there? You probably participated to some de-

When a man blames others
for his failures,
it's a good idea
to credit others
with his successes.

Howard W. Newton

gree in creating, promoting, or at least allowing them to be there. If it's your apartment and the pictures are still there five minutes from now, you are *allowing* them to remain by not taking them down.

Every so often we like to pretend we are the victim. We had nothing to do with it. We didn't want it. It just happened. That, in fact, is a good definition of a victim: a person to whom life happens. As someone said, "There are three kinds of people in the world: the ones who make life happen, the ones to whom life happens, and the ones who wonder, 'What happened?'" Victims fall (after slipping on a banana peel left there by some inconsiderate person) into the latter two categories.

Being a victim can become a habit—also the source of some of our best anecdotes. Most stand-up comics make a living from it. Stand-up comedy is mostly one "victim story" after another. Rodney Dangerfield has gained enormous respect telling stories about how little respect he gets.

Victim stories can be fun—although the victim may not think so (until much later). Here are some victim stories, taken from actual auto insurance accident reports:

> Coming home I drove into the wrong house and collided with a tree I don't have.
>
> The guy was all over the road. I had to swerve a number of times before I hit him.
>
> In my attempt to kill a fly, I drove into the telephone pole.
>
> I had been driving for forty years when I fell asleep at the wheel and had the accident.
>
> To avoid hitting the bumper of the car in front, I hit the pedestrian.
>
> An invisible car came out of nowhere, struck my vehicle, and vanished.
>
> The indirect cause of this accident was a little guy in a small car with a big mouth.
>
> The telephone pole was approaching. I was attempting to swerve out of its way when it struck my front end.
>
> The pedestrian had no idea which way to run, so I ran over him.

Faced with the choice
between changing one's mind
and proving there is no need to do so,
almost everyone gets busy on the proof.

JOHN KENNETH GALBRAITH

> I pulled away from the side of the road, glanced at my mother-in-law, and headed over the embankment.

Note the lack of accountability in these. That may be one reason they're so funny—we remember the lame excuses we've invented in the past. "The telephone pole was approaching," indeed.

It's fine to tell victim stories, but when we start to believe them, we get into trouble. Inherent in that belief are the underlying beliefs, "I have no control over my life," "I can't have things the way I want them," and "I'm not worthy of what I want."

Take a look at some occurrence—small, now—that you felt victimized by. Tell yourself the story as though you were telling it to a sympathetic friend, with all the bitter details.

Then take a look at the same story, and see if you can find some areas in which you were accountable—areas in which you helped, even in some small way, to create, promote, or allow whatever happened. You'll probably start seeing glimmers of, "Well, if I had followed my instinct and done this, the outcome would have been different." Or, "I made it even worse by . . . ." Or, "I could have left half an hour before."

To help find areas of greater response-ability in the story, here are some clues:

1. Go back in time. Usually we start a victim story at the point we can claim to be The Innocent. "I was just standing there, minding my own business when . . . ." If we go back in time, we often find the innocence fades. "I was all ready to go when Paul called and said he couldn't make it." If we go back in time, we might discover we canceled an appointment at the last minute with Paul the week before, or Paul had a history of being unreliable, or Paul had mentioned something else might come up. When we go back, we usually find we had some information or experience that takes the bloom off our innocence.

2. What were you pretending not to know? We all have an inner voice that gives us direction. Some people are more in touch with their voice than others are. It's not necessarily the loudest voice "in

I have been
a selfish being
all my life,
in practice,
though not in principle.

JANE AUSTEN

there," but it's consistent, and usually correct. (I call it the Master Teacher.) Often when something bad happens, people will spontaneously say, "I knew it!"—a highly accountable statement. But then they immediately revert to blame, accusations, and other forms of playing victim. What did our Master Teacher tell us about the situation? It might have been "Don't go" or "Be careful," yet we went and we weren't careful and—*voilà*—a victim story. Not that you should follow every voice inside your head, of course. If, however, you get a message from yourself, it's certainly worth checking out. Also, as you learn to listen to your Master Teacher, you'll be able to distinguish it from the voice of your lust, the voice of your discontent, the voice of your fear, and so on. (More on how to call upon this helpful inner voice later.)

3. What thoughts did you have about the situation? Did you, perhaps, through worry or doubt or unwillingness or some other negative thinking, contribute to what happened? Let's use the example of Paul canceling at the last moment. Maybe you had the thoughts: "I'm not sure I want to go to this place," or "I don't know if I want to spend time with Paul," or "I don't feel like going out," or "I wish I could watch TV tonight." Sometimes we think something, our wish is granted, and then we complain because we got what we wanted. The same is true of wanting to do something *so much* that our unworthiness surfaces. "I *really want* to go with Paul, but maybe I won't be good enough company for him," or "I never get to go to places with people I really want to, like Paul," or "If I were Paul, I wouldn't go out with me." Remember: what we fear can come upon us.

Are there some situations in which we really are victims? Of course. There are evil, destructive, deceitful people who will manipulate you into giving them what they want by promising whatever they think you need. In trusting, you get taken; by risking, you get took. Sharks are one of the dangers of swimming in tropical waters.

I am suggesting, however, that we have more choices than we realize in situations we would normally think of as choiceless. We are more powerful than the persona we've been programmed to believe is us.

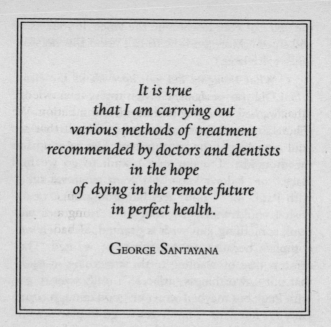

It is true
that I am carrying out
various methods of treatment
recommended by doctors and dentists
in the hope
of dying in the remote future
in perfect health.

George Santayana

The more you can look at all the incidents of your life—good and bad—from an accountable point of view, the more you'll reclaim the power you've given to the illusion of "random" situations "out there."

Remember the three magic words: Create, Promote, Allow—C. P. A.—Account-ability.

Continue exploring the concept by considering more and more important situations with the question, "How did I create, promote, or allow what's happening here?" And, "How can I create, promote, or allow more of what I want to take place?"

If you have trouble, consider it a creative puzzle—

"*What if* I were accountable?" Also, be *willing* to know. The willingness to know creates the opportunities to know.

There are three aspects to accountability:

1. Act-knowledgment. We simply acknowledge that we had *something* to do with the situation. We "act knowingly." We may not know all that we did—consciously or unconsciously—to set it up, but we're willing to take a look and, when we find some way we were accountable, to acknowledge it. This is not blame, criticism, condemnation, or guilt. (I'll get to guilt in a moment.) It's asking a simple question: "This happened to me, so if I had something to do with it, what was it?"

2. Response-ability is the ability to respond. How could you have more effectively responded to the situation? What effective responses can you take now? Realize that in *any* situation there are response options that will either lift you higher or drag you lower. Why not take the uplifting ones? Sometimes the response is physical; sometimes it's a change of attitude; sometimes it's both. You always have the ability to respond in an elevating way. Response-ability is not blame. People often ask, "Who's responsible for this?" in tones that clearly mean, "Who's to blame for this? Whom can we punish?" That's not how I use it here. Response-ability is simply looking at the response options available, and being willing to choose uplifting ones.

3. Corrective action. If we learn something, but it doesn't lead to a change in behavior, then we

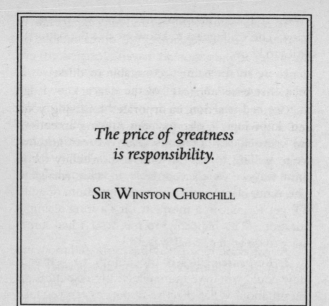

The price of greatness
is responsibility.

SIR WINSTON CHURCHILL

haven't really learned it. It's still a concept. It may be a nice concept, a well-thought-out and brilliantly described concept—but a just concept nonetheless. When genuine learning takes place, so does a corrective action. If we say, "Yes, we understand hammers are to be used for hanging pictures, not smashing frames," and we continue to smash frames, we haven't learned. We merely comprehend. To become truly accountable, one must be willing to take corrective action. We don't make plans with Paul, or next time we make plans with Paul, we have alternate plans in mind. Either of these would be corrective action.

To make plans with Paul and fully expect him to be there is (multiple choice): (a) unreasonable, (b) dumb, (c) an indication we haven't learned, (d) evidence we're not being accountable to ourselves in relationship to Paul, (e) all of the above.

Corrective action incorporates forgiving yourself and others. It also includes making amends. If we spill milk on a friend's floor, we can acknowledge we did it, we can take responsibility for it, but—to be truly accountable—we take corrective action: we clean up the milk.

As you continue to examine more and more important and "impossible" ("I couldn't *possibly* have had *anything* to do with that!") areas of your life from an accountable point of view, you'll start to get a sense of how powerful you truly are.

We use that enormous power to create—consciously and unconsciously, positively and negatively. As we look at our role in creating our life to date and see how much more we had to do with it than we thought, we can be more and more aware of our creative action. Then we can use it in more and more positive ways—such as healing.

For what I do
is not the good I want to do;
no, the evil I do not want to do
—this I keep on doing.

ROMANS

7:19

Guilt

Guilt is a miserable game we play with ourselves. It's the price we pay for not taking an honest, compassionate, realistic, forgiving look at our own reality. It's a game of make-believe with bitter consequences.

Guilt is anger directed at ourselves. We get angry with ourselves for something we should have done or shouldn't have done. It accumulates over time. Our self-punishment becomes worse with each repeated occurrence. ("I should have known better!")

Fear steps in. We become afraid of situations in which we might fail to live up to our personal expectations. We're afraid of what we might do to ourselves if we fail again. We're afraid of our own anger.

We avoid new people, situations, activities. We settle into a predictable rut, and then feel guilty we aren't doing more for ourselves. Some people become immobilized with guilt, afraid of doing anything lest they disappoint themselves again.

This cycle of negative energy—from ourselves to ourselves—can have devastating effects. It poisons relationships, inhibits growth, stifles expansion. And it hurts. It can become self-hatred. It puts enormous stress on the mind, emotions, and body.

Over time, it can kill.

Perhaps the most tragic part about guilt is that it is thoroughly unnecessary.

When lovely woman stoops to folly,
And finds too late that men betray,
What charm can soothe her melancholy?
What art can wash her guilt away?

The only art her guilt to cover,
To hide her shame from every eye,
To give repentance to her lover,
And wring his bosom,
is—to die.

OLIVER GOLDSMITH
1776

That's the bad news. Now, let's lighten up a bit and discuss the good news: after reading this chapter you'll never have to feel guilty again. You probably will, but you won't have to. Once you understand how guilt works, you don't have to let it do its dirty work on you.

We all have images, beliefs, and expectations about ourselves. They usually begin, "I am a good person, and good people . . . ." Most of these expectations are cultural and were "sold" to us when our sales resistance was particularly low—when we were children. We bought them. And we reconfirm the purchase every time we feel guilt.

To illustrate, let's take a fairly common example. We're on a diet. We want to lose some weight. Chocolate cake is not on our diet. We eat the cake. We feel guilty.

What images or beliefs about ourselves might have been violated by eating the cake?

"I am a good person, and good people take care of their body, keep commitments with themselves, have willpower, eat only things that are good for them, care about how they look, follow through on plans, meet goals, set a good example for others, and care about their loved ones." Something along those lines.

This is what good people do, but what did we do? When we describe our guilty actions to ourselves, we tend to exaggerate. Remember the fast-talking, bad-mouthing vulture? It has a field day. Squawk, squawk, squawk. Negative, negative, negative. Bad, bad, bad. Shame, shame, shame. It might sound something like this:

"I'm getting big as a house, and still I ate the fattening, empty-caloried piece of cake after having too much to eat at dinner anyway. I ignored all inner guidance to the contrary. I broke a solemn agreement with myself not to eat fattening foods. I have no willpower. I damaged my body by adding extra fat to it. I already look terrible, but now I'll look worse. I can't accomplish anything. I never do what I tell myself I'm going to do. I hurt my loved ones by setting a bad example of how to diet after I told them I was going to lose weight. If I don't care about myself, at least I could care about the people I love." And that's just round one.

The New England conscience doesn't stop you from doing what you shouldn't; it just keeps you from enjoying it.

CLEVELAND AMORY

The pristine image we have of ourselves is repeatedly violated by our despicable actions.

What to do? Well, the small print at the bottom of the "I am a good person . . ." contract reads, "And when I'm not, I'll feel *guilty.*" Feeling guilty lets us prove we're still a good person.

After all, who feels bad about doing bad things, bad people or good people? Good people, of course. Bad people *enjoy* doing bad things. Bad people feel *wonderful* doing bad things.

To prove we're good, we punish ourselves with guilt. This allows us to maintain the image that we *are* all of those wonderful things. By feeling guilty, we're saying, "I did it this time, but I'll never ever do it again. See how much this hurts me? I don't want to hurt this bad again. So I promise, cross my heart and hope to die, I'll never ever do it again."

Guilt allows us to pretend something is true about ourselves that, based on results, isn't. It lets us maintain an inaccurate image about ourselves, an image that does not match our actions.

Am I saying we're not good people? Not at all. That part's true. The falsity begins with ". . . and good people . . ." Do good people always, only, and exclusively do those things? Of course not.

Do good people sometimes not take care of their bodies? Sure. Do good people sometimes break commitments with themselves? Yes. Do good people sometimes lack willpower? Absolutely. Do they always eat things that are good for them? Ha! Do they always care about how they look? Hardly. Do they always follow through with their plans, always meeting their goals? Nonsense. Do they always set a good example for others? Of course not. And do they always care about their loved ones? Afraid not.

The truth is, good people *do* do all those good things *and sometimes they don't.*

You *are* a good person. You do a lot of good things. And sometimes you don't. Does that alter the fact that you're good? Not at all. It merely confirms the fact that you're *a human being.*

Guilt not only protects an erroneous gilt-edged image we have about ourselves; it *also lets us do the thing we felt guilty about doing again.* When we've

I have,
all my life long,
been lying till noon;
yet I tell all young men,
and tell them with great sincerity,
that nobody who does not rise early
will ever do any good.

SAMUEL JOHNSON

"paid the price" for our "crime," we're free to do it again *as long as we're willing to pay the price again.* The price? More guilt. "How badly do I want the cake? Is it worth two hours of guilt? No. I'll take a smaller piece and only feel guilty for an hour."

We plea-bargain with ourselves before we even commit the crime.

So, guilt as it's popularly practiced in our culture (a) feels lousy, (b) has devastating effects on our mind, emotions, and body, (c) maintains an inaccurate image of what "good people" are and do, (d) allows us to believe one thing about ourselves while doing something completely contradictory, and (e) lets us continue doing things that may not be in our best interests.

Talk about your nonproductive activities. And what good is there in guilt? Guilt is anger at ourselves. Anger is the energy for change. Therefore, guilt can be used as the energy for personal change. We can use the energy to change the image of how we should be *or* change the action we feel guilty about.

There is also the *twinge* of guilt we feel before taking part in the contrary action. The twinge is a much quieter sensation. Easier on the mind, body, and emotions. The twinge of guilt is our friend. Just as the warning light in our car reminds us to get gas, this twinge tells us when we're about to trigger a more painful form of guilt.

When you're about to do something—or even contemplating something—and feel the twinge of guilt, stop. The twinge of guilt is telling you you're off balance. You are about to take an action that would violate an image you have about yourself.

At this point, rather than plea-bargain or blindly rush ahead, do one of two things—*change the image or the action*. You can change the image you have about yourself, bringing it up to present-day reality, *or* you can not take the action that violates your image.

If you do either one, you will not have the punitive, painful, lasting guilt.

Take chocolate cake, for example. You have lots of options for changing the image. You could change your belief to include occasional forays into cakedom, or you could decide your weight is fine as

***MAE WEST:** For a long time*
I was ashamed
of the way I lived.

"Did you reform?"

***MAE WEST:** No;*
I'm not ashamed anymore.

it is and call off the diet, or you could promise to take a long walk after dinner, or any other alteration of the image that currently says, "Chocolate cake is always forbidden." Changing the action is simple: don't eat the chocolate cake. (Once again: simple, but not necessarily easy.)

If you do one of those two things—change the image or the action—you will not feel guilty about eating the chocolate cake. If you don't change the image or the action, it's back to the old cycle of crime and punishment.

In addition to the obvious physical, emotional, and mental benefits of breaking the cycle of guilt, here are three others:

1. Breaking the guilt cycle gives us a more realistic view of ourselves and humanity in general. One of the values of the "tell-all" biographies is that they let us see that good people—great people—who have accomplished laudable, extraordinary things, are human beings, too. We all have a full complement of quirks, foibles, preferences, habits, lusts, and temptations. Sometimes they serve us; sometimes they don't. And so what? It's the human condition. Nothing to get upset about.

2. It lets us set more reasonable goals. So we eat a piece of chocolate cake now and again. So we don't lose three pounds a week. Maybe we lose only one pound a week. That's still 52 pounds a year. We can take it easier on ourselves, taking time for what we once called "failure" and now call "diversion."

3. It lets us do things that are truly important. By not kidding ourselves and cluttering up the daily "agenda for action" with pipe dreams, we can focus more clearly and with greater determination on the truly important tasks at hand. If our mind is not cluttered with twenty or thirty things we "should" be doing, it's easier to do the two or three things that really must be done.

Freeing yourself from guilt is a gradual progression. Guilt, for most people, is an automatic response. When it goes off—and it will—please don't feel guilty about feeling guilty. And if you do feel guilty about feeling guilty, don't feel guilty about feeling guilty about feeling guilty. And if you do feel guilty about feeling guilty about . . . .

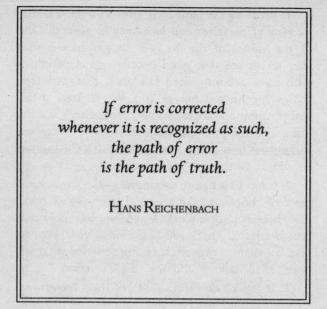

If error is corrected
whenever it is recognized as such,
the path of error
is the path of truth.

HANS REICHENBACH

Some people create a New Enlightened Image of themselves that says, "I am a good person and I no longer feel guilt." Please, change that image before you even create it. Probably the most accurate one you can have is, "I am a good person and I feel what I feel," because that's the way it seems to go. Sometimes it's guilt and sometimes it's glory.

If you're in a cycle of guilt, there are techniques to help you change your image or your actions. But first, let's talk about resentment.

Life teaches us
to be less harsh with ourselves
and with others.

Goethe

Man must evolve
for all human conflict
a method which rejects revenge,
aggression and retaliation.
The foundation of such a method
is love.

MARTIN LUTHER KING, JR.

Resentment

Resentment is a miserable game we play with ourselves and others. It's the price we pay for not taking an honest, compassionate, realistic, forgiving look at other people's reality. It's a game of make-believe with bitter consequences.

Resentment is anger directed at others. We get angry with others for something they should have done or shouldn't have done. It accumulates over time. Our punishment becomes worse with each repeated occurrence. ("They should have known better!")

Fear steps in. We become afraid of situations in which people might fail to live up to our personal expectations. We're afraid of what we might do to others if they fail again. We're afraid of our own anger.

We avoid new people, situations, activities. We settle into a predictable rut, and then feel resentful because we aren't doing more for ourselves. Some people become immobilized with resentment, afraid of doing anything lest they let others disappoint and anger them again.

This cycle of negative energy—from ourselves to others—can have devastating effects. It poisons relationships, inhibits growth, stifles expansion. And it hurts. It can become hatred. It puts enormous stress on the mind, emotions, and body.

Over time, it can kill.

Perhaps the most tragic part about resentment is that it is thoroughly unnecessary.

Hating people
is like burning
your own house down
to get rid of a rat.

HARRY EMERSON FOSDICK

I never hated a man
enough to give him
his diamonds back.

ZSA ZSA GABOR

Sound familiar? No, you weren't having an attack of *deja vu*. What I just said about resentment is the same thing I said about guilt a few pages ago.

Resentment and guilt are the same. With guilt, *we* don't live up to the images we have about how we should be; with resentment, *other people* don't live up to our images about how *they* should be.

The images are ours. The anger is ours. We're judge, jury, and executioner. With guilt, the judgment goes against us. With resentment, the judgment goes against others. (All that I'm about to say about resenting *people* is true of *things,* too—cars, VCRs, weather, nature, food, TV commercials. For the sake of clarity, I'll just talk about people. Please add "and things" at key points.)

When we resent others, we are protecting our image of how they should behave. Based on results, the image is false. But we protect the image because, after all, it's easier to keep our image and resent people for not measuring up than it is for us to change our image.

We have a lot invested in our image of how others should behave. We inherited the basic plan from our parents and teachers. Then we spent years refining it. Why should we change our shoulds, musts, and have-tos just because some inconsiderate people are too lazy to measure up?

The problem is, of course, the anger. Almost invariably, it does more harm to us than to the people we're mad at. Earlier I quoted, "The love I give you is secondhand—I feel it first." The same is true of hate. From a cardiovascular point of view, the most dangerous and damaging emotion is anger. It's one of the most unpleasant emotions, too.

The solution? Once again, the six magic words—change the image or the action. Except with resentment it's shortened to three—*change the image.*

With anger at ourselves (guilt), we have an option. We have, after all, the right to change our actions if we so choose. We do *not*, however, have the right to change anyone else's actions. We, therefore, have only one solution—change the image.

There are two situations in which you have the right to change another's actions—when you're the parent of a young child or when you're the boss. In those situations, you may have not only the right, but the obligation to change the child's or the em-

It is easier to fight
for one's principles
than to live up to them.

ALFRED ADLER

ployee's behavior. You will most likely find, however, that if you change your image of how people should be behaving before attempting to change their behavior, you will get better results and feel better in the process.

With resentment, *always* change the image, and *only* if you're a parent or the boss do you even consider changing the action.*

*Some people add an exception to the above list: "If I'm in a relationship, I get to change the other person's behavior." No. Especially no. Emphatically no. That's the cause of more disastrous relationships than probably anything else. Accept your

To eliminate resentment, add, ". . . and sometimes they're not" to all the images you have about other people. "Friends are always honest, and sometimes they're not." "Doctors are always meticulous, and sometimes they're not." "Waiters are always friendly, and sometimes they're not." When you feel resentment, you know the other person is in the ". . . and sometimes they're not" range of behavior.

When Jesus told his followers, "Love your enemies, bless them that curse you, do good to them that hate you, and pray for them which despitefully use you, and persecute you" (Matthew 5:44), do you suppose he said it primarily so those nasty persecutors could enjoy the benefits of his disciples' love, blessings, goodness, and prayers?

I think he advised his disciples to love their enemies because it was also good for *the disciples*. That way, no matter *what* happened to them, they would always be loving, blessing, doing good, and praying—not a bad life.

That the people around you will feel better when you stop resenting them is a secondary benefit. That *you* will feel better when you're not resenting others is the primary gain.

As with guilt, we have an inner friend to tell us when it's time to change our images. It's a twinge of resentment. The twinge of resentment is quiet, like the twinge of guilt. It will gently tug and

loved ones; don't change them.

If any of you is without sin,
let him be the first to throw a stone at her.

JESUS OF NAZARETH
JOHN 8:7

Fifty-four-year-old Ellsworth Donald Griffith told a Des Moines, Iowa judge that he was too old to go to prison, and asked instead for a public stoning for his conviction for terrorizing his former employer. His one condition was that only those without sin be allowed to cast stones. The judge sentenced him to 5 years in prison.

THE WORLD ALMANAC & BOOK OF FACTS

remind you, "It's time to change your image about . . . ."

If you don't change the image at that point, you'll probably be off on resentment, running the gamut from ticked off to seething. That's okay. As soon as you find yourself there, back off, take a deep breath, and take one (or all) of the steps listed in the next chapter.

When you realize that your resentment is based not on others' *actions,* but on your *reactions* to their actions, it's a day for celebration. Yet another "bad thing" you thought happened "out there" comes under your direct influence. You reclaim even more of your power. You have more mastery, more control over your life—not because you can control others' actions, but because you're learning to modify your own re-actions.

Another word for it is freedom.

BELINDA: *Ay, but you know we must return good for evil.*

LADY BRUTE: *That may be a mistake in the translation.*

SIR JOHN VANBRUGH

1698

Getting Out of Guilt and Resentment

Whenever you're caught in the cycle of guilt or resentment, a few techniques can help get you back on track. I'll be discussing most of these in detail later, but here's a summary:

1. ***Change the image.*** I know I've said this several times, but it bears repeating. Ask yourself, "What am I upset about?" Whatever it is, let it be okay. Accept the "transgression"—either yours or another's. Give yourself (and others) permission to do what you (or they) *have already done*. Let your image to adjust to reality. You don't have to *like* it, but you don't have to hate it either.

2. ***Forgive.*** Forgive the others and forgive yourself. Forgive yourself for whatever you did. Forgive the others for whatever they did. Then forgive yourself for judging yourself and others.

3. ***What's the payoff?*** Are you *enjoying* the intensity of it all? Are you feeling "right"? Is all the drama of it fun? What are you getting from this resentment?

4. ***Move.*** Do something physical. Run around the block. Clean a closet. Do aerobics. If you're in bed, move your arms a lot. Get your energy circulating, flowing, moving.

5. ***Refocus.*** Yes, once again I suggest: focus on something in your immediate environment that's more positive.

6. ***Is it worth dying for?*** If you had a choice—(a) defending the inaccurate image or (b) your life—

Humor is
a prelude to faith and
Laughter is
the beginning of prayer.

REINHOLD NIEBUHR

which would you choose?

7. Be grateful. Find something to be grateful for—anything. Right now.

8. Observe. Observe the anger or resentment. Observe the *feeling*. Don't do anything to it or with it. Don't pay attention to the thoughts feeding the feeling. Observe the feeling itself.

9. Breathe. Resentment and guilt are usually felt in the lower abdomen and chest. Take slow, deep breaths into these areas. Stretch the area as you breathe in. Imagine a white light going in with each breath and filling the area.

10. Surrender. Let go of the struggle. Don't *try*

to get rid of the feeling. Just surrender. Feel it; don't fight it.

11. Sacrifice. Give it up. If you thought sacrifice meant giving up good things, know that it can also mean giving up the not-so-good things. Sacrifice your judgments. Give them up.

Use any of these techniques, in any order, when you feel guilt or resentment.

The important thing is not getting rid of guilt and resentment as quickly as possible. Perhaps the most valuable aspect of guilt and resentment is what they can teach you about yourself. What "shoulds," "musts," and "have-tos" hold the most sway over you? Where did they come from? What can you do about them? What are you getting out of the guilt and resentment? What are the payoffs?

Guilt and resentment are the primary expressions of anger. Anger and fear are the primary "negative" emotions. Learning to master them can take time. Be patient. Tell yourself you're doing a wonderful job.

You are.

If you can't say anything
good about someone,
sit right here by me.

ALICE ROOSEVELT LONGWORTH

Monitor What You Say

Listen to yourself as you speak. Note especially any time you (a) let your words limit you, or (b) set something in motion you might not want in motion. Watch out for sentences along the lines of "I can't take this anymore," "I'll never get it right," "This is killing me," or even "It's to die for!"

We are powerful creators. What we say often enough can become reality. When it comes to pass, we say, "I *know* I didn't create this!" No? Remember six months ago when you said, "I need to lose ten pounds; I don't care how, but I need to lose ten pounds"? The "how" is extensive dental work that will keep you from eating very much for a few weeks. By the time it's over, you'll have lost ten pounds. "But I didn't want it *this* way!" "I don't care how," you said. This is the how.

If you find yourself saying something you don't necessarily want to take place, quickly say, "Cancel" or any other word you understand to mean, "Don't put what I just said in motion." Then say what you really want.

Put yourself on a one-minute time delay. Remember Yul Brynner as the Pharaoh in *The Ten Commandments*? Remember when he gave a command? "So let it be written," he would say in deep, pharaonic tones, "so let it be done." Give yourself sixty seconds to cancel an order before the scribe within you hears, "So let it be written, so let it be done."

Elysium is as far as to
The very nearest Room
If in that Room a Friend await
Felicity or Doom—
What Fortitude the Soul contains,
That it can so endure
The accent of a coming Foot—
The opening of a Door—

EMILY DICKINSON

Yes, as my swift days near their goal,
'Tis all that I implore:
In life and death a chainless soul,
With courage to endure.

EMILY BRONTE

Endurance

If something can't be removed, ask for the strength to endure it. There is an old saying, "That which doesn't destroy us makes us stronger." A life-threatening illness can be a strengthener, not necessarily to the body, but certainly to the character and to the spirit.

Robert Louis Stevenson prayed: "Give us grace and strength to forbear and to persevere. Give us courage and gaiety and the quiet mind."

If all of our tribulations were taken from us, we would never grow. It would be crippling. As Oscar Wilde said, "When the gods choose to punish us, they merely answer our prayers."

When we learned to walk, we stumbled, fell, struggled, fell again, bumped our heads—it went on for months. Our parents, who easily could have carried us, instead encouraged us. They comforted us when we fell, but put us back on our feet and stepped back, saying, "Come on, you can do it."

As infants we may have wondered, "Why are they doing this to me? Why are they putting me through all this torture? Without the "torture," however, we never would have learned to walk.

Perhaps there's a lesson we must learn that we don't understand, a lesson that requires this new "torture." If that's the case, then all we can ask for is the strength to endure.

"Weeping may endure for a night, but joy cometh in the morning" (Psalm 40:5).

Alas, I know
if I ever became truly humble,
I would be proud of it.

Benjamin Franklin

Part II: THE CURE

THREE:

LATCH ON TO THE A-FIRM-A-TIVE

Now we're ready for the really good stuff—the affirmations of living, loving, health, wealth, happiness, and joy.

I'm not sure what Johnny Mercer meant by "latch on to" in the lyric of his song. I doubt if he meant "become attached to." I certainly don't mean it that way. If joy, loving, and happiness become new "shoulds," "musts," and "have-tos," we are, once again, "doomed before we even take the vow."

Humans have a natural ability to want, desire, aspire, yearn, and long for. Any attempt to diminish this natural desire I find (a) counterproductive, (b) frustrating, and (c) so improbable it borders on the impossible.

Some people desire desirelessness with such a passion that it actually *increases* their ability to desire. What we do we become stronger in, and these

Ah, but a man's reach
should exceed his grasp,
Or what's a heaven for?

ROBERT BROWNING

people yearn so much and so often to have no more yearning that their ability to yearn becomes astronomical.

I see nothing wrong with the human trait to desire. In fact, I consider it integral to our success mechanism. Becoming *attached* to what we desire is what causes the trouble. If you *must have it* in order to be happy, then you are denying the happiness of here and now.

If, however, you're focusing on the positive aspects of the reality around you while traveling in the direction you want to go, I see no problem with that at all. In fact, it sounds to me like a pleasant, productive way to live.

Rather than trying to diminish desire, I suggest you desire what you really want more of. *Desire* happiness. *Aspire* to gratitude. *Long* for health. *Crave* compassion. *Seek* satisfaction. *Lust* after God (however and whatever you perceive God to be). *Want* to love yourself, others, and everything around you more and more each day.

These are laudable goals. They're also fun, challenging, exciting, and not only within your grasp, but also within your reach.

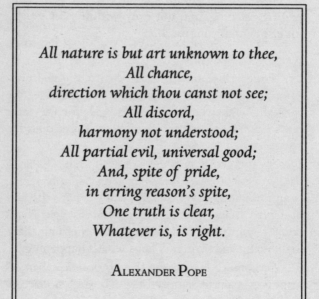

All nature is but art unknown to thee,
All chance,
direction which thou canst not see;
All discord,
harmony not understood;
All partial evil, universal good;
And, spite of pride,
in erring reason's spite,
One truth is clear,
Whatever is, is right.

Alexander Pope

A Is for Acceptance

Acceptance is such an important part of happiness, contentment, health, and growth that some people have called it "the first law of personal growth."

The world goes on, people do what they do, events come and go, and, for the most part, our only choice in all this is, "Do I accept it or not?" If we accept it, we flow with it. We allow life to do what it's already doing.

If we refuse to accept it, we usually feel pressure, pain, frustration, anxiety, and dis-ease. We struggle with what is. The struggle, for the most part, takes place within us—where it also does the most harm.

Acceptance is not the same as *liking,* or *being happy about,* or even *condoning.* It is simply seeing something the way it is and saying, "That's the way it is." It's seeing what's going on and saying, "That's what's going on." It's looking at something that's happening and saying, "That's what's happening."

Acceptance is realizing that to do *other* than accept is (a) painful and (b) futile. Through nonacceptance we try to control the world. We want our "shoulds," "musts," and demands to rule the world.

It doesn't work. It simply does not work.

To prove how futile the struggle to control the world, get up tomorrow at 4 a.m. and try to keep the sun from rising. Do *everything* you can to keep it from coming up. Struggle madly. Use all your power, influence, money, friends, and political con-

The more
the marble wastes,
the more the statue grows.

MICHELANGELO

nections to help. You won't be able to delay its scheduled ascension for so much as a millisecond.

Maybe you don't want to control the turning of the earth; you just want to control the world around you. Good luck on that one, too. The truth is, we sometimes can't even control ourselves—that part of the universe we have the most direct influence over. If we can't control our own thoughts, feelings, and physical reactions, how can we hope to control others?

Nature goes on being nature in its own natural way. We have very little control over it. What do we have control over? The space within the skin of our body. We can work to make that environment as loving, joyful, peaceful, and delightful as we like. That in itself is a lifelong project—and a worthy one, too.

The rest—the outer environment—does what it does. There's not much more to do than say, "It's doing what it's doing."

When we set out to change a small fraction of the outer universe we *do* have some ability to change, one of the best starting points is acceptance. The sculptor begins by accepting the block of marble as it is, and then removes everything that isn't a statue. When asked how to sculpt a horse, one artist explained, "I see the horse in the stone; then I take away everything that is not the horse."

Michelangelo's *David* was carved from a flawed block of marble. Another sculptor had begun work on the block and abandoned it. There was a deep gash in the side, making the stone "unacceptable" to sculptors for decades. Michelangelo, however, accepted the marble—gash and all—and created one of the marvels of humanity.

We begin with acceptance and move from there. This includes acceptance of ourselves. We are, please remember, a part of nature. We can be as contrary as a thunderstorm on a picnic. That "natural" part of us has its own rhythms, its own timelines, and its own agenda. While bringing this "animal" under control, we must learn to accept it.

This "natural" part of us most people call the body, and that's accurate, providing that you remember the body includes the brain that thinks the thoughts and the nerves that feel the feelings.

There is no good
in arguing
with the inevitable.
The only argument available
with an east wind
is to put on your overcoat.

JAMES RUSSELL LOWELL

Thoughts and feelings are a necessary part of the human animal.

The "natural" part of us thinks the Fight or Flight Response is *terrific*. Eons of genetics have told it so. We now must gradually convince "it" that the Love and Acceptance Response is more valuable for our survival as an animal.

This "convincing" we call *education*. The source of the word is *educare*, "to lead forth from within." It's the gradual process of leading from within rather than being led from without.

In that process of *teaching* acceptance, we must *practice* acceptance. Set a good example for yourself.

Learn to accept whatever you do. This, of course, is not *carte blanche* to run roughshod over others or to hurt yourself. It's just a realization that, being human, we're going to do things we're not going to like (and by "doing," I mean *all* levels of doing, including thoughts and feelings), and we might as well accept those, too.

Learn to accept even your lack of acceptance. When you're not accepting something, accept your nonacceptance of it. Can't accept your nonacceptance? Then accept the fact that you can't accept your nonacceptance. If the bad stuff like guilt can pile up in layers (feeling guilty about feeling guilty about feeling guilty), so can the good stuff (accepting the fact that you can't accept your nonacceptance).

Yes, it gets funny, and it certainly can be fun. That's one of the keynotes of acceptance: a sense of lightness. As you accept the heaviness, you begin to feel "the unbearable lightness of being." Accept that, too. No: welcome it.

With acceptance, you can't set some things aside and say, "I'll accept these, but not those." Acceptance is unconditional. You can *like* one thing more than another—that's preference—but acceptance means not excepting anything. Actually, it's easier that way. You don't have to *remember* what to and what not to accept. If it is, accept it. Simple.

Schedule acceptance breaks throughout the day. Give yourself an acceptance break right now. Accept *everything* around you, everything inside you, everything about everything. Accept your thoughts.

I travel light; as light,
That is, as a man can travel who will
Still carry his body around because
Of its sentimental value.

CHRISTOPHER FRY

Accept your thoughts about your thoughts. Accept your thoughts about your thoughts about your thoughts. Accept whatever feelings you have, the sensations in your body. Don't try to change any of it—trying to change is a form of nonacceptance.

Accept your surroundings, your physical environment. Accept your room, its furnishings, the smells, the sounds, and the occupants. Accept your thoughts about what's there and about what's not there. Accept your memories, fantasies, demands, and opinions about how it should be.

Accept all the things you did but wish you didn't do and all the things you didn't do but wish you did. Notice that these decisions about what's hot and what's not about an activity (or inactivity) are thoughts, too. Accepting thoughts—including the negative ones—is an important step toward greater joy.

And greater health.

To be conscious that we are
perceiving or thinking
is to be conscious
of our own existence.

ARISTOTLE

To become the spectator
of one's own life is to
escape the suffering of life.

OSCAR WILDE

Observe

Observation is a pathway to acceptance. To observe is to think, feel, taste, smell, see, and hear without attachment, without attempting to manipulate the outcome, without taking sides.

All you do is observe. Simply "be with" whatever information your senses present to you. If your mind goes off on judgments and evaluations, observe that. Don't get involved with the thoughts; don't try to change them; just observe them.

As you learn to observe, you become more in touch with that part of you that's *you*. When you stand back and observe, you'll begin to experience a *you* that isn't your mind and its thoughts, isn't the emotions and their feelings, and isn't the body and its sensations.

This existence of *you* is hard to communicate, because I have to use *words*, which are decoded by the mind, and the mind does not like to relinquish its authority or to admit that there's something more basic to you than it.

You'll understand by doing. After fifteen or so minutes of consciously observing, you may begin to notice the part that's doing the observing.

Give yourself a period of time in which you won't be disturbed. Decide for that period of time to do nothing but observe. Sit or lie comfortably. Now, be still and be.

The mind will present "good ideas" to do something else. Don't do anything about them; just observe them. The feelings will want something more

I am a camera
with its shutter open,
quite passive, recording,
not thinking.
Recording the man
shaving at the window opposite
and the woman in the kimono
washing her hair.

CHRISTOPHER ISHERWOOD

exciting to feel about. Don't fulfill them; observe them. The body will demand attention. Don't attend to it; just observe the demands.

If you want to change positions, don't. Just observe the desire to change positions. If you have an itch, don't scratch it. Observe the itch. Your mind, body, and emotions may throw little—and sometimes not so little—temper tantrums. Observe the tantrums. Observe the inner kicking and screaming. These (or the fear of these) may be what has controlled you for some time. Gain authority over them. You gain authority by doing none of the actions they demand you do. Just sit and observe.

The game is this: The mind, body, and emotions

say, "I'm going to get you to move before the fifteen minutes (or whatever time you set for yourself) is over." *You* say, "No, I'm not." And the game begins. You may say, "Oh, it's easy not to move for fifteen minutes." Most games look easy from the sidelines. Play the game and see.

If it's easy, congratulations! If it's not, don't be surprised. The things that trouble you during this process are probably the same things that trouble you in life: the "shoulds," "musts," "have-tos," and demands of your mind, body, and emotions.

The solution? Observation. Simply observe. You'll learn a lot about yourself. And, you'll learn a lot about the parts of yourself that aren't your self.

You can, if you like, extend the "sitting observation" to "moving observation." As you move through life, observe it. Observe your reactions.

Observation is a primary tool of awareness. The more you observe what you're now unaware of, the more aware you become.

Behold: consciousness.

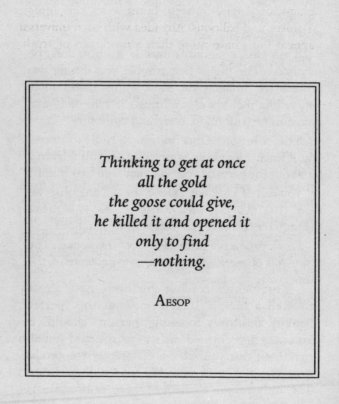

Thinking to get at once
all the gold
the goose could give,
he killed it and opened it
only to find
—nothing.

Aesop

Patience

There is a saying that has found its way onto plaques, posters, buttons, bumper stickers, mugs, T-shirts, and balloons. Any idea with such universal appeal must have more than a modicum of truth. This saying does.

Be patient. God isn't finished with me yet.

Patience is our compassion for the distance between what we are now and what we know we can be.

Because we have such fertile imaginations, we can envision ourselves scaling mountains one moment and swimming oceans the next. To get from the mountaintop to the beach, however, takes a certain amount of time. If we're on the mountain and want to go to the ocean, that's fine. But if we strike against ourselves for not being at the ocean *right now*, we're being impatient.

Most people reading this book have already formed a mental image of what the "perfect, healthy, positively focusing" person "should" be. You may have formed such an image, and you also may have cast yourself as the star of the production. Great! (Or, in show-biz terminology: Bravo!) The only minor challenge, then, is how we get from where we are to where we want to be.

But if you're putting undue pressure on yourself to achieve these goals of perfection, health, and positivity—impatience has crept in.

Relax. Life is a lifelong journey. You'll never get out of it alive. You'll never be "done." You're fine

No thing great is created suddenly,
any more than a bunch of grapes or a fig.
If you tell me that you desire a fig,
I answer you that there must be time.
Let it first blossom,
then bear fruit, then ripen.

EPICTETUS
50–120

Dear God,
I pray for patience.
And I want it right now!

OREN ARNOLD

just as you are. You're not finished with yourself, and never will be. I've yet to meet a person who has declared, "I'm done!" Humans have desires, dreams, and goals beyond their current reality, no matter how magnificent that reality might be. It's part of the human condition.

Realize, then, that the journey from here to there will never be completed. Such is life. Have compassion for the distance between where you are now and where you're going next. (Where you are now, remember, is the goal of a former moment in time.)

Patience is enjoying the journey. It's not climbing the mountain to get to the top; it's climbing the mountain to enjoy the climb. Enjoy the *process* of your life. The travel ads claim, "Getting there is half the fun," and as Robert Townsend corrected: "Getting there is *all* the fun."

Besides, if you don't have fun while getting there, you probably won't have much fun when you arrive. Your joy muscles will have atrophied. You will have learned to postpone fun so well that you'll postpone it until your *next* destination. ("I can't wait to go on vacation." "I can't wait to get home.")

Another popular saying is "Let go and let God." Letting go is relaxing. Letting God is being patient. Relax and be patient. What a great prescription for enjoying life.

When you learn patience with yourself, it's easy to extend it to others. When you learn patience with others, be sure to extend it to yourself.

Realize that, right now, everything is the way it "should" be, and when later comes, everything will be "perfect" then, too.

What is patience? Enjoying the moment. How does one enjoy the moment? By being patient. An endless loop? Sure. And you can jump in at any point.

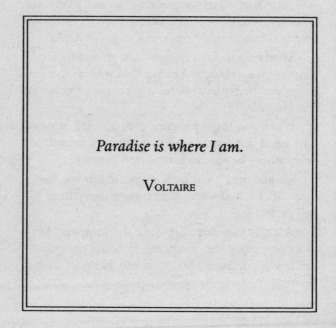

Paradise is where I am.

Voltaire

Altitude and Attitude

Another endless loop (I like to think of them *as upward spirals)* is the one of altitude and attitude. When "stuck" in something you don't like, you can either change the altitude or the attitude and, as Peter Pan would say, "U-u-u-u-up you'll go!"

Altitude is our viewing point, our perspective. The higher our viewing point, the more we can see. The more we can see, the more information we have. The more information we have, the better we can make well-informed decisions.

When the question arises, "Shall I think negatively about this moment or not?" I maintain that, with enough altitude, your spontaneous response will be "not."

Have you ever been in a situation that seemed awful at the time, but eventually led to something wonderful? If you knew, at the time, that the bad situation would eventually lead to a much better one, would you have wasted all that energy feeling bad about it? Probably not.

What if *all* situations in life were like that? What if there were a *reason* behind all movement, a *plan* behind the action? What if, with sufficient altitude, you could see the plan? Not necessarily the way in which every detail will come to pass—what a dull life it would be if we knew precisely what the future held—but more a general sense that "something good will come from this."

Attitude is the way we approach things—our point of view. Do you look at life as an adventure to

It is possible that our race may be an accident, in a meaningless universe, living its brief life uncared for, on this dark, cooling star: but even so—and all the more—what marvelous creatures we are! ¶ What fairy story, what tale from the Arabian Nights of the Jinns, is a hundredth part as wonderful as this true fairy story of simians! ¶ It is so much more heartening, too, than the tales we invent. ¶ A universe capable of giving birth to many such accidents is—blind or not—a good world to live in, a promising universe. We once thought we lived on God's footstool; it may be a throne.

CLARENCE DAY

be enjoyed, or a problem to be solved? There are infinite possibilities for living in either Adventureland or Problemville. The choice, as I've pointed out numerous times, is yours. The key is attitude.

The connection between attitude and altitude is easy to see. If we have a good attitude, our altitude will lift, and if we have an elevated altitude, our attitude will rise. (The reverse, by the way, is also true—spirals go up or down, and seem to be infinite in either direction.)

Altitude is raised through meditation, contemplation, prayer, spiritual exercises, creativity, service—connecting directly in some way with the uplifting energy of life.

Attitude lifts through inspiring lectures, reading, seminars, therapy, support groups, books, movies, TV shows—learning concepts and techniques that naturally lead to an enlightened view.

If you lift the attitude, the altitude will lift. If you raise the altitude, the attitude will lift. Either way, *comme tu veux* (it's up to you).

Of course, doing things to lift both attitude *and* altitude will put you on what is technically known as an *upward hyper-spiral,* or, as it's more commonly known, joy.

My religion consists
of a humble admiration
of the illimitable superior spirit
who reveals himself
in the slight details
we are able to perceive
with our frail and feeble minds.

ALBERT EINSTEIN

I could prove God statistically.

GEORGE GALLUP

Reach for God

I've dropped God's name quite a few times in these last few chapters. Maybe it's time to talk directly about the Deity.

I'm going to suggest you reach for God in two ways.

First, whatever your concept of God currently is, reach a little higher. Whatever you believe or perceive God to be is fine with me—from the bearded, omnipotent Father on the throne to the creative flowering of Mother Nature. Whatever it is, see if you can expand it just a little bit more.

Second, reach for God in whatever form you feel God to be. If God is the power that grows plants and moves planets, fine. If God is the creator behind all that, fine. If God is the part of us that beats our heart and breathes our breath, fine. Reach into that power, energy, and spirit for support, solace, direction, and love.

Relate to God in whatever way you choose, but do relate. Chat, ask for things, listen for guidance, give love, receive joy, or just say "thanks."

Give it a try. You have nothing to lose but your doubt. The following thoughts on God may stir a few of your own.

> Serve God, that He may do the like for you.—*The Teaching for Merikare (2135–2040 B.C.)*

> What is God? Everything.—*Pindar (518–438 B.C.)*

Has God forgotten
all I have done for him?

LOUIS XIV

(1709)

(Louis also said,
when a coach arrived precisely on time,
"I almost had to wait.")

Beauty is the gift of God.—*Aristotle*

Even God lends a hand to honest boldness.—*Menander (342–292 B.C.)*

I speak Spanish to God, Italian to women, French to men, and German to my horse.—*Charles V*

When God wounds from on high he will follow with the remedy. *Fernando de Rojas*

I treated him, God cured him.—*Ambroise Par (1517–1590)*

God is usually on the side of the big squadrons and against the small ones.—*Roger de Bussy-Rabutin*

Belief is a wise wager. If you gain, you gain all; if you lose, you lose nothing. Wager then, without hesitation, that He exists.—*Blaise Pascal (1623–1662)*

If God were not a necessary Being of Himself, He might almost seem to be made for the use and benefit of men.—*John Tillotson (1630–1694)*

Live innocently; God is here.—*Linnaeus (1707–1778)*

For I bless God in the libraries of the learned and for all the booksellers in the world.—*Christopher Smart*

The universe is the language of God.—*Lorenz Oken (1779–1851)*

Of course God will forgive me; that's his business.—*Heinrich Heine (Last words, 1856)*

In the faces of men and women I see God.—*Walt Whitman*

VISITOR: "Henry, have you made your peace with God?"
THOREAU: "We have never quarreled."

God forbid that I should go to any heaven in which there are no horses.—*Robert Bontine (1853–1936)*

God hid the fossils in the rocks in order to tempt geologists into infidelity.—*Sir Edmund Gosse*

The Lord God is subtle, but malicious he is not.—*Albert Einstein*

To believe in God is impossible—
not to believe in him is absurd.

VOLTAIRE

next to of course god america I love you land of the pilgrims' and so forth—*e. e. cummings*

God is a verb.—*Buckminster Fuller*

Isn't God special?—*Church Lady*

If only God would give me some clear sign! Like making a large deposit in my name at a Swiss bank.—*Woody Allen*

I could not say I believe.
I know!
I have had the experience
of being gripped by something
that is stronger than myself,
something that people call God.

CARL JUNG

It's good to be just plain happy;
it's a little better to know
that you're happy;
but to understand that you're happy
and to know why and how
and still be happy,
be happy in the being and the knowing,
well that is beyond happiness,
that is bliss.

HENRY MILLER

Nothing Is Too Good to Be True

Ready for a pop quiz? Okay. Consider this statement: "If something is too good to be true, it is."

Pop quiz question: What words will follow "it is"?

(a) "too good" (If something is too good to be true, it is therefore not true.)

(b) "true" (If something is too good to be true, it is true.)

BZZZZZZZ. Time's up.

The correct answer is (b): if something is too good to be true, it is true. The answer most people spontaneously arrive at, however, is (a).

LESSON: Negative thoughts lead to negative assumptions.

SCORING: Give yourself 50 points if you chose answer (a). Give yourself 50 points if you chose answer (b). Give yourself 100 points for taking the test.

GRADING: If you got more than 20 points, congratulations! You get an A. Give yourself a gold star. Excellent work. Superb. Bravo. Hurrah! Good for you.

That's the pop quiz. How did you do?

Too good to be true?

It is.

Mirth is like
a flash of lightning,
that breaks through
a gloom of clouds,
and glitters for a moment;
cheerfulness keeps up
a kind of daylight
in the mind,
and fills it with a steady
and perpetual serenity.

Joseph Addison

1672–1719

Uplifting Acronyms

If we have a life-threatening illness, sometimes the very sound of the name—or the condensed version of the name (CA for cancer, MS for multiple sclerosis, etc.)—can strike fear into our hearts.

So, change the meaning of the abbreviations. They're just letters. Assign other words to them, uplifting words. Then, whenever you hear people say the letters, you can smile. To them it means one thing; to you it means something else.

CA can be *Creating Always,* or *Carefree and Alive,* or *Caring for All.*

MS could be *Mighty Spiritual,* or *Making Success,* or *Mirthful Snuggle.*

AIDS might become *And I'm Doing Swell,* or *Always I'm Dancing and Singing,* or *Another Interesting Day in Spirit.*

You can also invent acronyms for treatments you don't like; shots, for example. *Sure Helps Overcome The Symptoms* or *Sure Heals Over The Seasons.*

You can do it with any words or abbreviations you don't like. They're just letters. Letters can represent anything you want. Might as well let them represent something uplifting.

Without this playing
with fantasy
no creative work has ever
yet come to birth.
The debt we owe
to the play of imagination
is incalculable.

CARL JUNG

Visualization

Creative visualization is holding an image of the direction we want to go, of what we want to achieve, of the things and people we want to be with, and of what we want to become.

Visualization is something we all do all the time anyway—we are always visualizing, either positively or negatively.

If I were to ask you to draw a square, a triangle, and a circle, you would probably be able to do that without "thinking" too much about it. You'd have an almost immediate image of each of those shapes. That image would come from visualization.

The use of the term *visual* in visualization is, perhaps, misleading. Yes, some people see clear, Technicolor images, but others have more a sense (a feeling) of what they're "visualizing," while for others, "visualization" is process of hearing. Visualization can take place through any one or any combination of the five senses.

Perhaps a better word might be *imagine*—to put an *image* of something *in* to your awareness. Either word is fine. I'll use *visualization* because that's the term that has generally come to describe using the mind and emotions as tools for consciously creating a positive reality.

I say "consciously" because we *un*consciously use visualization to create our lives. Almost everything we've done, we probably "thought about it" before we did it; that "thinking about it" included visualization. We project ahead in our imagination,

His imagination
resembled the wings
of an ostrich.
It enabled him to run,
though not to soar.

LORD MACAULAY

ON JOHN DRYDEN
1828

imagine what the situation will be like, imagine the way we would like it, and imagine all the things that might go wrong.

Therein lies the rub. Many people create their own *negative* reality through *negative visualization*. I've quoted a couple of times the saying, "What you fear may come upon you." Negative visualization is the process by which it comes about. We worry so much about something that we create an image of failure, terror, rejection, and destitution. Then we set about to fulfill our vision.

This process is not a total waste of energy—we do, after all, get to be "right." "I knew it!" we think. "That wasn't worry; that was *accurate perception.*"

The reality seldom turns out as bad as we imagined. We're relieved, then, when the other shoe finally drops and we discover catastrophe is merely disaster.

As Henry Ford said, "If you think you can do a thing or think you can't do a thing, you're right."

I, naturally, am suggesting you use this powerful tool of the imagination for your upliftment, healing, and joy; that you use it as yet another method of getting what you really want and, of course, not hurting anyone else in the process.

Positive visualization accomplishes the positive in the same way that negative thinking achieves the negative. It helps us "preview" goals, makes us comfortable with the reality we're creating, and lets us know when to say yes and when to say no as opportunities arise. (The ones that fulfill our vision, we follow; the ones that run counter to our vision, we let pass.) And, somehow, our thoughts seem to attract to us the realities our imagination creates.

For the balance of the book, when I use the word *visualization*, I'll be referring to *positive* visualization. I just wanted you to know that *all* thinking incorporates visualization and that all visualization tends to manifest itself in physical reality.

How do *you* visualize? What senses do you personally use? What's it like? It's easy to find out. Think of the Eiffel Tower. Now think of the Statue of Liberty. Now think of a lemon. Now think of a rose. What color is the rose? If it's red, make it yellow; if it's yellow, make it red. Think of a lake. Think of a glass of water. What does your bath-

The imagination
may be compared
to Adam's dream—
he awoke
and found it truth.

KEATS

room look like? What color is your car?

However you got those images, that's how *you* visualize.

One essential point about visualization: *Never lose in your imagination.* It is your imagination; you can have everything precisely the way you want. Have it that way. When visualizing, you're not limited to any physical reality. You can fly. You can be always joyful. You can be perfectly healthy. You can be loved. You can be loving.

So be it.

All that is comes
from the mind;
it is based on the mind,
it is fashioned
by the mind.

THE PALI CANON

500–250 B.C.

If we really want to live,
we'd better start
at once to try;
If we don't
it doesn't matter,
we'd better start to die.

W. H. AUDEN

For the Highest Good of All Concerned

Whenever asking for something (and visualization is a form of asking), you might find it a good idea to underwrite your request with an insurance policy.

The insurance policy I suggest: preface and/or follow all your requests with "for the highest good of all concerned."

We are powerful creators. We might ask for something—a solution to a problem, say—and, by the time that solution comes to pass, it has more problems attached to it than the problem it was intended to solve: it isn't the right color (or some other omitted detail), we no longer need it, we already have two others, or we simply no longer want it.

Sometimes putting requests in motion is like ordering room service at a bad hotel. We place the order at ten in the evening. By midnight nothing's come, so we give up and go to sleep. At 3:00 a.m., there's a pounding at the door, "Room service!"

"I don't want it anymore."

"But you ordered it."

"That was at ten o'clock."

"We were very busy tonight."

"Well, I don't want it now."

"Did you cancel your order?"

"No. The phone lines were busy."

There are
two tragedies in life.
One is to lose
your heart's desire.
The other is to gain it.

George Bernard Shaw

"How many times did you try?"

"Three."

"That wasn't enough."

"Well, I still don't want it."

"You ordered it. You've got to eat it."

"No, I don't."

"It'll be outside your door. You'll have to step over it in the morning."

"Fine. Now, leave me alone."

"And you have to pay for it."

"I'll do nothing of the kind."

"Then we won't bring you breakfast."

"Fine. Now, go away."

"What about my tip?"

"What tip?"

"It's customary to offer a gratuity when someone brings you room service. Especially at three o'clock in the morning."

"But I didn't want room service at three o'clock in the morning."

"Did you tell them that when you placed the order?"

"No."

"Then it's not our fault. It's certainly not *my* fault. I did my job. I deserve a tip."

"You're not getting a tip. Now, leave me alone."

"The maid's a friend of mine. I'll tell her not to clean your room tomorrow."

"I'm checking out tomorrow."

"The bellboy's a friend of mine, too. You'll have to carry your own baggage."

"Write yourself a tip on the bill. Now, let me get some sleep."

"Could you sign the bill, please?"

"What?"

"If you give a tip, you have to sign the bill."

"Why?"

"Hotel policy."

Sound familiar?

To get what we want—and only what we want, and all of what we want—it's good to be as specific as possible. But it seems that, no matter how many

The highest good.

CICERO

106–43 B.C.

details we include, the fickle finger of fate can add a few we never considered.

That's where "the highest good" comes in. Do all that you can; then ask for it in the name of the highest good of all concerned. That way, no matter what happens, what comes to you will be right, and the timing will be perfect.

This is especially true when making requests for others. We don't always know what would be the best for *ourselves,* so how can we hope to know what would be the best for someone else?

I was once told of an elderly woman who was in a coma. Her friends and family prayed, affirmed, and visualized unceasingly that she come out of the coma and live. The coma continued for weeks. The woman finally awoke from the coma and said in perfectly lucid tones to those gathered around her bed, "Let me go. I've seen what it's like on the other side. I want to go there. You're all holding me here. I love you. If you love me, let me go." She closed her eyes, returned to the "coma." A few hours later—after the message of "let go" was spread among her family and friends—she died.

If her friends had sent their prayers, affirmations, and visualizations to her for her highest good and the highest good of all concerned, she might have been able to make her transition with less struggle.

How often have we wished for our friends, "I hope he gets that job," or "I hope they stay together," or "I hope she sells her house"? Maybe the new job, staying together, and selling the house aren't for their highest good. Maybe later they'll say, "I sure hate this job," or "We should have broken up years ago," or "I wish I had my house back." At this point we usually tell ourselves, "But that's what they *said* they wanted."

What people say they want and what they really want when it actually comes to pass are often two different animals. Usually two different species.

What we don't know, fully and absolutely, is the future. We don't know what will happen or how things will be different or how we will have changed. What we ask for today, we may not want tomorrow. This is why it's a good idea to make a list

The tendency of
man's nature to good
is like the tendency of water
to flow downwards.

MENCIUS
372–289 B.C.

of all the things you're asking for—your list of goals. When you no longer want something (maybe because you got something better), cross it off your list. Tell yourself, "Thank you, but I no longer want this."

When asking for things, some people also like to add, "this, or something better." If we want ten million dollars, but we get twenty million, that would be okay, wouldn't it? Some people put an upper limit on their receiving by how they ask. "This, or something better, for my highest good and the highest good of all concerned" encompasses all variables, changes, and extremes.

You can relax after asking. (Relax from worrying, that is. You'll still have to get busy to make your dreams a reality.)

"For my highest good and the highest good of all concerned" trusts that there is some Higher Power—Mother Nature, Father God, or whatever you care to call It—who is taking care of us, who is there to nurture and support us, who knows what we want before we even know it, and who is happy to give it to us.

In the beginning
God created the heaven and the earth.

And the earth was without form, and void;
and darkness was upon
the face of the deep.
And the Spirit of God
moved upon the face of the waters.
And God said,

Let there be light:
and there was light.

THE FIRST BOOK OF MOSES,
CALLED GENESIS

1:1–3

Light

The concept of *light* as a gift from "someplace greater" to humanity seems to be ageless and universal. It spans time, geography, and belief. It's central to almost every religion, a great many philosophies, and is at the very core of atomic physics—which means at the very core of life itself.

In approximate historical order, let's look at how *light* is viewed by the major religions of the world.

Hinduism, one of the oldest religions in the world, was founded around 1500 B.C. One of Hinduism's sacred texts, the *Brihadaranyaka Upanishad,* states (1.3.28):

> Lead me from the unreal to the real!
> Lead me from darkness to light!
> Lead me from death to immortality!

Light is equated both with reality and immortality. "En*light*enment" is a Hindu's highest goal.

Judaism was formally founded around 1300 B.C.E. (Before the Common Era). Jewish scripture is abundant with references to light, starting with "In the beginning," quoted on the facing page.

The Old Testament of the Bible—the sacred texts as well as the story of the Chosen People—includes some of the most beautiful references to light ever written.

> And the Lord went before them by day in a pillar of cloud, to lead them the way; and by night in a pillar of fire, to give them light. (Exodus 13:21)

Ye are the light of the world.
A city that is set on a hill
cannot be hid.
Neither do men light a candle,
and put it under a bushel,
but on a candlestick;
and giveth light unto
all that are in the house.
Let your light
so shine before men,
that they may see your good works,
and glorify your Father
in heaven.

MATTHEW

5:14–16

Lord, lift thou up the light of thy countenance upon us. (Psalm 4:6)

The Lord is my light and my salvation; whom shall I fear? the Lord is the strength of my life; of whom shall I be afraid? (Psalm 27:1)

Arise, shine; for thy light is come, and the glory of the Lord is risen upon thee. (Isaiah 60:1)

I shall light a candle of understanding in thine heart, which shall not be put out. (II Esdras 14:25)

The light that cometh from her [wisdom] never goeth out. (Wisdom of Solomon 7:10)

Buddhism was founded by Gautama Buddha around 525 B.C. Buddha is often referred to as "The Light of Asia." "En*light*enment," in fact, is what transformed the endarkened Siddhartha Gautama into "Buddha" ("the Enlightened One").

Christianity. Jesus said of himself, "I am the light of the world: he that followeth me shall not walk in darkness, but shall have the light of life" (John 8:12).

He told his followers, "Yet a little while is the light with you. Walk while ye have the light, lest darkness come upon you" (John 12:35).

After he physically left the earth, Jesus sent "an advocate" in the form of the Light of the Holy Spirit, which first appeared to the disciples as tongues of fire (light).

Islam was founded by the prophet Mohammed in 622 A.D. The sacred text of Islam is the Koran. This passage from the Koran (24:35) leaves little doubt as to Islamic beliefs about light:

> God is the light of the heavens and of the earth. His light is like a niche in which is a lamp—the lamp encased in glass—the glass, as it were, a glistening star. From a blessed tree it is lighted, the olive neither from the East nor of the West, whose oil would well nigh shine out, even though fire touched it not. It is light upon light. God guideth whom He will to His light, and God setteth forth parables to men.

The Native Americans of both North and South America had many religions, but most have a common thread—The Great Spirit, Mother Earth, and

Beyond plants are animals,
Beyond animals is man,
Beyond man is the universe.
The Big Light,
Let the Big Light in!

JEAN TOOMER

the colors of Light. This North American Indian song illustrates the latter.

May the warp be the white light of morning,
May the weft be the red light of evening,
May the fringes be the falling rain,
May the border be the standing rainbow.
Thus weave for us a garment of brightness.

Or from the poem "The Flight of [the Aztec] Quetzalcoatl":

It ended
With his body changed to light,
A star that burns forever in that sky.

Now, if all this talk about God and light isn't quite up your avenue, how about ancient philosophers?

The Greeks liked light. Pindar (518–438 B.C.) wrote, "Creatures of a day, what is a man? What is he not? Mankind is a dream of a shadow. But when a god-given brightness comes, a radiant light rests on men, and a gentle life."

The Romans were fond of light, too. "On a dark theme I trace verses full of light," wrote Lucretius (99–55 B.C.), "touching all the muses' charm."

The pagan gods used light. "The evening is come; rise up, ye youths," spoke Catullus (87–54 B.C.). "Vesper from Olympus now at last is just raising his long-looked-for light."

Not happy with Greeks, Romans, and pagans? How about *poets*?

Dante, in the early 1300s, declared that Beatrice ". . . shall be a light between truth and intellect." Three hundred and fifty years later, Henry Vaughan calmly informed us,

> I saw Eternity the other night
> Like a great ring of pure and endless light.
> All calm, as it was bright;
> And round beneath it,
> Time in hours, days, years,
> Driv'n by the spheres
> Like a vast shadow moved;
> in which the world
> And all her train were hurled.

A hundred-or-so years later, Wordsworth advised us, "Come forth into the light of things,

There are two ways
of spreading light:
to be the candle
or the mirror
that reflects it.

EDITH WHARTON

/ Let Nature be your teacher." And Lord Byron either heard a song from without or (as I like to think) a sound from within when he wrote:

A light broke in upon my brain—
It was the carol of a bird;
It ceased, and then it came again,
The sweetest song ear ever heard.

Emily Dickinson enjoyed one of the qualities of light: "*Phosphorescence.* Now, there's a word to lift your hat to," she wrote. "To find that phosphorescence, that light within, that's the genius behind poetry."

Closer to our time, Theodore Roethke pointed out, "The word outleaps the world, and light is all." On a more personal note, he wrote, "Light listened when she sang."

Which brings us to one of the favorite poetical uses of light—to describe one's beloved. The most famous, perhaps, is Shakespeare's "But, soft! what light through yonder window breaks? / It is the east, and Juliet is the sun!"

Robert Burns was a bit more, well, Scottish with the light of love:

> The golden hours on angel wings
> Flew o'er me and my dearie;
> For dear to me as light and life
> Was my sweet Highland Mary.

Tennyson, at the tender age of thirty-three, remarked upon seeing the gardener's daughter,

> Half light, half shade,
> She stood, a sight to make an old man young.

All right. Enough poets. How about *artists*? Michelangelo wrote, "I live and love in God's peculiar light." During an interview, Marc Chagall once made this comment: "Do not leave my hand without light."

And of light and death? Goethe's last words were "More light!" while Teddy Roosevelt requested, "Put out the light." Herder's self-written epitaph was "Light, love, life." Longfellow seemed to accept the notion that light is to be found on either side of death: "The grave itself is but a covered bridge / Leading from light to light, through a brief darkness."

It is eternity now.
I am in the midst of it.
It is about me in the sunshine;
I am in it,
as the butterfly
in the light-laden air.
Nothing has to come;
it is now.
Now is eternity;
now is the immortal life.

RICHARD JEFFERIES

THE STORY OF MY HEART (1883)

All this too airy-fairy for you?

What about good old psychology? Jung wrote in *The Practice of Psychotherapy:*

> The unconscious is not just evil by nature, it is also the source of the highest good: not only dark but also light, not only bestial, semihuman, and demonic but superhuman, spiritual, and, in the classical sense of the word, "divine."

If you're not interested in religion, philosophy, poetry, art, parting words, or psychology, I'll just have to appeal to your *patriotism!**

> Oh, say, can you see
> by the dawn's early light,
> what so proudly we hailed
> at the twilight's last gleaming?

Why have I gone through all this? Isn't this book long enough already? Well, this was just my meandering way of illustrating that there are many kinds of light. My suggestion? Whichever kind you like, use it.

Imagine, if you will, a pure, white light surrounding, filling, and protecting you, all of your activities, everyone and everything around you. Ask for this light for your highest good and the highest good of all concerned.

Just as darkness is merely the absence of light, not a real thing in itself, negativity, another form of darkness, is simply the absence of another kind of light.

Where does the darkness go when you turn on the light? What happens to your fist when you open your hand? Where does your lap go when you stand up? If you work with the light (and ask the light to work with you), you may find yourself asking the question, "What happens to negativity when I ask for the light?"

You can think of light as an acronym: *Luxuriating In Good Happy Times*, perhaps, or *Loving Intensely*

*As George M. Cohan—who should know—pointed out, "Many a bum show has been saved by waving the flag."

There was a young lady
named Bright,
Whose speed was far
faster than light;
She set out one day
In a relative way,
And returned home
the previous night.

ARTHUR BULLER

Gives Higher Thinking, or *Laughing Internally Gets Hilarious Teachings.* Invent any others you choose.

If there is a power in light you can call on, you might as well use it. If not, you're not losing much except the few seconds it takes to think, "I ask the light to surround, fill, and protect me and everyone and everything around me for my highest good and the highest good of all concerned." (In a pinch, you can shorten it to: "Light! Highest Good!")

It's one of those you-have-little-to-lose-and-a-lot-to-gain suggestions. Try it. Play with it. See what happens. I'm not asking you to believe; just experiment. Based on your results, you'll know if there's something to it for you or not.

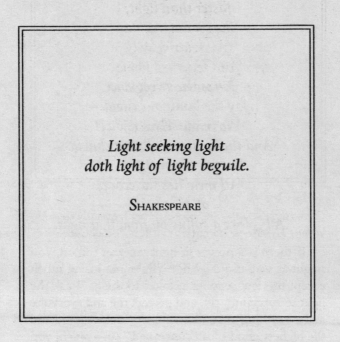

Light seeking light
doth light of light beguile.

SHAKESPEARE

Joy is the sweet voice,
Joy the luminous cloud—
We in ourselves rejoice!
And thence flows all that charms
or ear or sight,
All melodies the echoes
of that voice,
All colors a suffusion from that light.

COLERIDGE

The Colors of Light

As long as I've suggested you experiment with light, let me tell you about the colors of light, too. Certain colors have certain effects on many people.

This is probably not surprising. You may have felt a difference between walking into, say, an all-yellow room and walking into an all-blue room. The investigation of color and its effects on people is now considered by many a legitimate scientific study.

The white light contains all colors. With paints, all colors mixed together form a sort of murky green-brown. When you combine all colors of direct light, however, it makes white. On a color TV, for example, when the screen is white, all the primary colors are on. The *absence* of all colors is black.

You've probably seen light go through a prism and become the colors of the rainbow. Rainbows are formed, in fact, by water molecules in the air acting as billions of tiny prisms.

When you want the benefit of all colors, use white. When you're looking for specific results, you can use specific colors.

Red is the color of intense, physical energy. When you need a powerful burst of energy, imagine red or look at something red. Coke does not put caffeine in its cola and paint the cans bright red for nothing. They're selling *energy*—raw, physical energy. The Real Thing! The Pause That Refreshes! Coke Is It!

For memory has painted
this perfect day
With colors
that never fade,
And we find at the end
of a perfect day
The soul of a friend
we've made.

Carrie Jacobs Bond

This powerful physical energy, if overemphasized, sometimes leads to delusions of grandeur. As Edmond Rostand noted, "I fall back dazzled at beholding myself all rosy red, / At having, I myself, caused the sun to rise."

When the red gets rowdy, it's often associated with mischief: "Three jolly gentlemen, / In coats of red, / Rode their horses / Up to bed" (Walter de la Mare). If the physical actions go too far, red becomes associated with crime: "caught red-handed" or "My case is bad. Lord, be my advocate. / My sin is red: I'm under God's arrest" (Edward Taylor).

The intense physical energy is also why red is the color often associated with sexuality: red-light districts and scarlet letters. As John Boyle O'Reilly wrote, "The red rose whispers of passion / And the white rose breathes of love; / O, the red rose is a falcon, / And the white rose is a dove."

Orange is the next color in the spectrum. Orange is a color of energy, too, but a quieter, more sustaining energy. You'd use red if you needed a burst of energy; orange, for more enduring physical strength.

"The red earth" of the South is really more orange in color. ("The orange earth of Tara" doesn't sound too romantic.) Edward Markham's description of Abraham Lincoln incorporates the orange quality of abiding strength: "The color of the ground was in him, the red earth, / The smack and tang of elemental things."

Yellow is the color of the mind, of joyful, purifying, mental energy. It's the color of lemons (so what?), smile buttons, and Joy dishwashing detergent. (Lily Tomlin: "A friend of mine asked her four-year-old daughter, 'Do you know what joy is?' and the daughter answered, 'Yes. It's what gets your dishes so spotlessly clean you can see yourself.'") Yes, yellow light *does* bring clarity.

The thing we most often associate with yellow is the sun. The sun has been described as "glorious" (Shakespeare or Coleridge, take your pick) and "colossal" (Wallace Stevens)—qualities we could certainly apply to the mind (on a good day).

As Daniel Webster observed, "Knowledge, in truth, is the great sun in the firmament. Life and power are scattered with all its beams." Or, as

Dear friend,
all theory is gray,
And green
the golden tree of life.

Goethe

Theodore Roethke said, "The sun! The sun! And all we can become!"

Green is the color of healing and the color of learning—brilliant, emerald green. "The Lord is my shepherd; I shall not want. He maketh me to lie down in green pastures: he leadeth me beside the still waters" (Psalm 23: 1–2). "That happy place, the green groves of the dwelling of the blest" (Virgil).

Andrew Marvell marveled (sorry) in 1651, "Annihilating all that's made / To a green thought in a green shade." The "annihilation" is that of illness when the ease of green confronts dis-ease, or when the green of learning confronts ignorance. "Keep a green tree in your heart," states the Chinese proverb, "and perhaps the singing bird will come."

Of course, healing and learning are active processes. When you think of green, think of actively healing yourself, through physical action and active visualizations. Think of vigorously learning all you can about yourself and your life. "April prepares her green traffic light and the world thinks Go" (Christopher Morley).

"Blue color is everlastingly appointed by the Deity to be a source of delight." John Ruskin said it in 1853 better than I could today. Blue is a color of spirit, of calm, of peace. "Blue, darkly, deeply, beautifully blue" (Robert Southey).

As the sun is yellow and usually associated with sunny thoughts, so the sky is high and blue, and the sea is deep and blue. High and deep: two good descriptions of a life fully lived. "The spacious firmament on high, / With all the blue ethereal sky" (Joseph Addison). "The sea! the sea! the open sea! / The blue, the fresh, the ever free" (Barry Cornwall).

The Apache have a chant: "Big Blue Mountain Spirit, / The home made of blue clouds / I am grateful for that mode of goodness there." And the final word on blue will go to Coleridge (dear Coleridge), who reminds us that "Saints will aid if men will call: / For the blue sky bends over all!"

Purple is the color of royalty—the inner royalty that is you and the outer royalty of the divine. We seem to associate purple with kings, queens, and the main color in stained-glass windows.

Use purple when you want to feel cloaked in the

And God smiled again,
And the rainbow appeared,
And curled itself
around his shoulder.

James Weldon Johnson

grand, majestic, stately One of the universe, or the grand, majestic, stately presence within you.

It's also fun mixing colors. If you have, say, "the blues," you might add the physical energy of red, which would make a more active purple. Or you could add to blue some mental energy (yellow), which would give you the green of healing.

If you were being a little too yellow—thinking too much at the expense of action (cowards, who sacrifice action for fearful thoughts, are often called "yellow")—you could add some highly physical red, which would give you steady, reliable orange to help carry out your physical tasks. Or you could add blue to the yellow to make green and be ready for some active healing or learning.

If you add too many colors, don't worry: unlike mixing paints, when you overmix light, the worst you can end up with is white.

Use the colors you feel drawn to. Think about them surrounding and filling you with their energy. You can also look at sheets of colored paper, or wear clothes of the colors you want to imbue yourself with. As always, ask for them to impart their energy for your highest good and the highest good of all concerned.

My special place.
It's a place no amount
of hurt and anger
Can deface.
I put things
back together there
It all falls right in place—
In my special space
My special place.

Joni Mitchell

Make a Sanctuary

If you wanted to learn wood crafting, you'd probably want not just tools, but a workroom. If you wanted to become an artist, you'd probably want not just paints, but a studio. If you wanted to become a gourmet cook, you would probably want not just pots and pans, but a kitchen.

If you want to become a "gourmet visualizer," you might want not just the techniques of visualization, but also a place for you to use them. I call this place a sanctuary.

A sanctuary is a place you build in your imagination. It's an inner place for you to go to visualize, contemplate, meditate, affirm, do spiritual exercises, solve problems, get advice, heal yourself, relax, have fun, hang out, and communicate with yourself and others.

I call it a *sanctuary* because the word seems to incorporate the qualities of preciousness *(sanctity)*, retreat, getting away from it all, safety, and refuge. You can call your inner place whatever you choose. Some call it a workshop; others, a shrine or an inner sanctum. The name is not important. Building and using it is.

You build a sanctuary in your imagination. The nice thing about building in your imagination is that the wait between design and construction is nonexistent. You can try something out, see how you like it, change it, see how you like that, and change your changes, all in a very short time.

To show you how quickly this can happen:

A harbor,
even if it is a little harbor,
is a good thing,
since adventures come into it
as well as go out,
and the life in it
grows strong,
because it takes something
from the world and
has something to give in return.

SARAH ORNE JEWETT

imagine the Statue of Liberty. See the right arm holding up the torch and the left arm holding the tablets.*

Imagine that Lady Liberty has gotten tired of holding up her right arm all these years. (She is a she, by the way—the artist's mother posed for the

*In the United States, by the way, the Statue of Liberty's tablets have July 4, 1776, engraved on them, the date of the signing of the Declaration of Independence. In France, the tablets of a much smaller Statue of Liberty have July 14, 1789, engraved on them, the date of the Storming of the Bastille. Knowing that, don't you wish Trivial Pursuit would become popular again?

statue.) Imagine her switching the tablets to her right arm and the torch to her left. Then see her holding aloft the torch in her left hand while holding the tablets in her right.

That didn't take long. Can you imagine how long that would have taken to do in real life? Heck, it took them two years and Lee Iacocca just to *clean* the thing.

As I mentioned earlier, some people see clear pictures; others have a vague sense; while others don't see much, but listen carefully and "know" something happened.

If I asked you to draw a very rough sketch of the Statue of Liberty with the torch in her left hand, you could probably do it, even though you had never seen a left-handed Liberty before. You would be drawing your visualization of it, from your creative imagination.

In constructing your sanctuary, keep this in mind: Moss Hart, the playwright and director, bought an estate outside New York and began landscaping it. He moved a large hill from one location to another, redirected the course of a stream, and rearranged trees so the effect would be aesthetically pleasing. When George S. Kaufman came to visit and saw the changes Hart had made, he commented, "This is what God would do if He only had money."

When building your sanctuary, be a god with lots of money—because in your imagination, *you are*.

You can have as many workers as you want, or

Can success change
the human mechanism so completely
between one dawn and another?
Can it make one feel taller,
more alive, handsomer,
uncommonly gifted
and indomitably secure
with the certainty
that this is the way life will always be?
It can and it does!

Moss Hart

you can snap your fingers and things will just appear. Want to change the color of the whole place? Snap your fingers, it's done. Want to make it twice as large? Snap, it's larger.

I'll give you the basic outline for a sanctuary. Keep in mind that it's *your* sanctuary. You can add anything else you like. There are no limitations other than the ones *you* place there. I, naturally, recommend limitlessness.

I'll suggest uses for the sanctuary later, but for now I'll just describe their basic function. Their size, shape, design, and so on, are entirely up to you. Ready? Here we go.

Location. Your first choice is location. Where would you like your sanctuary to be? It can be anyplace, real or imagined: on a mountaintop, floating over the ocean, on the moon, in a valley.

Outside. What do you want the outside of the sanctuary to look like? Choose a size (from enormous to moderate to cozy), shape (cathedral to cottage to geodesic dome), color (the full spectrum, plus colors we can't physically see). Landscape it as you please: add rivers, rock formations, galaxies, and shrubbery galore.

Entry Way. The entry way to your sanctuary permits *only* you to enter. How does it know it's you? Do you have a special key? Does it read your handprint? Do you have secret words, such as "Open sez me"? Or does it just automatically recognize you?

White Light. Just inside the doorway, create a perpetual white light. Whenever you enter or exit your sanctuary, automatically pass through a column of pure, white light. As you do, you are surrounded, filled, protected, and healed by this light, and only that which is for your highest good and the highest good of all concerned takes place while you're in your sanctuary.

Main Room. How would you like the main room of your sanctuary to be? Large? Small? Carpeted? Wood floors? Grass? How about the walls, ceiling, windows? How is it decorated? Snap into place whatever you want. If you're not entirely satisfied, snap your fingers and create something else.

Three things are to be
looked to in a building:
that it stand on the right spot;
that it be securely founded;
that it be successfully executed.

GOETHE

Information Retrieval System. This can be in the main room or in a special room by itself. It's a way of getting information on whatever you want to know. It could be a computer terminal, a staff of researchers, a telephone, or anything else. All you need is a method of asking questions and getting the answers.

Video Screen. Again, this can be in the main room or in its own room. It can be any size, from hand-held to wall-size. Have some comfortable chairs in front of it so you can relax and watch. What will you watch? Mostly the story of your life. You're the star; everyone else is just bit players. You can also use the video screen to play videos from the information retrieval system. Surround the screen with a white light that can go off and on.

Ability Suit Closet. For every ability you have or would like to have—painting, flying, being rich, playing piano—there's a suit that, when you put it on, instantly gives you that ability. When you're done with the suit, throw it on the floor. It automatically hangs itself back in the closet. That's just a minor ability of the ability suits.

Ability Practice Area. This is where you can try different abilities on for size. You put on the ability suit for, say, gourmet cook, and the ability practice area becomes a master chef's kitchen. You can also use this area to practice abilities as you develop them.

People Mover. This is the way to invite others into your sanctuary. (Remember, only you can come and go by way of the main entrance.) It can be an escalator, a conveyer belt, one of those beam-me-up-Scotty devices from *Star Trek*, or whatever people-moving you can imagine.

White Light by People Mover. Place a perpetual white light over the entrance of the people mover. In this way, anyone who comes into your sanctuary is automatically surrounded, filled, and protected by the white light, and only that which is for his or her highest good and the highest good of all concerned can take place. Anyone visiting your sanctuary passes through this white light both on entering and on leaving.

Healing Center. This can be a multi-room wing of your sanctuary. Here, all the healing arts are

We must reserve
a back shop all our own,
entirely free,
in which to establish
our real liberty
and our principal
retreat and solitude.

MICHEL EYQUEM DE MONTAIGNE

1580

practiced. You are attended by all known and imagined healers—past, present, and future. The latest and most ancient technologies are available, as of course are all future discoveries.

Sacred Room. This is a special room for you to commune with yourself—to meditate, contemplate, do spiritual exercises, visualize, or just be. If you like, you can invite special friends into this room of communion.

Master Teacher. A special feature of your sanctuary is the presence of a special teacher, a friend, someone who knows everything about you, who cares for you totally, and who loves you unconditionally. How do you discover your Master Teacher?

Easy. Just stand in front of the people mover and say, "Would my Master Teacher please come forth?" From the column of white light in front of the people mover will emerge your Master Teacher. Take some time. Get acquainted. Show off your sanctuary. Enjoy together the sacred room.

I'll leave you two alone for a while. See you both—whenever you get around to it—in the next chapter.

By means of an image
we are often able to hold on
to our lost belongings.
But it is the desperateness of losing
which picks the flowers of memory,
binds the bouquet.

COLETTE

MRS. MALAPROP:
Illiterate him, I say,
quite from your memory.

RICHARD SHERIDAN
1775

Healing Memories

Most of us have memories of past hurts, disappointments, and fears that keep returning. When this happens, we're letting a memory of something that happened *then* negatively affect us *now*. Fortunately, memories—like any other part of our being—can be healed.

Here's a simple technique for healing memories. Go into your sanctuary, making sure you pass through the white light at the entry way. You may want to ask your Master Teacher to join you. If so, stop by the people mover and pick up your Master Teacher. Have a seat in front of your video screen.

The white light surrounding the screen is off. On the screen, see the situation you feel upset about. Let it play itself out. Watch it as you would a movie. After it's over, go back and freeze-frame a moment you found particularly upsetting.

Imagine you have a large paintbrush full of black paint in your hand. Take the paintbrush and make a large, black *X* across the upsetting image on the screen. Let the image and the paint fade.

Now, the white light around the edges of the video screen begins to glow. On the screen, see the situation again, but this time let it happen *exactly the way you would have liked it to happen*. Remember, never lose in your imagination. Ask your Master Teacher for suggestions on winning *big*.

This process *replaces* the painful or fearful memory with a joyful, contented one. With some memories, you may need to repeat the process a few times; with others, once will do.

Neither a lofty degree
of intelligence
nor imagination nor both together
go to the making of genius.
Love, love, love,
that is the soul of genius.

MOZART

Healing Your Body

The healing center of your sanctuary is a powerful place. There, healing can take place instantly. Some people like to have their Master Teacher come along when they go for healing. (Some people keep their Master Teacher with them all the time. Your sanctuary and Master Teacher are only a thought away.)

How to heal your body in your healing center is limited only by your imagination. You can be given the Miracle Shot (painlessly, of course), shot with the Magic Bullet (which cures whatever ails you), or cured with the Miracle Pill. You can have healers heal you by placing their hands on you. You can lie under different colors of light and be healed in that way.

In your healing center is an infinite supply of replacement body parts, especially stocked for your body. You can snap out any part that's not quite up to par and snap in a perfect part. It only takes a second. You can do it yourself or have a whole team—like the pit crew at the Indianapolis 500—do it for you.

If you know you're having trouble with, say, your liver, snap out the old liver and snap in a new one. Heart? Snap out, snap in. (You can also replace your whole circulatory system—blood and all—while you're at it.) Immune system? Easy. Snap, snap.

You might want to look at some color drawings of various organs and where they're located. The

It is not enough
to have a good mind.
The main thing
is to use it well.

RENE DESCARTES
1637

more vivid the image and knowledge of the replacement body part, the better. You may have to replace a particularly recalcitrant part a hundred times, but that's okay. Whatever it takes, right?

You can bring in for consultation, on your people mover, the greatest medical experts in the world (any world). They're always available, always have plenty of time, and never charge a cent. You can invite healers from the past, present, and future—real and imagined—to do work and to give advice.

Some people like to have a Master Healer to organize the comings and goings of all the other healers. Some people like to imagine their Master Teacher in a white coat and stethoscope. Others like the variety of new and different experts.

Anytime you hear of a new healing method or technique that interests you, go to your healing center and try it out. Let it work perfectly for you. Create new techniques. And feel free to visit the healing center even when you're not sick. You don't have to be sick to enjoy getting better.

As I've stated before, none of the inner work you do should replace the outer work of proper medical treatment. If your outer treatment reaches an impasse, however, the inner work might help the outer along.

Some people ask their inner doctors for help in diagnosing certain "mysterious" ailments. When they go to their regular (outer) doctor next, they say, "Just for the heck of it, why don't you check out __________." It's amazing how often __________ has something to do with the ailment.

If you have any spiritual or religious beliefs, be sure to invite the healers of your tradition—via the people mover—into your sanctuary. And don't accept some assistant—go for the Top, the Head Honcho, the Big Enchilada.

You're worth it.

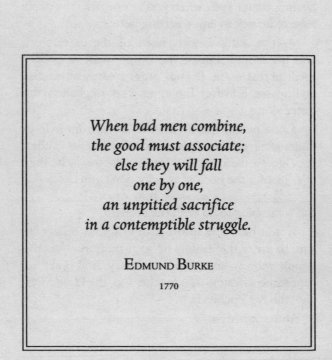

When bad men combine,
the good must associate;
else they will fall
one by one,
an unpitied sacrifice
in a contemptible struggle.

EDMUND BURKE

1770

Visualize Health

The technique of visualization I'm about to describe can be done in your sacred room, if you like, or in a special room of the healing center. You can, as always, have your Master Teacher come along. (The Master Teacher, naturally, has the ability to join you in any inner journeys you take; makes a great guide, in fact.)

The technique is one made popular by Dr. Carl Simonton.* For years, Dr. Simonton has been using nontraditional methods for treating cancer patients who were diagnosed as untreatable and "terminal." (When new patients enter his clinic for an initial consultation, Dr. Simonton looks them straight in the eye and asks, "When did you decide to die?")

Imagine whatever is *not* healthy as the Bad Guys and your healthy body parts as the Good Guys. Then imagine them slugging it out. The Good Guys *always, always, always* win.

If, for example, you have cancer cells in your body, you can see those as, say, cowboy villains in black hats and your white blood cells as heroes in white hats. They meet at the OK Corral for a showdown. Much punching and gunplay later, the "black hats" are in jail or boot hill, and the "white hats" are riding off into the sunset or going upstairs with

*You can receive a catalog of Dr. Simonton's books and tapes by calling 1–800–338–2360. Outside the U.S.: 1–817–575–2420.

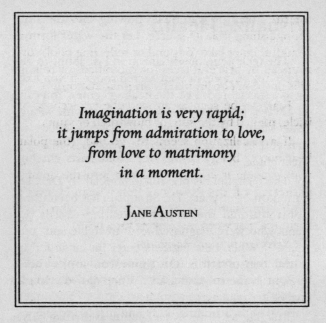

Imagination is very rapid;
it jumps from admiration to love,
from love to matrimony
in a moment.

JANE AUSTEN

Miss Kitty or doing whatever your white hats enjoy doing.

You can imagine the nasty cells being dog biscuits and the good cells dogs; whenever a dog sees a biscuit, naturally he eats it. Or imagine the good cells as Pac-Man (or Ms. Pac-Man) and the bad cells as the little white dots Pac-People devour. (Am I revealing my age by mentioning Pac-Man?)

The negative emotions often connected with life-threatening illness (fear, anger, guilt, blame, unworthiness, helplessness) can be visualized away.

You can see anger, for example, as a fire (or burning embers or fire-breathing dragon) and rivers (or fire hoses or waterfalls) flowing into the fire, extinguishing it at its source. Let the water form a beautiful inner lake (or pond or reflecting pool) surrounded by peaceful trees (or mountains or rolling hills or—don't be limited by *my* imagination).

Fear can be seen as an ice cube (or iceberg or icicle) melted by the sun (or blowtorch or sauna).

If a visualization seems to "go bad" (the polar bear you've been chasing turns and starts chasing you), change it *at once.* (You run into the annual gathering of the National Polar Bear Hunter's Club—thousands of hungry hunters who have spent the past week just *looking* for a bear.)

Never lose in your imagination.

Another option is to imagine the harmful cells in your body mutating into non-life-threatening ones. They mutate to a point where they no longer want to be in a human body and just leave. (There are all sorts of viruses, bacteria, and parasites that want nothing to do with the human body.)

If you have an organ that's not functioning properly—a heart, say—visualize it operating perfectly. See it doing its job flawlessly. In your imagination, hear and feel it beating with strength, regularity, and vigor. If you have, for example, clogged arteries, see them open, clear, and healthy.

These visualizations can be done anywhere, anytime. Let boredom and impatience be the reminders to do some inner work. The checkout line at the supermarket or a dull passage on the radio can be the perfect time to heal yourself.

You see things;
and you say, "Why?"
But I dream things
that never were;
and I say, "Why not?"

GEORGE BERNARD SHAW

The options, as you may have noticed, are endless. Be creative. Have fun. If you learn to enjoy the process of healing, you'll find your health more enjoyable, too.

The mind,
in proportion as it is cut off
from free communication with nature,
with revelation,
with God,
with itself,
loses its life,
just as the body droops
when debarred from
the air and the cheering
light from heaven.

William Ellery Channing

It would be a great thing
to understand pain
in all its meanings.

Peter Mere Latham

Listen to Your Pain

What if pain were really your friend? What if it were giving you important advice about your life and, once you listened to and followed that advice, the pain would go away?

We learned that guilt and resentment could be used to keep us from traveling down pointless and destructive pathways of negative thinking. The same is true of pain.

Let's define pain as anything in your mind, body, or emotions you wish weren't there. It might be a physical pain (headache, sore muscles, upset stomach), an emotional pain (hurt, anger, fear), or a mental pain (confusion, doubt, rigidity).

All you have to do is talk to your pain. Ask it some questions. Listen to the answers. If the answers seem to make sense, follow the pain's advice.

Go into your sanctuary—gathering your Master Teacher at the people mover, if you like—and go to the sacred room. Imagine the pain leaving your body and sitting in a chair opposite you. Give the pain some human characteristics. How would Walt Disney animate it? What kind of Muppet would Jim Henson make of it?

Then ask the pain some questions. Make them up as you go along. Here are some possible starters: Do I embarrass you by talking to you? What payoff am I getting from having you? How am I using you? Is there anything I avoid by having you around? Is there some excuse you give me? What other information do you have for me? What would I have to

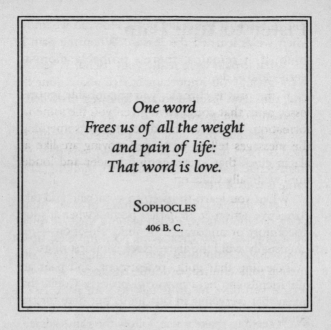

One word
Frees us of all the weight
and pain of life:
That word is love.

SOPHOCLES
406 B. C.

do in order to let you go? Do you have any other advice for me?

You may be amazed how knowledgeable the pain is. After you've made note of the information, say good-bye to the pain and imagine it surrounded by a white light. See the pain disappear into this light, smiling and waving good-bye, newly freed energy, happy to be going on to other projects.

Then put the pain's advice in motion. If you do the things you've been avoiding, you'll probably find that the pain doesn't need to be there reminding you anymore.

When we've learned the lesson the pain was

sent to teach, it generally goes. How do we know when we've learned the lesson? When the pain is gone. If it remains, there's probably more to learn—and to do.

If the pain is chronic, you've probably ignored lesser pains that could have given you the same information. When we need to change something, the messages telling us to get moving are like an alarm clock that keeps getting louder and louder until we finally wake up.

When you learn to listen to your pain and take corrective action at an earlier point—when it's just discomfort or annoyance or mild sensations—you can usually avoid the alarm clock's loudest rings.

Learning that guilt, resentment, and pain are our friends can be a powerful process. Could that mean that *everything* in our life is put here for our good?

Good question.

Sometimes
I sits and thinks,
and sometimes I just sits.

SATCHEL PAIGE

Meditate, Contemplate, or "Just Sits"

In addition to visualization, you might like to try any number of meditative and contemplative techniques available—or you might just want to sit quietly and relax.

Whenever you meditate, contemplate, pray, do spiritual exercises, or "just sits," it's good to ask the white light to surround, fill, and protect you, knowing only that which is for your highest good and the highest good of all concerned will take place during your quiet time. You may want to do your meditation in your sanctuary.

Before starting, prepare your physical environment. Arrange not to be disturbed. Unplug the phone. Put a note on the door. Wear ear plugs if noises might distract you. (I like the soft foam-rubber kind sold under such trade names as E.A.R., HUSHER, and DECIDAMP.) Take care of your bodily needs. Have some water nearby if you get thirsty, and maybe some tissues, too.

Contemplation is thinking *about* something, often something uplifting. You could contemplate any of the hundreds of quotes or ideas in this book. Often, when we hear a new and potentially useful idea, we say, "I'll have to think about that." Contemplation is a good time to "think about that," to consider the truth of it, to imagine the changes and improvements it might make in your life.

Or, you could contemplate a nonverbal object,

Most of the evils in life arise from man's being unable to sit still in a room.

BLAISE PASCAL

1623–1662

such as a flower, or a concept, such as God. The idea of contemplation is to set aside a certain amount of quiet time to think about just *that,* whatever you decide "that" will be.

Meditation. There are so many techniques of meditation, taught by so many books and organizations, that it's hard to define the word properly.

You might want to try various meditations to see what they're like. With meditation, please keep in mind that *you'll never know until you do it.* We may like to think we know what the effects of a given meditation will be by just reading the description, but I suggest you try it and *then* decide.

Breathing Meditation. Sit comfortably, close your eyes, and simply be aware of your breath. Follow it in and out. Don't "try" to breathe; don't consciously alter your rhythm of breathing; just follow the breath as it naturally flows in and out. If you get lost in thoughts, return to your breath.

Mantras. Some people like to add a word or sound to help the mind focus as the breath goes in and out. Some people use *one* or *God* or *AUM (OHM)* or *love*. These—or any others—are fine. As you breathe in, say to yourself, mentally, "love." As you breathe out, "love." If you don't like synchronizing sounds to breath, don't. It doesn't matter.

It's not so much the *sound*, but the *meaning you assign* to the sound. You may use a mantra such as "Ummmm" just because it sounds good—satisfying and relaxing. Or you may say "Ahhhh" represents the pure sound of God. Because you *say* it does, it will.

Affirmations. Brief affirmations can be used in meditation. My favorites include "God is within me" and "I love myself."

Some people think meditation takes time *away* from physical accomplishment. Taken to extremes, of course, that's true. Most people, however, find that meditation *creates* more time than it *takes*. Meditation is for rest, healing, balance, and information. All these are helpful to attain a goal.

One of the primary complaints people have about meditating is, "My thoughts won't leave me alone." Well *naturally*—that's what the mind does; it *thinks*. Rather than fight the thoughts (good

A powerful agent
is the right word.
Whenever we come upon
one of those intensely right words
the resulting effect
is physical
as well as spiritual,
and electrically prompt.

MARK TWAIN

luck), you might *listen* to the thoughts for nuggets of information. If a thought reminds you of something to do, write it down (or record it on a tape recorder). Then return to the meditation.

As the "to do" list fills, the mind empties. If the thought, "Call the bank," reappears, you need only tell yourself, "It's on the list. I can let that one go." And you will. It is important, however, to *do* the things on the list—or at least in a nonmeditative state to consider doing them. If you don't, you will continue to think about them, again and again.

When finished meditating, not only will you have had a better meditation, you will also have a "to do" list that can be very useful. One insight gleaned during a few minutes of meditation might save *hours,* perhaps *days* of unnecessary work. That's what I mean when I say—from a purely practical point of view—meditation can make more time than it takes.

The currents of the Universal Being
circulate through me;
I am part and parcel
of God.

EMERSON

Affirmations

An affirmation is a statement of positive fact. It's always worded in the present and usually begins with "I am." Affirmations are designed "to make firm" the positive things about yourself.

Affirmations may be truer in the future than they are now, but the affirmation is always claimed *here and now.* Affirmations can be said anywhere, silently or out loud. The more often they're used, the more real, true, solid, and "firm" they become.

Setting aside periods of time especially for affirmations is valuable. Go to your sanctuary, sit in the sacred room, and say a selected affirmation over and over again. After a while, go to the video screen and watch yourself living that affirmation fully.

Then go to the ability closet and put on the ability suit for that affirmation. Go to the ability practice area and live the affirmation.

Affirmations are very powerful. When you repeat them in front of a mirror while looking into your eyes, all the negative thoughts and feelings that keep you from fulfilling your affirmation will surface. Let them surface; let them float away. Beneath all the limitations is a part of you that knows the truth of the affirmation.

Create affirmations to suit your particular situations. Remember to keep them positive statements of the *present.* "I am healthy, wealthy, and happy," not "I want to be healthy, wealthy, and happy," or "Pretty soon, with enough luck, I'll be healthy, wealthy, and happy."

I am the maker
of my own fortune.
I think of the Great Spirit
that rules this universe.

CHIEF TECUMSEH

Here are some affirmations to get you started. Pilfer these, and then go on to create your own.

Affirmations others have used . . .

I am one pure of mouth, pure of hands.
(The Address to the Gods, 1700–1000 B. C.)

I am nearest to the gods.
(Socrates)

I am ready for Fortune as she wills.
(Dante)

I am not only witty in myself, but the cause that wit is in other men.
(Shakespeare)

I am coming to that holy room.
(John Donne)

I am in love with the world.
(Swift)

I am content.
(John Quincy Adams)

I am on the side of the angels.
(Benjamin Disraeli)

I am the master of my fate; / I am the captain of my soul.
(William Ernest Henley, 1888)

I am as strong as a bull moose.
(Theodore Roosevelt)

Every day, in every way, I'm getting better and better.
(Emile Coue, 1857–1926)

I am absorbed in the wonder of earth and the life upon it.
(Pearl S. Buck)

I am the greatest.
(Muhammad Ali)

I am strong, I am invincible, I am woman.
(Helen Reddy)

And here are some others you might try . . .

I feel warm and loving toward myself.

I am worthy of all the good in my life.

I am one with the universe, and I have more than I need.

I always do the best I can with what I know and I always use everything for my advancement.

I forgive myself unconditionally.

I am grateful for my life.

I love and accept myself and others.

I treat all problems as opportunities to grow in wisdom and love.

I am relaxed, trusting in a higher plan that's unfolding for me.

I automatically and joyfully focus on the positive.

I give myself permission to live, love, and laugh.

I am creating and using affirmations to create a joyful, abundant, fulfilling life.

. . . this, or something greater for my highest good, and the highest good of all concerned. (A good ending to all affirmation sessions, by the way.)

I love me.

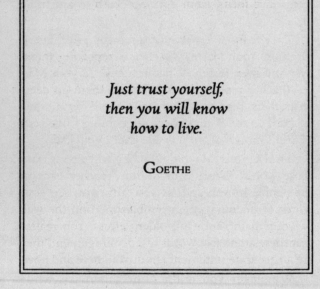

Just trust yourself,
then you will know
how to live.

GOETHE

Words of Encouragement

Go to your sanctuary and invite your Master Teacher in. Together, go to the sacred room. Sit down, close your eyes, and relax. Imagine your Master Teacher kneeling behind your chair and whispering gently into your ear a few words of encouragement, words you will use often on your path from illness to health, from negative thinking to positive focus, from desiring death to affirming life.

They're just a few words: three, four, five. Listen carefully. Your Master Teacher is repeating them, over and over. Listen. What are they? As your Master Teacher repeats them, relax; let them go deep. Hear them repeated, over and over. After a while it's hard to tell if the words are coming from your Master's mouth or from inside your own head.

Thank your Master Teacher for giving you those words. Escort your Master Teacher back to the people mover, and, as you turn, you see your words of encouragement emblazoned on the wall of your main room in golden letters. You realize that these aren't just words of encouragement; they are an accurate statement about you, here and now.

Whenever you enter your sanctuary, while standing under the white light of your entry way, pause for a moment; read your words of encouragement. Let the words touch your heart. Whenever you feel challenged on your path, remember that those are not just words, but a fundamental truth about you.

Always
forgive your enemies—
nothing annoys
them so much.

Oscar Wilde

Forgiveness

Yes, I am saving the best for last. The information in any one of these final three chapters, if applied with a genuine desire to heal, is more than enough.

The first of these is forgiveness. Forgiveness may be the greatest healer. As Charles Fillmore said:

> Here is a mental treatment guaranteed to cure every ill that flesh is heir to: sit for half an hour every night and mentally forgive everyone against whom you have any ill will or antipathy.

We hold so much against ourselves and against others; then we hold it against ourselves that we hold things against ourselves and others. Judging ourselves and others for not measuring up is painful. (PAINFUL = PAY-IN-FULL.)

The way out? Forgiveness. The process of forgiveness is such a simple one. It's so easy, most people don't realize how effective it can be, so they don't try it and don't find out how well it works.

To forgive yourself, all you have to do is say, "I forgive myself for ____________ (transgression)," or "I forgive ____________ (another) for ____________ (transgression)," and fill in the blanks.

Notice that the forgiveness is unconditional. Be willing to let go of any hurt, guilt, resentment, or attachment.

That's part one.

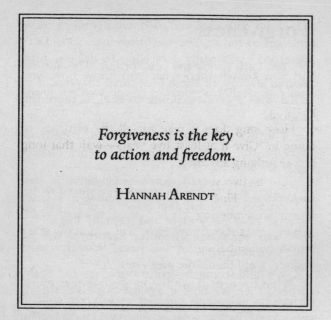

Forgiveness is the key
to action and freedom.

HANNAH ARENDT

Part two is, "I forgive myself for judging myself for ____________ (transgression)," and "I forgive myself for judging ______________ (another) for ____________ (transgression)."

What we or someone else did is of little concern. The real problem *for us* began *when we judged* what happened as wrong, bad, improper, hurtful, mean, nasty, etc. It's our *judgment* we need to forgive. The action was just the action. Our *judgment* about the action caused our difficulty.

If you're going to judge something, wait until all the evidence is in. Yes, so-and-so walked out on you, but two years later you met such-and-such, and thanks to so-and-so's departure you were free to take up with such-and-such, who is much more fun than so-and-so ever was; therefore, so-and-so's "desertion" was really a blessing in disguise and, had you known then what you know now, you would certainly have thrown so-and-so a *bon voyage* party.

How long does it take for all the evidence to come in? Give it at least five years—wait that long before judging anything.

"But in five years I won't remember this even took place." Fine. Then forget it now. If it's not worth remembering for five years, it's not worth getting upset about now. How will you know if it's worth remembering for five years? Wait five years and see. Until then, "the jury's out."

What happens if we forget the five-year moratorium on judgments (and, of course, we will)? If you forget, then as soon as you remember, forgive yourself on the spot. Knowing it was the judgment—not the action—that caused the hurt, pain, and separation, forgive yourself for judging.

Just say those forgiveness sentences to yourself. Try it. See what happens. It's one of those techniques that works by rote: you do it, it works. When should you do it? Whenever you're upset. All upset is caused by our judgment. Forgive the judgment, and the upset tends to fade.

You may have to repeat the forgiveness sentences several times, because you may have judged something several times. How many times does it take? You know the answer to that one by now: when the upset goes away, it was enough.

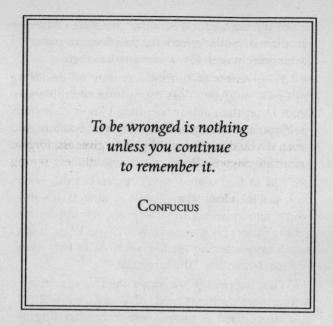

> *To be wronged is nothing*
> *unless you continue*
> *to remember it.*
>
> CONFUCIUS

There's another element to forgiveness, and that's forgetting. When it's forgiven, it's forgotten. Let it go. It's not worth holding on to. Some people would rather have the righteousness of their vindictiveness than health. That's their choice.

Use the white light, your sacred room, and your Master Teacher in your forgiveness process. Learn to forgive fully and completely. If you want health, wealth, and happiness, you can't afford the luxury of lugging around all those unforgiven, unforgotten past events. Let them go.

Declare regular periods of General Amnesty during the day. Forgive yourself and everyone else for everything that happened (or failed to happen) since the last General Amnesty. Schedule one every few hours. Nothing from the past is worth polluting your present with for any longer than that.

Forgiveness is simply a matter of declaring yourself forgiven. That can surface worthiness issues faster than almost anything I know. Tell yourself you are worthy of being forgiven. You are. And even if you don't *feel* worthy of forgiveness, forgive yourself anyway. Prove your unworthiness wrong again.

And then forgive it.

Thank God for tea!
What would the world
do without tea?
—how did it exist?
I am glad I was not
born before tea.

SYDNEY SMITH
1771–1845

The Attitude of Gratitude

As you learn to focus on the positive things in your current environment, take it one step further: be *grateful* for everything in your life.

Start with the outstanding things, then the good things, then the mundane things, then the not-so-good things, then the very not-so-good things, then the terrible things.

Why should you be grateful for the terrible things? First, meet terrible things with feelings of gratitude, because gratitude feels so good. Second, the terrible things are part of your life—there must be some reason why they're there. You might not know the reason yet, but, sooner or later, if you're open to it, the reason will appear. So, be grateful until it does, and when it does, be grateful.

Negative thinking simply cannot coexist with gratitude. If a nasty thought tries to take hold, the attitude of gratitude says, "Thank you for that thought!" Such appreciation diffuses negative thinking almost at once.

Remember to be grateful for what we often take for granted—our awareness, our senses, our bodies, our lives. Sure, we have things we could complain about, but we also have so much to be grateful for.

Whom or what should you be grateful to? It doesn't matter. Take your choice. You can be grateful to the power company for the electricity, or Edison for inventing the light bulb, or the designer of the lamp, or for the money to pay the power bill,

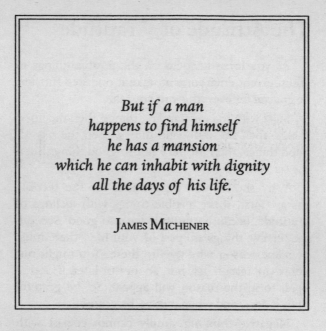

But if a man
happens to find himself
he has a mansion
which he can inhabit with dignity
all the days of his life.

JAMES MICHENER

or to God for the energy behind it all, or any combination. And that's for just a *lamp.*

Who gets the gratitude is not as important as *your feeling* the gratitude. Gratitude is such a free, abundant, happy attitude. That's why I'm suggesting you find things to be grateful about—not so the electric company gets thank-you notes, but so you'll feel the joy of being grateful.

In his cassette tape *Meditation of Gratitude: A Key to Receptivity* ($12 postpaid from The Cosmos Tree, 301 E. 78th NY, NY 10021), Roger Lane asks you to imagine yourself as a sweater, a simple wool sweater. He then goes through everything even a simple sweater has to be grateful for: the sheep, the spinners, the knitters, the people who grow the food to feed the knitters, etc.

And how much more we have to be grateful for than a sweater! If we were truly grateful for everything in our lives, we wouldn't have *time* for a single negative thought.

Throw an inner gratitude party. Invite the people from your past and present into your sanctuary and thank them for all they've contributed to your life: teachers, lovers, friends, brothers, sisters, spouse(s), children, and, of course, parents. See them come in, one by one, through the white light of the people mover. Express your gratitude. Then point them to the bar and buffet and welcome your next guest. (Your Master Teacher knows a great Master Caterer.)

Gratitude opens the place in you to receive. Whom do you prefer giving to: people who truly appreciate your gifts, or those who find fault with every little detail? The universe probably thinks as you do: let's give to the grateful.

And it does.

If I have the gift of prophecy
and can fathom all mysteries
and all knowledge,
and if I have a faith
that can move mountains,
but have not love, I am nothing.
If I give all I possess to the poor
and surrender my body to the flames,
but have not love, I gain nothing.
Love is patient, love is kind.
It does not envy, it does not boast,
it is not proud.
It is not rude, it is not self-seeking,
it is not easily angered,
it keeps no record of wrongs.
Love does not delight in evil
but rejoices with the truth.
It always protects, always trusts,
always hopes, always perseveres.
Love never fails.
And now these three remain:
faith, hope and love.
But the greatest of these is love.

I CORINTHIANS 13

Loving

There are three magic words in healing—*I Love You*. When we say them, to others or to ourselves, all are healed.

I prefer the word *loving* to *love*. Loving includes the action necessary to bring about the qualities of love. Love is nice, of course, but love-in-action gets a lot more done.

Loving feels wonderful, but it's more than just a *feeling;* loving is a choice. We *choose* to be loving toward ourselves and others. This moment we choose. The next moment, we choose again. We always have a choice.

We can be lost in the gravity of our bad habits and negative thinking, but with each moment comes a new opportunity to choose loving. Now and now and now again.

It's usually not a grand choice preceded by golden trumpets and a chamberlain heralding, "Do you choose the joy of loving, or do you choose the quagmire of negative thinking?" Usually it's small choices: How do I respond to this information? Should I focus on the positive or the negative? Would eating this be taking care of myself? Would doing my exercises be loving myself?

There may not be a "loving feeling" behind the choice to take a loving action, but we take the action anyway; that's part of the *decision* to be loving. The loving action often produces the loving feeling. When we act in a loving way—either toward ourselves or others—we usually start to feel loving. If

If you call him
your Master will hear you.
Seven bars on the door
will not hold him
Seven fires burning bright
only bring him delight.
You can live
the life you dream.

JUDY COLLINS

we wait for the loving feeling before we take a loving action, we might take only two or three loving actions a week.

Who is there to love? Ultimately, you. As the song declares, "Learning to love yourself is the greatest love of all." You're the only person you'll be with *constantly* for the rest of your life. Why not make it a loving time?

Choose to love yourself. *Do* loving things for yourself. *Act* toward yourself in a loving way. *Forgive* yourself for *everything. Be easy* on yourself. *Love* yourself *unconditionally.* When you learn to love yourself—warts, bumps, bald spots, love handles, habits, negative thinking, illness, and all—you can love anyone or anything. Then you'll always be "in loving."

Did I say love the illness? Yep. Love it so much that it wouldn't even *dream* of harming you. Love it so much that if you told it, "I love you, but I could love you better if you were over there," it would go over there. Love it so much that that you won't have any hate left in you about anything.

As Dale Evans pointed out, "I'm so busy loving *everybody,* I just don't have time to hate *anybody.*"

What's the answer? Loving. What's the question? It doesn't matter; the answer is still loving.

It's the last word I want to leave you with, the first word in healing, the antidote to stress, the ease that dissolves dis-ease, the Magic Bullet of Joy, the vaccine against hatred, the positive action we can take when negative thinking flares, what we can always be grateful for, proof positive that the blessings already are, and the heart of forgiveness—

Loving.

Stay at home
in your mind.
Don't recite
other people's opinions.
I hate quotations
Tell me what you know.

Emerson

Other Books by Peter McWilliams

You Can't Afford the Luxury of a Negative Thought Audio Tapes

The unabridged text of this book, read by the author. **Six cassettes. $24.95.**

Focus on the Positive

Exercises, processes, journal space, drawing room, and more—all designed to complement the material in the preceding book. 200 pages. **Trade paperback, $11.95.**

LIFE 101 Everything We Wish We Had Learned About Life In School—But Didn't

The overview book of the *LIFE 101 SERIES*. The idea behind *LIFE 101* is that everything in life is for our upliftment, learning and growth—including (and, perhaps especially) the "bad" stuff. "The title jolly well says it all," said the *Los Angeles Times*—jolly well saying it all. 480 pages. **Trade paperback, $5.95. Audio tapes** (unabridged, five cassettes), **$22.95. Wristwatch, $35.00.**

The Portable LIFE 101

179 essential excerpts plus 177 quotations from the *New York Times* bestseller *LIFE 101*. Think of it as the Cliff Notes to life. **Trade paperback, $5.95.**

DO IT! Let's Get Off Our Buts

This is a book for those who want to discover—clearly and precisely—their dream; how to pursue that dream, even if it means learning (and—gasp!—practicing) some new behavior; and who wouldn't mind having some fun along the way. 500 pages. **Paperback, $5.95. Audio tapes** (unabridged, six cassettes), **$24.95.**

The Portable DO IT!

A collection of reminders and quotes to encourage you to continue getting off your buts. The perfect pocket companion on the road to fulfilling your dreams. 208 pages. **Trade paperback, $5.95.**

LOVE 101 Loving Oneself is the Beginning of a Lifelong Romance

If you were arrested for being kind to yourself, would there be enough evidence to convict you? If not, this book (or audio tape set) is a must. It explores improving the most important relationship in your life—your relationship with yourself. After all, you're the only person you'll be eating with, watching TV with, bathing with, and sleeping with for the rest of your life. 400 pages **Trade paperback,** $11.95. **Audio tapes** (unabridged, eight cassettes, includes Meditation tape), $24.95

How to Heal Depression

by Harold H. Bloomfield, M.D., and Peter McWilliams

The first companion book of the eighteen-year bestseller, *How to Survive the Loss of a Love.* In simple, clear, direct prose (with quotes on every other page) it explains what depression is, what causes it, and what the most effective treatments are. **Hardcover,** $14.95. **Audio tapes** (unabridged, six cassettes, read by the authors), $19.95.

How to Survive the Loss of a Love

by Melba Colgrove, Ph.D., Harold H. Bloomfield, M.D., and Peter McWilliams

A directly helpful guide to recovering from any loss or major change in life. 212 pages. **Hardcover,** $12.95 **Trade paperback** (rack size), $5.95. **Audio tapes** (unabridged, two cassettes, read by the authors), $11.95.

Ain't Nobody's Business If You Do

The Absurdity of Consensual Crimes in a Free Society

The idea behind this book is simple: As an adult, you should be allowed to do with your person and property whatever you choose, as long as you don't physically harm the person or property of another. 818 pages. **Hardcover,** $11.47. **Paperback,** $5.95.

Surviving, Healing and Growing

The How to Survive the Loss of a Love Workbook

Exercises, processes, and suggestions designed to supplement *How to Survive the Loss of a Love*. Lots of room to write, draw, doodle, survive, heal & grow. 200 pages. **Trade paperback,** $11.95.

LIFE 102:
What to Do When Your Guru Sues You

This book is presented as a moral tale—the journey of a New Age Candide—exploring the dangers of uninvited programming. It even includes lessons on how to counter-program and reprogram destructive programming, be it from a cult leader, a relative, the Tobacco Institute, or yourself. Peter McWilliams explains what we can do to obtain and maintain our personal freedom—a difficult but rewarding task. 424 pages. **Hardcover, $19.95.**

Come Love With Me & Be My Life

The Complete Romantic Poetry of Peter McWilliams

Touching, direct, emotional, often funny, this is the best of Peter McWilliams's romantic poetry. 250 pages. **Hardcover,** $12.95. **Audio tapes** (unabridged, two cassettes, read by the author), $12.95.

I Marry You Because . . .

Poetry and quotations on love and marriage. 192 pages. **Trade paperback,** $5.95.

PORTRAITS: A Book of Photographs

The first published collection of Peter McWilliams's photographs, focuses on portraits of people. The book is a large format (9x12) and features more than 200 black & white and color photographs, exquisitely printed. 252 pages. **Hardcover,** $34.95.

To order any of these books,
please check your local bookstore, or call

1–800–LIFE–101

or write to

Prelude Press
8159 Santa Monica Boulevard
Los Angeles, California 90046

Please write or call for our free catalog!

Saul and Jonathan—
in life they were loved and gracious,
and in death they were not parted:
they were swifter than eagles,
they were stronger than lions.

II Samuel

1:23

ABOUT THE AUTHOR

PETER McWILLIAMS has been writing about his passions since 1967. In that year, he became passionate about what most seventeen-year-olds are passionate about—love—and wrote *Come Love With Me & Be My Life*. This began a series of poetry books which have sold nearly four million copies.

Along with love, of course, comes loss, so Peter became passionate about emotional survival. In 1971 he wrote *Surviving the Loss of a Love*, which was expanded in 1976 and again in 1991 (with co-authors Melba Colgrove, Ph.D., and Harold Bloomfield, M.D.) into *How to Survive the Loss of a Love*. It has sold more than two million copies.

He also became interested in meditation, and a book he wrote on meditation was a *New York Times* bestseller, knocking the impregnable *Joy of Sex* off the #1 spot. As one newspaper headline proclaimed, MEDITATION MORE POPULAR THAN SEX AT THE *NEW YORK TIMES*.

His passion for computers (or, more accurately, for what computers can do) led to *The Personal Computer Book*, which *TIME* proclaimed "a beacon of simplicity, sanity and humor," and the *Wall Street Journal* called "genuinely funny." (Now, really, how many people has the *Wall Street Journal* called "genuinely funny"?)

His passion for personal growth continues in the ongoing LIFE 101 SERIES. Thus far, the books in this series include *You Can't Afford the Luxury of a Negative Thought: A Book for People with Any Life-Threatening Illness—Including Life*; *LIFE 101: Everything We Wish We Had Learned About Life In School—But Didn't* (a *New York Times* bestseller in both hardcover and paperback); *DO IT! Let's Get Off Our Buts* (a #1 *New York Times* hardcover bestseller); *WEALTH 101: Wealth Is Much More Than Money*, and *We Give To Love: Giving Is Such a Selfish Thing.*

His passion for visual beauty led him to publish, in 1992, his first book of photography, *PORTRAITS,* a twenty-two-year anthology of his photographic work.

Personal freedom, individual expression, and the right to live one's own life, as long as one does not harm the person or property of another, have long been his passions. He wrote about them in *Ain't Nobody's Business If You Do: The Absurdity of Consensual Crimes in a Free Society.*

After successfully being treated for depression, he wrote with Harold H. Bloomfield, M.D., *How to Heal Depression.*

His fifteen-year sojourn through John-Roger's destructive cult, the Church of the Movement of Spiritual Inner Awareness (MSIA), is documented (with a surprising degree of humor) in *LIFE 102: What to Do When Your Guru Sues You.*

All of the above-mentioned books were self-published and are still in print.

Peter McWilliams has appeared on *The Oprah Winfrey Show, Larry King* (radio and television), *Donahue, Sally Jessy Raphael,* and, a long time ago, the *Regis Philbin Show* (before Regis met Kathie Lee—probably before Kathie Lee was *born).*

When I want
to read a book,
I write one.

BENJAMIN DISRAELI

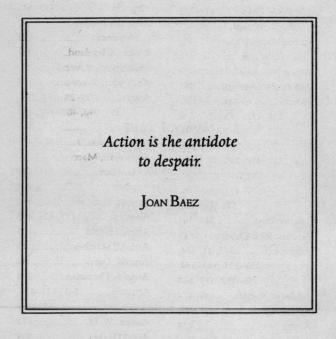

Action is the antidote
to despair.

JOAN BAEZ

Index

A

B

Gladness of heart
is the life of man,
and the rejoicing of a man
is length of days.

APOCRYPHA
Ecclesiasticus 30:22

The world has a way of giving
what is demanded of it.
If you are frightened and look
for failure and poverty,
you will get them,
no matter how hard
you may try to succeed.
Lack of faith in yourself,
in what life will do for you,
cuts you off from the good
things of the world.
Expect victory
and you make victory.

PRESTON BRADLEY

Happiness is
the most powerful of tonics.

HERBERT SPENCER

Happiness consists in activity:
such is the constitution of our nature:
it is a running stream,
and not a stagnant pool.

John M. Good

L

M

A merry heart doeth good like a medicine.

PROVERBS 17: 22

Is life not a hundred times too short for us to stifle ourselves?

FRIEDRICH NIETZSCHE

S

It is the chiefest point of happiness that a man is willing to be what he is.

ERASMUS

A first rate soup is better than a second rate painting.

ABRAHAM MASLOW

You have delighted us long enough.

JANE AUSTEN